Between the Brown and the Red

Ohio University Press Polish and Polish-American Studies Series

Between the Brown and the Red

*Nationalism, Catholicism, and Communism
in Twentieth-Century Poland—
The Politics of Bolesław Piasecki*

Mikołaj Stanisław Kunicki

OHIO UNIVERSITY PRESS

ATHENS

Ohio University Press, Athens, Ohio 45701
ohioswallow.com
© 2012 by Ohio University Press

To obtain permission to quote, reprint, or otherwise reproduce or distribute material
from Ohio University Press publications, please contact our rights and permissions
department at (740) 593-1154 or (740) 593-4536 (fax).

Printed in the United States of America
Ohio University Press books are printed on acid-free paper ∞ ™

First paperback printing in 2013
Paperback ISBN 978-0-8214-2073-7

HARDCOVER 20 19 18 17 16 15 14 13 12   5 4 3 2 1
PAPERBACK   21 20 19 18 17 16 15 14 13   5 4 3 2 1

Library of Congress Cataloging-in-Publication Data

Kunicki, Mikołaj Stanisław.
    Between the brown and the red : nationalism, Catholicism, and communism in
twentieth-century Poland : the politics of Bolesław Piasecki / Mikołaj Stanisław Kunicki.
        p. cm. — (Ohio University Press Polish and Polish-American studies series)
    Includes bibliographical references and index.
    ISBN 978-0-8214-2004-1 (hc : alk. paper) — ISBN 978-0-8214-4420-7 (electronic)
    1. Piasecki, Bolesław. 2. Politicians—Poland—Biography. 3. Communism and
Christianity—Poland. 4. Catholic Church—Poland—History—20th century.
5. Poland—Politics and government—1918–1945. 6. Poland—Politics and
government—1945–1980. I. Title.
    DK4435.P54K86 2012
    943.805'5092—dc23
    [B]
                            2012009339

Publication of this book in the Polish and Polish-American Studies Series has been made possible in part by the generous support of the following sponsors:

Polish American Historical Association and the
Stanley Kulczycki Publication Fund of the Polish American
Historical Association,
   New Britain, Connecticut

Stanislaus A. Blejwas Endowed Chair in Polish
and Polish American Studies,
   Central Connecticut State University,
   New Britain, Connecticut

The Polish Institute of Arts and Sciences of America, Inc.,
   New York, New York

The Kosciuszko Foundation,
   New York, New York

Thomas Duszak,
   Harrisburg, Pennsylvania

The Institute for Scholarship in the Liberal Arts,
   College of Arts and Letters, University of Notre Dame,
   Notre Dame, Indiana

Contents

Illustrations

Series Editor's Preface

In *Between the Brown and the Red: Nationalism, Catholicism, and Communism in Twentieth-Century Poland—The Politics of Bolesław Piasecki,* Mikołaj Stanisław Kunicki views the tangled political history of postwar Poland through the machinations of a pivotal, if relatively minor, political figure, Bolesław Piasecki. Part chameleon, part visionary, part political manipulator, and part bureaucratic functionary, Piasecki was the perfect opportunist and the quintessential political survivor.

In his student days in the 1930s, Bolesław Piasecki was a founder and member of a Catholic fascist youth group. Though stridently anti-Semitic, Piasecki also feared and disliked the Germans, which made him an admirer of Mussolini and fascist Italy but not of Hitler and the Nazis. Piasecki envisioned for Poland an authoritarian Catholic-fascist-nationalist state that would establish moral values and promote corporatist social progress. After the outbreak of World War II, Piasecki led an underground military faction that fought against both Nazi and Soviet forces. Arrested by Soviet authorities after the war, he escaped execution and rehabilitated himself by denouncing his prewar anti-Semitism (a hollow pledge, and one that Polish communist authorities did not enforce as it served statist purposes) and grafted his Catholic-nationalist vision onto pro-Soviet socialism. Thereafter, as head of an organization called PAX, he became a tool of the regime, trying to mobilize Catholic support for the communist government and serving as a foil to the anticommunist Polish Church and its leader, Stefan Cardinal Wyszyński. Meanwhile, Piasecki tried to transform his usefulness to Poland's communist rulers into political and economic advantage for himself, which he hoped eventually would pave the way for the conversion of PAX into a formal political party and, in turn, inject Catholic values into Poland's communist ideology. In neither of the latter did he succeed. Eventually, Piasecki became completely marginalized in Polish political life. As a Polish minister of culture commented, "Piasecki concentrate[d] on reforming socialism in the spirit of Catholicism rather than Catholicism in the spirit of socialism." In the eyes of his communist masters, this was his undoing, and they dropped him when he was no longer useful.

Kunicki's comprehensive political biography, interwoven with a deft exploration of postwar Polish political themes, paints a picture of an intriguing —if frankly rather despicable—figure who even as the swirling milieu of prewar, wartime, and postwar Polish politics repeatedly turned the political order upside down, attained remarkable political longevity. Piasecki (to quote the author), was "the only Eastern European fascist leader to continue his political career in a communist-dominated environment"; his story illuminates the complex relationship between communism and nationalism in postwar Poland and the relationship of Roman Catholicism and anti-Semitism to both. Indeed, Kunicki has written a courageous book that exposes dark authoritarian currents that, as he argues, pervaded postwar Polish politics and continue to enable a resurgent Polish Right in the post-Solidarity era. Kunicki thus examines hugely significant problematics in modern Polish history.

Publication of the Ohio University Press Polish and Polish-American Studies Series marks a milestone in the maturation of the Polish studies field and stands as a fitting tribute to the scholars and organizations whose efforts have brought it to fruition. Supported by a series advisory board of accomplished Polonists and Polish-Americanists, the Polish and Polish-American Studies Series has been made possible through generous financial assistance from the Polish American Historical Association and that organization's Stanley Kulczycki Publication Fund, the Stanislaus A. Blejwas Endowed Chair in Polish and Polish American Studies at Central Connecticut State University, the Polish Institute of Arts and Sciences of America, and the Kosciuszko Foundation, and through institutional support from Wayne State University and Ohio University Press. Publication of this particular volume also has been aided by a grant from the University of Notre Dame, the author's home institution. The series meanwhile has benefited from the warm encouragement of a number of other persons, including Gillian Berchowitz, M. B. B. Biskupski, the late Stanislaus A. Blejwas, Thomas Duszak, Mary Erdmans, Anna Jaroszyńska-Kirchmann, Brian McCook, James S. Pula, and Thaddeus Radzilowski, and from the able assistance of the staff of Ohio University Press. The moral and material support from all of these institutions and individuals is gratefully acknowledged.

John J. Bukowczyk

Preface

THE CONCEPT OF THIS BOOK began taking shape in the fall of 1998. At that time, I was pursuing a doctoral degree in European history at Stanford University. My advisor, Norman Naimark, suggested to me a dissertation topic. Out of my interest in the relationship of nationalism and communism in Eastern Europe came the idea of writing a biography of Bolesław Piasecki (1915–79), a prominent Polish nationalist politician who started his career as a fascist in the 1930s and ended it as a procommunist Catholic activist in postwar Poland.

In reassessing Piasecki's political career, I introduce to the reader one of the most fascinating figures in the history of twentieth-century Poland and the communist world. I narrow the scale of historical observation to an individual case, which I use to discuss the role of nationalism in modern Polish history and to analyze the entanglement of communism and fascism. In broader terms, I present an example of the ideological affinity between communism and nationalism. The end result of the party-state's gradual ideological demobilization and the growing reliance on ethnocentric nationalism was its transformation into a populist-nationalist regime, which unintentionally turned the cultural sphere into a pluralist and polyphonic realm. Parallel to this official nationalism promoted by the regime, communist Poland nurtured an organization that functioned as an incubator for the nationalist Right, Bolesław Piasecki's Catholic PAX association, socialist in its involvement and nationalist in its worldview.

A biography of a seemingly marginal figure always runs the risk of being too narrow or hardly relevant. If properly contextualized, however, it can broaden our understanding of larger phenomena. Throughout his long political career, Piasecki had to deal with Poland's political and religious leaders, Marshal Józef Piłsudski's entourage and heirs, commanders of the wartime resistance movement, Stalinists, Władysław Gomułka's national communists, and Edward Gierek's self-proclaimed technocratic experts and managers. Studying Piasecki's encounters with these contemporaries allows me to examine and illuminate the important relationships between authoritarianism, nationalism, communism, and religion.

This book is based on formerly classified materials from Polish archives, including the files of the former security police from the Institute for National Remembrance (Instytut Pamięci Narodowej, IPN), communist party and government files from the New Documents Archive (Archiwum Akt Nowych, AAN), and collections from the Archive of the Catholic Association Civitas Christiana (Archiwum Katolickiego Stowarzyszenia Civitas Christiana, AKS CC), PAX's successor institution. Archival sources include confidential reports, official and personal correspondence, meeting minutes, transcripts of private conversations, and court evidence. I have also drawn on the holdings of the Hoover Institution Archives (HIA) at Stanford and the Open Society Archives in Budapest.

In addition to archival sources, I have used political pamphlets, collections of published documents, published and unpublished memoirs, and voluminous press sources. Press sources and pamphlets published before the war provide genuine opinions of and convictions about Piasecki and his comrades, unlike postwar press materials, which were released under the supervision of communist censors. Many of the memoirs that I consulted were written by Piasecki's former associates.[1] Some of these authors parted with Piasecki after political disagreements or as a result of war and exile. Others are exceptionally sycophantic toward Piasecki and self-laudatory. I have drawn on these accounts with great caution.

This study is based on my doctoral dissertation, and I thank my mentors and colleagues in the Department of History at Stanford for their help. I am particularly grateful to my advisor, Norman Naimark, who supported me through all these years and gave me much confidence in this project. Thomas W. Simons, Jr., Amir Weiner, and John Connelly influenced my initial approach and offered useful criticism of the manuscript. Several friends and colleagues helped me with initial drafts, among them Holly Case, Caitlin Murdock, Paul Stronski, and Marci Shore. Ruth Homrighaus was an excellent developmental editor. At Notre Dame, Thomas Kselman took time off from his busy schedule to read drafts and offer invaluable suggestions on the subject of political Catholicism. Marc Rodriguez gave me helpful, practical tips about editing. Most of this book was revised while at Notre Dame, and I thank all my colleagues from the Department of History for their unwavering support. This work has profited immensely, moreover, from conversations with Brian Porter-Szűcs, Jerzy Borejsza, Timothy Snyder, Jan T. Gross, Antony Polonsky, and Laurie Koloski. I am very grateful to the two anonymous readers for Ohio University Press, who provided excellent feedback for the final version of the manuscript.

The completion of this book would have been unthinkable without several research trips to Poland, where I gained access to previously classified documents. I thank the archivists of the Institute for National Remembrance, the Archive of the Catholic Association Civitas Christiana, the New Documents Archives, and the Archive of the Institute of Military History. I am also grateful to the staff of the Hoover Institution Archives and the Open Society Archives. I thank Jarosław Piasecki, who supplied me with information about his father. Jan Engelgard kindly provided me with important facts and details. Andrzej Paczkowski and Krzysztof Persak of the Institute of Political Studies of the Polish Academy of Sciences offered invaluable logistical support in Warsaw. I also express my warmest thanks to friends, colleagues, and members of the staff at the Institute for Human Sciences in Vienna for making me feel so welcome there and supporting me during my research fellowship in 2005–6.

Portions of this book were presented at the national conventions of the American Association for Advancement in Slavic Studies in 2002 and 2007, as well as at seminars at the Institute for Human Sciences in Vienna. An earlier version of chapter 6 was published as "The Red and the Brown: Bolesław Piasecki, the Polish Communists, and the Anti-Zionist Campaign in Poland, 1967–1968" in volume 19 of *East European Politics and Societies* (Spring 2005).

This project would not have been possible without support and grants from several institutions and programs, including a Weter Dissertation Fellowship, a Mellon Foundation Dissertation Fellowship, an O'Bie Shultz Fellowship, the Graduate Research Opportunities Program, and Summer Research Grants at the Center of Russian and East European Studies, all at Stanford University; a Józef Tischner Fellowship at the Institute for Human Sciences in Vienna; and grants from Institute for Scholarship in the Liberal Arts at Notre Dame.

My greatest debts are to my parents, who nurtured my interest in history. I dedicate this manuscript to my mother, Wiktoria Kunicka, and to the beloved memory of my father, Bogumił Maciek Kunicki.

Abbreviations

AK	Home Army (Armia Krajowa)
KN	Confederation of the Nation (Konfederacja Narodu)
KPP	Communist Party of Poland (Komunistyczna Partia Polski)
NKVD	People's Commissariat for Internal Affairs (Narodnyy komissariat vnutrennikh del)
ONR	National Radical Camp (Obóz Narodowo-Radykalny)
OPN	Political Organization of the Nation (Organizacja Polityczna Narodu)
OWP	Camp of Great Poland (Obóz Wielkiej Polski)
OZN	Camp of National Unity (Obóz Zjednoczenia Narodowego)
PPR	Polish Workers' Party (Polska Partia Robotnicza)
PPS	Polish Socialist Party (Polska Partia Socjalistyczna)
PSL	Polish Peasant Party (Polskie Stronnictwo Ludowe)
PZPR	Polish United Workers' Party (Polska Zjednoczona Partia Robotnicza)
RNR	National Radical Movement (Ruch Narodowo-Radykalny)
ZBOWiD	Union of Fighters for Freedom and Democracy (Związek Bojowników o Wolność i Demokrację)
ZMP	Union of Young Poland (Związek Młodej Polski)
ZWZ	Union for Armed Struggle (Związek Walki Zbrojnej)

Guide to Pronunciation

The following key provides a guide to the pronunciation of Polish words and names.

a is pronounced as in *father*

c as ts, as in *cats*

ch as guttural h, as in German *Bach*

cz as hard ch, as in *church*

g (always hard), as in *get*

i as ee, as in *meet*

j as y, as in *yellow*

rz as hard zh, as in French *jardin*

sz as hard sh, as in *ship*

szcz as hard shch, as in *fresh cheese*

u as oo, as in boot

w as v, as in *vat*

ć as soft ch, as in *cheap*

ś as soft sh, as in *sheep*

ż as hard zh, as in French *jardin*

ź as soft zh, as in *seizure*

ó as oo, as in *boot*

ą as a nasal, as in French *on*

ę as a nasal, as in French *en*

ł as w, as in *way*

ń as ny, as in *canyon*

The accent in Polish words always falls on the penultimate syllable.

Between the Brown and the Red

Introduction

IN A CLIMACTIC SCENE from Andrzej Munk's 1960 film *Bad Luck* (*Zezowate szczęście*), the protagonist, Jan Piszczyk—a young, shy, clumsy man studying law at Warsaw University—finds himself at the forefront of a political demonstration. The year is 1938, and proregime students are urging Poland's strongman, Marshal Edward Rydz-Śmigły, to "march on Kaunas," the capital of Lithuania. Suddenly, Piszczyk notices new faces in the crowd around him. "These new colleagues were very vocal," he observes, "but their chants were somehow different." From the shouts of the new arrivals—Jews to Madagascar! Down with Sanacja!—it becomes clear that fascist thugs have infiltrated the crowd. A born coward and an opportunist, Piszczyk chants alternately "On Kaunas!" and "Jews to Madagascar!" thereby gaining an enthusiastic response from both parts of the crowd. In the end, the fascists vandalize Jewish shops, while the police club all the demonstrators indiscriminately.

Warsaw in the late 1980s reminded me of the city from Munk's film: It was a dangerous yet fascinating place. Communism's fin de siècle was a season of intellectual debates, political demonstrations, street clashes, and anxiety mixed with hope. As party comrades from the Central Committee started looking for an exit strategy from historical determinism, we university students engaged in various journeys of political self-discovery. I was genuinely annoyed each time I saw a student wearing a miniature Chrobry Sword, the emblem of the nationalist Endek movement from before the war.[1] I also disliked the gangs of skinheads roaming the streets, assaulting "odd" or defiant young people and shouting, "Poland for the Poles!" All such behavior smacked of a return to the 1930s, with its fascist thugs, nationalist students, and chauvinist rhetoric. It was as if anti-Semitism, fascism, and nationalism had thawed from the deep freeze of a communist ice age. Fortunately for Poland, what seemed to be a return of old demons turned out to be only a small part of a brief and chaotic political transition: skinheads did not take over the streets, fascists did not rise to power, and neo-Endeks transformed themselves, however reluctantly, into democratic politicians.

Indeed, the metaphor of a communist ice age is somewhat misleading. The nasty parts of Polish nationalist mythology were not dormant during this period, and some even flourished under the party's rule. They survived the communist interregnum and emerged in the late twentieth century in the form of a preoccupation with the ethnic backgrounds of public figures and with the notions of *Żydokomuna* (a Jewish-communist conspiracy) and of the "true Pole" (*prawdziwy polak*) and his antithesis, the Jew (*żyd*). Conspiracy theories purporting to unmask the enemies of the Polish nation also continued to attract new adherents.

Polish communism reinforced the ethnocentric self-definition of Polishness. World War II, the Nazi extermination of Polish Jews, and the postwar territorial settlement had cleansed Poland, in large part, of its ethnic minorities. By presiding over this process of ethnic homogenization, Polish communists fulfilled the dream of earlier Polish nationalists—the creation of "a Poland for the Poles," as the old battle cry went. After the end of Stalinism, the communist regime used aggressive nationalism as a powerful tool to single out internal and external enemies. In parallel to this official nationalism, communist Poland also nurtured an organization that functioned as an incubator for the nationalist Right: Bolesław Piasecki's Catholic PAX association, socialist in its commitment and nationalist in its worldview.

Only recently has the relationship between communism and nationalism in twentieth-century Eastern Europe and Poland begun to receive the attention that it deserves, and these studies reveal a number of common themes.[2] First, they undermine the Cold War construct of totalitarianism as an approach to understanding twentieth-century Eastern Europe, especially during the period of communist rule. They portray nationalism as a living and diverse phenomenon subject to evolution through everyday life practices rather than as a rigid set of beliefs enforced by ideologues. They also break with the mainstream scholarship of nationalism by disputing the connection between the rise of nationalism and the creation of nation-states, on the one hand, and the secularization of society and the demise of religion, on the other. Instead, some of these works argue that the birth of organic nationalism often has roots in religious renewal and fervor. Finally, these studies often tap historical sociology to present the Soviet bloc states as heterogeneous polities open to various forms of negotiation and dialogue between societies and party regimes on the political, intellectual, and social levels. To date, only a handful of Western scholars have attempted to produce book-length studies on the entanglement of religion, nationalism, and communism. Although this work is not a history of nationalism and Catholicism under Polish communism, it attempts to respond to this demand.

This study provides a comprehensive political biography of the Polish nationalist politician Bolesław Piasecki. Before World War II, as the leader of the National Radical Movement, a small fascist group, Piasecki envisioned Poland as a prototialitarian state integrated on the basis of ethnicity, Catholicism, and mass organization. The cornerstones of his doctrine were the notions that God was the highest destiny of man and that striving to increase the might of the nation was the path to God.[3] During the war, Piasecki gained control of a right-wing combat organization, the Confederation of the Nation, which in 1943 merged with the Home Army. Arrested by the communists in November 1944, he was released within the year and soon founded a procommunist movement of progressive Catholics, later known as PAX (the Latin word for "peace"). He pledged to build a Catholic-Marxist alliance and to mobilize the nationalist Right in the establishment of a socialist Poland.[4] Piasecki proposed the creation of a dual political system embodied by a communist-Catholic ruling coalition. He believed that under the ideological guidance of PAX, Catholics, communists, and nationalists would be united in the service of God, socialism, and nation.[5] Piasecki's concept was socialist in its form and nationalist in its content, since he always viewed Catholicism as central to Polish national identity. He remained the sole leader of PAX until his death in 1979.

In reassessing Piasecki's political career, I narrow the scale of historical observation to an individual case, which can be useful in discussing the ideological affinity between nationalism and communism and posing questions about the nature of this relationship.[6] Piasecki's biography is important not only for its uniqueness—Piasecki was the only Eastern European fascist leader to continue his political career in a communist-dominated environment—but also because it overturns conventional wisdom about communism. I contextualize this story against the background of Poland's interwar politics and anti-Nazi resistance, the communist takeover and Stalinist period, the post-Stalinist period, and communism's belle époque of the 1970s.

It is my hope that this political biography will prompt historians to reevaluate the way in which twentieth-century Polish history has been understood. I propose that under certain conditions, not only did the communists make use of nationalism, but—as Piasecki's case proves—they also prolonged the existence of the nationalist Right. Indeed, I argue that PAX *was* the nationalist Right under communism. Piasecki's story, therefore, calls into question the commonly accepted view that fascism in Eastern Europe was wiped out by the victory of the Red Army and by the subsequent communist takeover.

I explore Piasecki's postwar career against the background of the nationalization of the Polish United Workers' Party and argue that "Left" and "Right" are elusive concepts in modern Poland and in Eastern Europe as a whole. On the one hand, Piasecki's prewar ideology included traditional elements of the Right, such as xenophobia, an exaltation of the ethnically homogenous community, religious fundamentalism, and a paramilitary movement led by a charismatic ideologue. On the other hand, Piasecki shared with the extreme Left an embrace of anticapitalism—here overlapping with the rejection of the West—glorification of a centralized state, cultivation of collective identities, and historical determinism. More important, both Piasecki and the communists believed that their destiny was to construct a new society.

For Polish communists, the recruitment of Catholic nationalists like Piasecki provided a chance to mobilize nationalism and Catholicism. Facing a predominantly hostile country with a strong Right and a powerful Roman Catholic Church, they needed allies from outside their ranks—people who, while not Marxists, would support their cause. Therefore, Piasecki's value lay precisely in the fact that he was not a communist: Piasecki's PAX could channel his nationalist-Catholic clientele into the regime's camp. Later, while aiming to legitimize the party's flagging rule in the aftermath of de-Stalinization, the regime of Władysław Gomułka gradually incorporated—even if selectively—elements of the Polish nationalist canon: namely, the glorification of the national past, Germanophobia, and anti-Semitism. The ultimate outcome of the process was the so-called Polonization of the Polish United Workers' Party. This process culminated in the 1967–68 anti-Semitic campaign, in which Piasecki played a vital role, contributing to the evolution of the Polish communist state into a nationalist-populist regime.

Here, I would also emphasize the similarity between Piasecki and Gomułka, his communist doppelganger: while the former attempted to reconcile his nationalism with socialism, the latter sought to reinforce communism with nationalism. Hence, their political relationship, which lasted for two decades, should come as no surprise. Both of them—sometimes jointly, but more often separately—tried to cross the boundary between two ideologies. And both of them ultimately failed. Their red-brown kinship, which fully manifested itself in 1968, backfired, contributing to the ideological demobilization of Polish communism during the following decade and the emergence of the advocates of civil society.

I also seek to capture the multifaceted nature of church-state relations in communist Poland, relations that oscillated between mutual confrontation, accommodation, and dialogue rather than stagnating in a state of constant struggle.[7] Because of the ethnically homogenous makeup of postwar Poland, the lack of legitimacy of the communist regime as a national state, and the relatively soft form that religious persecution assumed in Poland—at least in comparison to other Soviet satellites—the Church gradually succeeded in monopolizing national identity and its symbolic projections. Nevertheless, what happened in Poland, especially after the end of Stalinism, went beyond the historical duel between the religious and the secular, the clerical and the atheist, the domestic and the alien. Under communism, the bond between religion and nation grew stronger, despite the regime's attempt to play the nationalist card to present itself as Polish rather than communist—or perhaps because of it.

Piasecki's PAX was one of several Catholic organizations that advocated a Marxist-Christian dialogue. Some of these groups, like PAX, were staunchly procommunist. Others were ready to recognize party rule without endorsing its ideological system and weakening the Church. Here, Piasecki's biography addresses the dilemma of Catholic intellectuals who witnessed and often took part in a competition to define and own Polish national identity. His involvement in the government highlights various processes that characterized uneasy church-state cohabitation and eventually led to the victory of the Church.

In his superb novel *The Spell*, Hermann Broch wrote, "Fate is merely the subordination of the mind to a specific conceptual world."[8] The point I would like to emphasize is that the fate of the politician—at least prior to the technocratic age—was determined by the power of convictions, by personal charisma, and by the ability to respond to the fluctuations of mass politics in an age of rival ideologies. Piasecki did subscribe to specific political concepts, including the ethnocentric vision of nationalism and a peculiar Polish raison d'état. His remarkable consistency may explain his ultimate failure: while the politician always strives to win power, Piasecki never achieved this goal, at least in part because he refused to reform his worldview. Fate, in its classical Greek meaning, implies the inability of the individual to control his own destiny against teleological forces defining the universe. But unlike the unfortunate protagonist of Munk's film, Piasecki was not a pawn. During the forty-five years of his political career, not only did he answer to history, but he also contributed to the course of twentieth-century Poland.

1 ||| The Early Years, 1915–35

REBORN IN 1918 AFTER MORE than 120 years of foreign rule, independent Poland faced a number of challenges. The extent of its territory was not finally determined until 1921, with the signing of a peace treaty with Bolshevik Russia and a ceasefire agreement with Germany following the third Silesian uprising.[1] In the new Polish nation-state, ethnic minorities, including Ukrainians, Jews, Belorussians, and Germans, constituted 35 percent of the population. Ethnic differences overlapped with social and religious distinctions. The minorities' attitude toward the Polish state varied from outright rejection (Ukrainian nationalists), to perception of Poland as a "seasonal state" (Germans), to acceptance coupled with demands for greater autonomy (Jews). The Polish ruling elites often behaved as if the country were a one-nation state and frequently trampled the political, religious, and cultural rights of ethnic minorities.

In domestic politics, the main conflicts and rivalries arose from three major political movements of the pre–World War I period: the independence movement led by the Polish Socialist Party (Polska Partia Socjalistyczna, PPS) and Józef Piłsudski; the right-wing nationalist movement of Roman Dmowski's National Democrats (Narodowa Demokracja, known by the acronym Endecja); and the peasant movement dominated by the Polish Peasant Party (Polskie Stronnictwo Ludowe, PSL) and its leader, Wincenty Witos. Before 1914, these groupings had adopted differing approaches toward the partitioning powers of Russia, Germany, and Austria-Hungary and toward the idea of nation building: armed struggle and social progress (PPS), loyalism and ethnonationalism (Endecja), and socioeconomic emancipation

(PSL). World War I forced them to conclude temporary alliances, and from 1918 to 1920, the camps of Piłsudski, Dmowski, and Witos often cooperated. But once territorial consolidation had taken place, they resumed their political confrontation.

During the first years of its existence, the Polish republic attempted to define its political system. The result was a bitter conflict between the Right and the Left, between the Piłsudskiite Legionnaires and Dmowski's nationalists, between those who favored a stronger executive and those who clung to the supremacy of a parliament elected on the principle of universal suffrage. The 1921 constitution promoted the legislative branch over the executive. But as political parties proliferated, successive ruling coalitions failed to secure a lasting majority in the fragmented parliament. The rifts among the main political forces deepened in 1923, following the assassination of President Gabriel Narutowicz by a nationalist fanatic in December 1922, Piłsudski's voluntary political retirement, and the brutal pacification of workers' strikes by the center-right government of Witos.[2] For the next three years, Poland saw a parade of short-lived coalition governments. In May 1926, when the center-right alliance of Endecja, the Christian Democrats, and the PSL formed yet another cabinet headed by Witos, Piłsudski launched a military coup d'état.

The internal divisions mentioned here did not necessarily correspond with pro- or antidemocratic persuasions. The nationalist Right, which frequently had the largest parliamentary representation, was hardly a proponent of a democratic state. In fact, Piłsudski's coup d'état of May 1926 could be interpreted as a preemptive strike against the Right rather than a proto-fascist onslaught on democratic institutions. The Left backed Piłsudski. What became clear to nearly all politicians in 1926 was that Poland stood at a crossroads. Piłsudski's supporters and opponents alike searched for fresh organizational models, preached the gospel of national rebirth, and embraced new political and cultural currents ranging from feminism and secularism to militant Catholicism and fascism.

By the early 1930s, Piłsudski's Sanacja (Purification) regime had proved unable to implement far-reaching reform measures or to move beyond its initial vague appeal to morality, virtue, and activism. Instead, it became increasingly authoritarian. The National Democrats, the main right-wing organization, meanwhile experienced an influx of young militants who radicalized the party and eventually brought about its split. The climate favored political radicalism, and it nourished militants of all sorts. Radicalism, voluntarism, and anti-Semitism—pitched as a remedy for the country's socioeconomic problems—all manifested themselves in Polish politics. Finally, a new generation, brought up in independent Poland, was coming of age. This generation adhered to "discipline of thought and strong solutions" as well as to the heresy of "collective thinking" in the words of Henryk Dembiński, a young Catholic activist who later would join the communist movement.[3]

The advent of militancy in Poland was hardly unique in the European context. The immediate post–World War I period witnessed the growth of political activism bolstered by suffrage reforms, violence propelled by the experience of brutalizing combat, anxieties raised by the threat of revolution, and the partial delegitimization of the liberal and conservative politics that had dominated the pre-1914 landscape. Coupled with certain domestic attributes, most notably the belated modernization and half-baked liberalization of political systems, these challenges soon resulted in the division of the continent into a northwestern democratic tier, Latin/Mediterranean and eastern and central European authoritarian zones, and a border territory comprising Germany and France, where democratic and authoritarian forces clashed.[4]

It is against this complex background that one must read the story of the early years of Bolesław Piasecki. As a member of the younger generation, he embraced political radicalism and preached revolution. As a member of the Polish nationalist Right, he first followed and then began to modify the dynamics of the political era in which he came of age.

The Polish Nationalist Right: A Historical Overview, 1926–30

After his 1926 military coup, Józef Piłsudski pursued a moderate course, dubbed a "semi-constitutional guided democracy" by Antony Polonsky.[5] By creating a government party, the Nonpartisan Bloc for Cooperation with the Government (Bezpartyjny Blok Współpracy z Rządem), to embrace a broad coalition of groups, the marshal hoped to keep parliament under control.[6] But offering a program that included a coherent ideological credo and specific reforms was another issue altogether. The Piłsudskiites' vagueness on this matter—what Eva Plach calls their "utopian open-endedness"—coupled with a dynamic rhetorical invocation of "imponderables," moral cleansing, and a strong state, garnered considerable support among members of the military and the intelligentsia.[7] But Sanacja's increasing statism eventually conflated state and regime, so that all critiques of the government became assaults on the Polish state and nation.[8] Still, this statism did possess elements of a multicultural approach to the process of nation building, including minority and women's rights, secularism, and above all a new concept of national identity, one more inclusive than the ethnoreligious integral nationalism employed by the Right.

Piłsudski was not alone in his disillusionment with parliamentary government. While the Left applauded the coup, the nationalist Right contemplated its own alternatives to parliamentary governance. In 1924 and 1925, the National Democrats had proposed numerous constitutional amendments, including increasing presidential power and curtailing the liberal franchise.[9] The party leader, Roman Dmowski, also esteemed Italian Fascism.[10]

Although the success of Piłsudski's coup shocked the National Democratic movement, Dmowski did not consider the situation hopeless. In a letter to Enrico Corradini, a prominent Italian Fascist, he described the coup as the beginning of a crisis that eventually would elevate the National Democrats to power. According to Dmowski, Piłsudski's regime was the work of the Masons, who in the long run were too weak to hold power. Following a National Democratic victory, the party would impose a system based on limited political representation and fully controlled by a nationalist party on a fascist model.[11] Dmowski's actions in the following months demonstrated his strong desire to reform the movement along protofascist lines. On December 4, 1926, he set up a new mass organization, the Camp of Great Poland (Obóz Wielkiej Polski, OWP).

The OWP was originally conceived as a broad anti-Sanacja front open to the Polish Peasant Party and the Christian Democrats.[12] These prospective partners declined to participate, however, fearing domination by the nationalists. The organization's political program was designed by veteran Endeks Roman Rybarski, Bohdan Wasiutyński, and Dmowski himself, who adopted a radical approach, hoping to rejuvenate Endecja.[13] In fact, a rejuvenation movement or national revival to vie with that offered by Sanacja was at the heart of the OWP's program. The founding declaration professed the camp to be "an organization of the conscious strengths of the nation" committed to fostering the Roman Catholic faith, eradicating Jewish influences in the country, and upholding "a high level of morality and moral discipline."[14]

But these were hardly new constructs. Authoritarianism had been a dominant undercurrent of the National Democratic movement since the turn of
the century, when Dmowski and his comrades had grown preoccupied
with authority, discipline, strict social and political hierarchies, and quasi-
colonialist expansion. Democracy, or rather democratic rhetoric, constituted
the most effective means of controlling the masses.[15] Dmowski's integral
nationalism also negated class struggle among ethnic Poles; the Endeks therefore tended to abstain from supporting workers' grievances and grew ever
more conservative.[16]

The OWP particularly appealed to young activists eager to replicate
Italian models.[17] Dmowski set the tone in the summer of 1926 when he
published a series of enthusiastic articles on Fascism and Mussolini's Italy
and in the following year when he described the camp as organized on the
basis of hierarchy and discipline.[18] At the top of the OWP was the Great
Council, a construct borrowed from Fascist Italy, with Dmowski as its chairman (*wielki oboźny*). The majority of recruits came from the Endeks' student union, the All-Poland Youth (Młodzież Wszechpolska). By 1929, the
youth segment of the OWP, the Youth Movement (Ruch Młodych), supplied half of the thirty-five thousand sworn members of the camp.[19]

Who were these militants? Founded in 1922, the All-Poland Youth
quickly dominated student government institutions and became active beyond the confines of academia. In December of that year, they joined the
campaign against Narutowicz. In 1923, they participated in the pacification
of workers' strikes. The following year, their demands for a *numerus clausus*
for Jewish students were barely defeated in parliament. During the 1926
coup d'état, eight members of nationalist student organizations who joined
the government's troops died in combat.[20] The nationalist students believed
not only that Sanacja was killing Poles but that it also had concluded an alliance with the hated Jews. Such views dominated the agenda of the student
periodical *Akademik polski*, founded and edited by Jan Mosdorf.[21]

The OWP's anti-Jewish rhetoric and violence were consistent with the
line of the National Democratic leadership: anti-Semitic and chauvinistic,
the party advocated a repressive policy toward all ethnic minorities. In the
Endeks' view, these "foreigners" threatened the country's unity and sabotaged the process of nation building. As non-Christians who held to their
own language and customs, Jews occupied a place of special importance

in nationalist discourse. Portrayed as parasitic, alien, and profoundly anti-Polish, they were also blamed for "blocking" the aspirations of Polish society. Their assimilation was swiftly ruled out. In fact, as early as 1902, Dmowski had concluded that they had to be eliminated.[22]

Violent anti-Semitic outbursts in academia were not accidental. As Irina Livezeanu proposed in her study of cultural politics in interwar Romania, another country that experienced a rise in student anti-Semitism, the nationalists "were concerned not only with the ethnic balance of the universities, but with that of society at large," and "since the universities produced the leadership stratum, these were their most immediate targets."[23] In this respect, anti-Semitism in Polish academia constituted part of a regional phenomenon that manifested itself even more strongly in Romania and Hungary.

The activities of the OWP did not prevent the Endeks' defeat in the March 1928 parliamentary elections, however: the National Democrats won only 8.4 percent of the vote, despite Dmowski's efforts to mobilize Catholics to the party's cause.[24] In a 1927 pamphlet titled *Church, Nation, and State,* Dmowski had set about constructing a nationalist-Catholic synthesis. "Catholicism is not an appendix to Polishness . . . but to a large extent constitutes its essence," he claimed. "Any attempt aiming at separating Catholicism from Polishness and the nation from the Church and religion amounts to the destruction of the Polish nation."[25] Essentially, Dmowski sought to discredit Sanacja's followers as agents of a secular assault on the link between Polishness and Catholicism. In 1928, Dmowski's party adopted a new name, the National Party (Stronnictwo Narodowe, SN), to indicate its all-Polish, universal character, in terms of both program and constituency.

Dmowski's attempt to reconcile nationalism with Catholicism had a huge impact on the younger generation of the Polish nationalist Right, which rapidly adopted militant Catholicism. Notwithstanding the domestic cultural war against Sanacja, the initiative also reflected the broader European phenomena of new religious nationalism and Catholic revival in the first two decades of the twentieth century. Whereas World War I had weakened the nineteenth-century liberalism of Europe's nation-states and brought about more political activism, the Bolshevik Revolution and other postwar left-wing rebellions raised the specter of the atheist anti-Christ, communism. The social teaching of the papacy, articulated in Leo XIII's *Rerum novarum* of 1891 and reiterated by Pius XI in the 1920s and 1930s, expressed opposition to the free-market capitalist economy for its promotion of selfishness and materialism, but also to socialism and communism for their atheism and subversion of family life. Catholic political action received a great boost from the election of Pius XI in 1922.[26] Older nationalists like Dmowski, often coming from the nineteenth-century secular school, had to acknowledge that political Catholic militancy had become a powerful political tool. The fate of Charles Maurras, the leader of the Action Française and an agnostic, demonstrated how much a papal intervention could hurt even nationalist, anti-Semitic, and nonliberal politicians. In 1926, Pius XI did not hesitate to put some of Maurras's writings on the Vatican's index of forbidden books and to condemn his movement.

Nationalist-Christian consensus manifested itself across the political map of Europe in the 1920s and early 1930s. In Admiral Miklós Horthy's Hungary, traumatized by military defeat, the humiliation of Trianon, and Béla Kun's revolution, religious nationalism became the battle cry of the day, as both conservative nationalists and members of the new protofascist Right declared themselves Christians and crusaded for the elimination of anti-Christian forces by casting their counterrevolution as a struggle for national and religious revival.[27] In Romania, a new extremist nationalist movement, the Iron Guard, based its ideology on religious mysticism. In Spain and Portugal, young Catholic militants distanced themselves from older Catholic leaders and soon drifted toward the authoritarian and fascist Right. In Austria, Engelbert Dollfuss of the Christian Social Party established an authoritarian state that blended corporatism, elements of Italian Fascism, and the social teachings of the papacy. In Croatia and Slovakia, political Catholicism rallied to the nationalist cause, while in Belgium, young Catholic students and intellectuals led by Léon Degrelle set up the Christus Rex movement, which eventually embraced Fascism and Nazism.

In Fascist Italy, Benito Mussolini reached an understanding with the papacy when he signed the Lateran Pacts in 1929. To be sure, the Church fared badly under some fascist religious policies, particularly the banning of Catholic youth organizations in 1931, but it clearly understood that a compromise benefited both sides. The Vatican finally recognized the territorial settlement of Risorgimento, which it had denied to all previous governments of united Italy. After all, Mussolini was hailed as the gravedigger of atheist socialism. Pius XI described the Italian dictator as the "man whom providence has sent us." Later, the pontiff even talked of "Catholic totalitarianism" and applauded Fascism for representing "order, authority and discipline; none of them contrary to Catholic ways of thinking."[28]

In Poland, Dmowski's young adepts followed their leader in advocating nationalist authoritarianism, which the sovereign elite or a "governing party" would implement, with or without social consent, organizing the nation along hierarchical lines.[29] They also believed that a nation was the community of past, present, and future generations.[30] By attacking the notion of citizen political sovereignty and endorsing the idea of elitist dictatorship, the young nationalists were drawing on Dmowski's teachings as well as on Italian Fascist thought, which combined organic nationalism, radical statism, and paramilitarism. This militarization also reflected the increasing authoritarianism of the Sanacja government.

In September 1930, the government crushed the center-left opposition alliance known as Centrolew, detained its leaders in the military fortress at Brest, and dissolved parliament. In the November elections, Sanacja easily defeated its truncated opponents. Having destroyed Centrolew, the regime then concentrated its attack on the nationalist Right, the strongest remaining opposition force. This historical context is key to understanding the beginning of Bolesław Piasecki's political career.

Political Baptism, 1915–32

Bolesław Piasecki was born on February 18, 1915, in Łódź.[31] He was the first child of Ludomir Piasecki and Pelagia Kotnowska. Both parents belonged to impoverished Polish noble families from the Russian partition. In 1917, the family moved to Warsaw, where, shortly after World War I, Ludomir entered state service as an employee of the Ministry of Justice. He gradually rose to the rank of administrator of prison farms and forests. Piasecki's younger brother, Zdzisław, was born on February 11, 1922.

The Piaseckis enjoyed a standard of living that enabled them to send Bolesław to the prestigious Zamoyski private high school for boys. Raised in a national-Catholic atmosphere at home, the young man entered a school where sympathy for Endecja prevailed.[32] In the fall of 1929, he joined the National High School Organization (Narodowa Organizacja Gimnazjalna), an illegal association set up by the National Democrats to gain a foothold among students.

During the last two years of his high school education, Piasecki led the student government and regularly contributed to the school newspaper, writing on patriotic anniversaries as well as philosophical subjects.[33] These early publications reveal traces of his strong anti-individualism, which probably came from readings of Plato and the nineteenth-century Polish philosophers Józef Maria Hoene-Wroński and August Cieszkowski, whose views combined millenarian Christianity, romanticism, and nationalism. Piasecki's interest in philosophy was aroused by his uncle, Rev. Franciszek Bolesław Kotnowski.[34]

Piasecki graduated from high school in May 1931 and in the autumn of the same year entered the Department of Legal Studies at Warsaw University. He immediately joined the academic section of the OWP, possibly the most active student section of the movement in Poland.[35] As elsewhere in central and eastern Europe, law was the largest and the most popular department in Polish universities. In a country where education emphasized humanistic training and university graduates more often sought jobs in the civil service than in the professions, law could secure prestigious and relatively well-paid bureaucratic employment. The department offered courses in political theory, philosophy, and history, and it had been a hotbed of nationalist militancy since the 1920s. The provisions of the 1920 university bill that banned political organizations from academia were never truly observed.[36] In his memoirs, Wojciech Wasiutyński explained that after the harsh discipline of high school, the university's flexible and undemanding schedule left students with little work and too much free time, making politics a natural choice for many.[37]

Piasecki was a mediocre student whose grades grew worse every year.[38] At the same time, his status in the OWP progressed from commander of a basic cell to chief of the academic section in 1933. He also joined the editorial board of *Akademik polski*. In the course of his numerous activities, Piasecki met the people who later would be associated with his name and movement: Marian and Adolf Reutt, Olgierd Szpakowski, Włodzimierz Sznarbachowski, and Wojciech Wasiutyński, whose father, Bohdan, was a prominent Endek politician and friend of Dmowski. Marian Reutt and Piasecki formed the backbone of the youngest and most aggressive generation of prewar Poland's far Right. Raised in families of noble origins in which a nationalist upbringing was combined with a strong Catholicism, they came of age in independent Poland. It was precisely their militant Catholicism that separated them from older nationalist leaders. Membership in the OWP quickly turned them into protofascist radicals.

During their formative years, the men of Piasecki's entourage lived and studied in Warsaw, a city of more than a million inhabitants.[39] The bustling capital of a young state, Warsaw was the center of Polish politics. It was also the home of more than 350,000 Jews, who constituted 30 percent of the city's population. Anti-Semitism was particularly prevalent among the ethnic Polish middle class. Piasecki and his comrades witnessed xenophobia in their day-to-day lives, absorbed the anticommunism of the political establishment, experienced the Great Depression, and took part in a religious revival that was sweeping the country. Steeped in these influences, they came out as anti-Semitic, antileftist, antiliberal, and ultra-Catholic.

Marian Reutt's erudition and intellectual curiosity were exceptional, and his influence on Piasecki's circle is undisputable, particularly in the phrasing of various programmatic statements. Reutt was an admirer of Russian culture and was the first Polish translator of Nikolai Berdyaev's *The New Middle Ages* and *The Origin of Russian Communism* as well as Jacques Maritain's *Science and Wisdom*.[40] He witnessed the Bolshevik Revolution in Russia and, despite his rightist political views, read Lenin. According to Wasiutyński, Reutt was fascinated by Soviet communism.[41] Reutt fully shared Berdyaev's view of communism as the product of Russian nihilism and the embodiment of political religion, which strived to build God's kingdom on Earth both without and in opposition to God and truth.[42] Like Berdyaev, he also believed that all historic development was the work of God, who acted through man. God determined the progress of history, in which the coming of Christ signaled both the end and the beginning. On one level, history constituted the mystical reunion of God and man; on another, history was a myth, a tale or legend preserved in the memory of nation, as in the myths of the Reformation, the French Revolution, and the twentieth-century vision cherished by Hitler.[43] Berdyaev's critique of Marxism as a political atheistic religion; of modern German, French, and Italian nationalisms as pagan; and of democracy as detrimental to national community and identity probably sat well with the young Polish nationalist. But Berdyaev did not preach nationalism or theocracy as a panacea for the world's cultural crisis. Instead, he called for the establishment of a Christian state and Christian society that, if realized, would obliterate traditional state models, including that of the nation-state. We do not know whether Reutt noticed this conflict later, in the latter half of the 1930s, when he parted ways with Piasecki. The question is worth considering, however, given that both Berdyaev and Maritain eventually became advocates of Christian existentialism and universalism, moving away from the Right and toward the positions of critics of totalitarian solutions.

In September 1932, Piasecki became the secretary of the editorial board of *Akademik polski* with the support of Jan Mosdorf.[44] His youth—Piasecki was not even eighteen years old—was no obstacle. Tall and slender, blond-haired and blue-eyed, and always immaculately dressed, Piasecki had a likable appearance. Women and men adored him. Piasecki impressed people with his self-assurance and carefully chosen phrases, though he was a poor orator.[45] He certainly had personal charisma.

In November 1932, Piasecki contributed to the pamphlet *Guidelines on the Issues of Jews, Slavic Minorities, German Policy, and the Principles of Economic Policy* published by the academic section of the OWP. The section on the Jews is the longest, and its proposals are reminiscent of various anti-Jewish laws contemplated and implemented by the radical Right throughout Europe. As an alien, mafialike race, the Jews were to be excluded from any form of assimilation. They were to lose their citizenship rights in exchange for resident (*przynależny*) status. The principle of *numerus nullus* would end Jewish enrollment in public schools and universities as well as participation in the liberal professions, government, and military. Confined to ghettos and selected regions, they would have no right to own property outside these enclaves. A prohibition on mixed marriages would eliminate the problem of religious conversion. Jewish-owned estates were to be confiscated without compensation and redistributed in a program of land reform, while Jewish employment in industry would diminish to reflect their proportion in the country's population.[46]

Slavic minorities, specifically Ukrainians and Belorussians, did not constitute separate nations, but "tribal groups of the Polish nation": as such, they would be subjected to forced assimilation. With the help of the Roman Catholic Church, the culturally superior Poles would civilize and absorb the eastern Slavs.[47] The pamphlet's coverage of the German question was restricted to a brief historical overview and the presentation of Polish territorial claims. Upper Silesia, together with the northern parts of Lower Silesia, as well as Gdańsk, East Prussia, and Pomerania, were to be Poland's first territorial acquisitions, with further annexations in the future. The authors did not specify how these border shifts would take place, offering only the estimate that Polish expansion westward would take place in the span of one generation.[48]

The chapter on economics praised national and moral solidarity against class divisions and rejected the principles of liberal capitalism. Poland, in this vision, had to develop economic self-sufficiency and free itself from foreign capital. A shift toward medium and small enterprises would facilitate the growth of the middle class. The pamphlet's most radical economic proposal was the diffusion of private ownership under the supervision of the state. The state also would adopt a more aggressive policy against big capital and its foreign shareholders. Property ownership would cease to be a class privilege. That the program's authors prioritized nationalist ethics over economic interest is particularly apparent in its proposal that the mechanization of production would be limited in order to fight unemployment.[49]

The novelty of the socioeconomic and political solutions proposed by the *Guidelines* was twofold. First, the scope of its proposed anti-Jewish measures sealed the fate of Jewish converts to Catholicism: since they were not ethnic Poles, but Jewish Catholics, their road to assimilation and citizenship was effectively closed. The pamphlet's lack of references to emigration was not accidental. In the face of such universal discrimination, Jews were expected simply to depart. Secondly, the *Guidelines'* anticapitalist economic program stood in opposition to the Endek old guard's reluctance to abandon laissez-faire. It conveyed what Michael Mann calls a "statist third way between capitalism and socialism," seeking accelerated development through an integrated dictatorship in which economy and ideology were completely interwoven.[50]

Working on the *Guidelines* was a crucial experience in Piasecki's political training. In addition, his camaraderie with the other editors soon developed into a political collective under his command. Within three years, *Akademik polski*'s editorial team made up the leadership of the National Radical Movement.

The Collapse of the OWP and the Road to the ONR, 1932–34

In 1932, the government made clear that it would not tolerate the OWP, which by then claimed 120,000 members.[51] In the autumn of that year, local authorities banned the organization in the western provinces of Poznań and Pomerania and in the Kielce region. The camp did not take any action until January 1933, when it used the controversy over a new university law to show its strength.

The boycott of higher tuition fees no doubt reflected genuine and legitimate concerns on the part of students badly hit by the Great Depression in Poland. Initially, the action united nearly all student societies, from the procommunist Life (Życie) to the various pro-Sanacja and nationalist groups. Still, no broad alliance ever materialized because of the separatist stance taken by the nationalists, who quickly dominated the boycott and transformed it into a chauvinistic carnival in November 1932, when a Polish student lost his life in a brawl with Jewish apprentices in Lwów.[52] Nationalist students vandalized Jewish shops, clashed with progovernment groups, and stormed police lines in Lwów, Warsaw, and Poznań.[53]

The mobilizing effect of the student action seemed a boon for the OWP. By preserving the autonomy of academia from state control, the young militants also could shield the endangered organization from the government. Contrary to these expectations, however, the collapse of order at the universities provided the Sanacja regime with an opportunity to destroy the student section of the camp through a reform of university governance.

In many respects, the proposed university reform aimed at unifying and modernizing the academic system, which was proving itself unable to cope with the effects of the Great Depression. The project was hardly groundbreaking: university self-rule was to be modified but not taken away. The political elements of the bill consisted mostly of placing student associations under the control of a rector, whose appointment would require government approval, and giving the state control over 20 percent of all grants and stipends. Yet these innovations, as well as fears that the state-controlled portion of stipends would likely go to Sanacja supporters, turned many students and academics against the project.[54]

On February 21, 1933, the Sejm, or lower house of the Polish parliament, accepted the reform bill and forwarded it to the Senate. The appeals of university rectors to refrain from drastic measures had no effect on nationalist students. A student strike began in Lwów on February 23 and soon spread to Kraków, Warsaw, Wilno, and Poznań, leading to street demonstrations, scuffles with the police, and anti-Jewish brawls. In parallel to the student strike, OWP militants instigated pogroms against Jews in parts of the Polish countryside.[55] The strike collapsed on March 13. Two days later, parliament accepted the new university law. On March 28, the government dissolved the OWP throughout the country.

The controversy gave momentum to Piasecki's political writings, but he quickly went beyond the university crisis and began laying out his own nationalist-Catholic doctrine. In one of his texts, he openly declared that nationalists drew their inspiration from Catholicism. Just as in the Middle Ages, when Catholics had launched wars and crusades against the enemies of Christianity, now religion would mobilize the Poles to cleanse the country of alien and immoral elements.[56] Piasecki reached the same conclusion that other east and central European fascists and protofascists were advancing in countries like Hungary, Romania, and Austria: religion could and did reinforce organic nationalism.[57]

Piasecki refuted the claims of critics who believed that the two systems were incompatible—Catholicism with its notions of charity and universalism, and nationalism with its tenets of ethnocentrism, exclusion, and violence. His Catholicism was a religion of action and expansion, militant and unforgiving of its enemies, almost militaristic. In this model, only the nationalist was capable of passing judgment on believers. If nationalism and religion were one, those who rejected the fusion were stripped of their identity, be they professing Catholics or committed political nationalists. For Piasecki, the goal was to create a new Pole.[58] He contrasted the principle of *similarity* between men with the notion of their *sameness*. Democratic equality, he argued, operated on the premise of sameness, which led to a utopian confusion wherein illiterates had the same rights as intellectuals and an honest man's vote counted as much as that of a con artist. In Piasecki's view, only a political system based on hierarchy could secure a flow of competent individuals into the nation's ruling elite.[59]

For Endecja, the death of the OWP was a catastrophe. For Piasecki and like-minded young radicals, it was a point of departure. Disillusioned with the passive attitude of the National Party and the rapidity with which the camp had collapsed, the group around *Akademik polski* decided to seek new forms of political action and to push forward their agenda. Three months after the collapse of the OWP, Piasecki published in the *Akademik polski* his political manifesto, "The Principles of National Political Order."

These principles invoked a vision of a nationalist state based on ethnicity, hierarchy, and fascist organization. Slavic minorities were to be forcibly Polonized, while Jews and Germans would lose their citizenship. All political parties that reflected class or professional divisions were to be abolished, along with the existing electoral system. Only two organizations would be allowed: the Education and Political Organization of the Nation (Organizacja Wychowawczo-Polityczna Narodu), membership in which was to be compulsory for all Poles between the ages of ten and twenty-one, and the Political Organization of the Nation (Organizacja Polityczna Narodu, OPN), the movement of power. Elections were to be replaced by consultations between organization members and the government, eliminating the possibility of conflict between the state and society. The legislative and executive branches of government would become one in the same. A high council would elect the head of the OPN for a five-year term, and he in turn would appoint members of the government. In the case of a major disagreement within the high council, the government would be obliged to stage a popular referendum among OPN members. Votes would not bear equal weight, however, since their value would depend on the voter's position in the organization's hierarchy.[60]

Piasecki elaborated on the structure of the OPN in a supplementary article published in *Akademik polski* on October 10, 1933, under the title "The Outline of the Political Order of National Poland." It was hardly surprising that Piasecki, who viewed the youth as the nation's life force, began his outline with a description of the youth organization. It was to integrate all children, regardless of class, in a cycle of training that consisted of three stages. From the age of ten to fourteen, children would participate in games and shows that illustrated the history of Poland. In the second stage, adolescents would be subjected to compulsory military and ideological training. The final stage, lasting until the age of twenty-one, would require members to master knowledge of the national program. Only then would the selection of OPN members take place.

The OPN itself was to be divided into four classes of activists. The lowest level would include all Poles who passed through the ranks of the youth organization and did not commit any legal offenses. Advancement to the second level required a ten-year period of proper conduct in the previous group and a high school degree. A university education or outstanding participation on the second level, combined with model behavior, constituted the criteria for advancement to the third category. Members of the highest order would constitute the ruling class. As in the previous groups, education would be one of the requirements, a Ph.D. being deemed appropriate for membership in this class. Advancement on levels one and two was to be monitored and sanctioned by local OPN cells. In the case of the third and fourth orders, advancement decisions would have to be made by special commissions at the county and provincial levels. Committing a crime would result in degradation or expulsion.[61]

Piasecki did not explain the relationship between the OPN and the executive branch. On the one hand, he favored having a small group of leaders in charge of the country. On the other hand, he supported the OPN's superiority and contemplated the existence of strong local government. He failed to explain the mechanisms of the government's operation, and he left equally unspecified the institutional relationship between the church and the state.

Despite its numerous inconsistencies and gaps, "The Principles" incorporated all of the crucial elements that would inform Piasecki's doctrine for years to come. It was a mixture of fascism, nationalist collectivism, radical statism, and corporatism. It sketched out a project that bridged the traditional platform of the Polish nationalist Right with the fascist principles of radical nation-statism, cleansing of enemies from the body of nation, and transcendence of social conflict, the political order, and the economy.[62]

Piasecki presented his views at a meeting of young Endecja activists in Błota Karwieńskie in July 1933. The meeting was dominated, however, by an organizational agenda focusing on the status of the former OWP cells. While Tadeusz Bielecki, Dmowski's man, argued for a merger with the National Party, Piasecki and Mosdorf proposed that the OWP should go underground and steer itself toward direct confrontation with Sanacja. The militants lost this battle.[63] Nonetheless, Bielecki's victory was illusory: by absorbing young rebels into the party, the National Democrats created an opposition faction within its own ranks.

From that point on, secessionist tendencies among the young nationalists rapidly increased. In his memoirs, Wojciech Wasiutyński reported on the condition of the National Party in 1933–34: "At the time of the split in 1934, the National Party had an official 'parliamentary' program that did not address the situation under the conditions of dictatorship. . . . The party did not want a united opposition or any revolutionary action; nor did it contemplate a compromise with Sanacja. The Jewish question was the only binding issue."[64]

The revolt was led by Mosdorf, Piasecki, and Henryk Rossman. In October, the dissidents launched *Sztafeta,* a weekly newspaper in which political essays coexisted with pieces composed in the language of the street. In the fall of 1933, the rebels presented Dmowski with a list of demands that included the profound reform of the National Party as well as the removal of the unpopular Tadeusz Bielecki from the youth branch of the party. Rossman, who instigated this move, remained skeptical about the chance of any compromise, predicting that Dmowski would not yield.[65] Rossman's pessimism turned out to be correct. Dmowski rejected the proposals. According to Bielecki, Dmowski opposed the demands out of an aversion to their socioeconomic radicalism.[66] Wasiutyński, however, seemed unconvinced by this explanation. Was it not Dmowski, after all, who had supported the influx of young radicals into the OWP and thus contributed to the radicalization of the movement? His final rejection of the demands of the rebels, Wasiutyński argued, derived from personal pride and fears of dividing Endecja into too many factions.[67] In March 1934, Dmowski recalled Mosdorf and Rossman from their party posts. From that moment, a split within the party became unavoidable. On April 14, 1934, the rebels declared the creation of the National Radical Camp (Obóz Narodowo-Radykalny, ONR).

The First ONR, 1934–35

The founding declaration of the ONR was signed in the dining hall of Warsaw Technical University.[68] Piasecki was the author of one of the five drafts that served as the basis for the ONR program. It was Jan Mosdorf who edited these texts into the final version.[69]

The declaration consisted of three parts: an introduction, which presented an overview of the situation in Poland; a description of the ONR; and nine points that constituted the program of the organization. It proclaimed the ONR as the only force capable of reforming a declining economy, abolishing the ineffectual political system, and ending moral decay. The organization was unaffected by class divisions, it asserted, and was both ardently Catholic and deeply committed to the struggle against Jewish influence in Poland. It claimed to respect all groups participating in the struggle for independence and emphasized the unbreakable bond between the military ethos and the national spirit. Citizenship rights were to be granted to those inhabitants who consciously identified themselves with Polish culture and civilization. The Ukrainian and Belorussian minorities would enjoy full political rights, whereas Jews would receive resident status. The

ONR insisted on the nationalization of big industry and natural resources and on a land reform program that would liquidate large estates and redistribute arable land into small and medium-sized farms. It sought a national and collective model for the economy, with limitations on private property. The full employment of all Poles was a stated goal. The unemployed would find jobs in cities and towns cleansed of Jews (*odżydzenie*). Based on the principles of self-sacrifice, hierarchy, and unity between citizens and the state, the system would operate through the hierarchy of the Political Organization of the Nation.[70]

As this summary suggests, the ONR's declaration largely stemmed from the OWP's 1932 *Guidelines.* Its fervent critique of traditional parties suggested the camp's divorce from the National Democrats. Conversely, its emphasis on Poland's cleansing and the creation a political platform free from old conflicts and divisions bore some resemblance to the message of Sanacja. The homage paid to all veterans of the independence movement, regardless of their political persuasions, may have been a coded conciliatory message to the ruling camp. The radicals clearly sought to portray themselves as standing above political, social, and cultural divisions.

The emergence of the ONR drew various responses. The National Democrats were less united in their criticism than might have been expected. Bielecki brought the youth sections of the National Party into line. The position taken by Dmowski was more ambiguous: although he declared the ONR an irresponsible initiative that undermined the unity of the nationalist movement, he did not condemn it as harshly as other senior Endeks did.[71] The Endek press also displayed mixed attitudes. While *Kurier warszawski* pointed out that there were no genuine political differences between the secessionists and the National Party, only a generation gap, *Myśl narodowa* treated the ONR far more seriously by declaring it a new political entity with a distinct program.[72]

There were no similar hesitations on the Left. The Polish Socialist Party press organ *Robotnik* declared: "Finally, we have a legal Polish organization of a Hitlerian sort."[73] Far more complex was the response of Sanacja's leading journalist, Wojciech Stpiczyński, who expressed sympathy: "We can join a discussion table with youth that pays homage to the blood shed in the defense of independence and invokes a military spirit."[74] Although it would be wrong to assume that this attitude was shared by Piłsudski and Sanacja moderates who eschewed fascism and anti-Semitism, some supporters of the marshal showed strong nationalist and protofascist inclinations. Bronisław Pieracki, minister of internal affairs, whose authoritarian views earned him the nickname "Bronito" (from the combination of "Bronisław" and "Benito"), looked forward to making accommodations with the nationalist youth. He was among those government officials who admitted that the regime had lost the battle for the nation's youth to the nationalist opposition.[75] Shortly after the creation of the ONR, Pieracki began conferring with Rossman and Mosdorf about the possibility of creating a centralized, proregime youth organization.[76] In the spring of 1934, however, National Radical leaders did not have much to offer.

The ONR lacked strong leadership and internal discipline. Warsaw was the only location where the ONR possessed any organizational network. Although Mosdorf remained the titular ONR leader, the real power lay in the hands of Rossman, who chaired the group's conspiratorial structures. This organizational chaos fostered internal divisions. The main line of conflict ran between Rossman's and Piasecki's groups.[77] Mosdorf arguably did his best to ease these tensions.

The ONR numbered between two and five thousand members. The bulk of the membership came from Warsaw, where the National Radicals claimed nearly two thousand adherents, mostly students and proletarian youth.[78] Recruitment, training, and mass demonstrations were the domain of Piasecki. He was especially keen on recruiting students, as well as young workers and apprentices, and apparently met with some success. These recruits formed Piasecki's storm troopers, known under the rather misleading name of Various Universities (Uczelnie Różne). Under the command of Zygmunt Dziarmaga, they carried out acts of physical violence and intimidation.[79] The group's first rally took place on May 3, 1934, on the national holiday commemorating the Polish constitution of 1791. Twenty-five hundred ONR men marched in military fashion through the streets of Warsaw to be received by Piasecki in front of Saint Alexander's Church in the heart of the capital.[80] The ONR's actions did not go unopposed: the Warsaw Socialist Party openly urged its members to use physical violence against the National Radicals.[81] Shots were fired when the socialist squads besieged the editorial office of *Sztafeta*.[82] Liberal segments of Sanacja began pressuring the government to ban the ONR. The prospect of dissolution persuaded

Mosdorf and other leaders to appeal to their followers for calm and abstention from any street gatherings.[83] Nevertheless, Włodzimierz Sznarbachowski, one of Piasecki's deputies, defended armed confrontation: "Aiming our guns at Sanacja alone and signing nonaggression agreements with its opponents would be suicidal. Such a move would deprive us of our integrity and [would discourage] those members for whom activism constitutes the essence of our existence."[84]

Indeed, violence appealed to some youth, whose political views were far from being crystallized. Such was the case for Zygmunt Przetakiewicz, who greatly admired discipline, military choreography, and violence. He joined the ONR after witnessing the May 3 parade. He recalled many years later: "From the direction of the Botanical Garden, the columns of young people marched through Ujazdowskie Avenue. They were preceded by an honor guard, dressed in light-colored shirts and carrying two Chrobry swords.[85] They wore green bands with the symbol of the ONR, a hand holding a sword. They proudly marched in military fashion. I stood dazed."[86]

As the appeal of the ONR grew, the government watched it with a growing concern. On June 13, the authorities shut down the printing press of *Sztafeta*. The following day, Mosdorf called the office of Pieracki to plead for a lifting of the ban, but Pieracki was out. His secretary advised Mosdorf to contact the minister on Monday, June 18. Mosdorf replied: "It will be too late."[87] His words proved ominous—on June 15, Pieracki was shot dead as he was leaving a club for government officials.

Pieracki's assassin came from the ranks of the Ukrainian nationalists. Some government officials connected the murder with Mosdorf's phone call, however, and with a confiscated article by Sznarbachowski that lamented the lack of a tradition of political crime in the history of Poland.[88] Sanacja politicians who disapproved of Pieracki's flirtation with the nationalist opposition used the tragedy to crack down on the infant National Radicals. It is worth noting, however, that in 1934 the regime showed some interest in reconciling with its democratic opponents. Colonel Walery Sławek, for example, conducted secret talks with the Peasant Party. The government also released some Centrolew politicians from the Brest fortress. Hence, the attack on the ONR might have been an act of goodwill toward the center and the Left. Hours after the assassination, the police arrested some six hundred National Radicals, including Piasecki. Mosdorf escaped and went into hiding in eastern Poland.[89] On July 10, the government banned the ONR on charges of posing a threat to public security, inciting racial hatred, and inspiring antistate unrest.[90]

One month earlier, President Ignacy Mościcki had signed a special decree setting up detention camps for subversive individuals. The decree provided that the detainees could be held for up to three months without trial at the request of a district attorney. The government had the right to extend the detention to six months. The camp was opened in the small town of Bereza Kartuska in the eastern province of Polesie. On the night of July 6, Piasecki, nine other ONR activists, and one communist boarded the train for Bereza Kartuska.[91]

In the summer of 1934, the ONR's short period of legality came to an end. As the political writer Stanisław Cat-Mackiewicz put it, "The ONR had a good debut, because within three months after its creation it went to Bereza; the fire of repression forged its fighting spirit."[92] Though its leaders were in prison, the ONR would continue to be a factor on the political map of Poland. The nationalist Right would never regain its unity.

The Road to the RNR, 1934–35

ON THE MORNING OF JULY 7, 1934, the ONR prisoners marched into the camp at Bereza Kartuska in an atmosphere of romantic adventure, singing nationalist songs. They saw themselves as another generation of revolutionaries for whom incarceration in the dungeons of Castello Sant'Angelo, Kufstein, Petropavlovsk, or Warsaw's Cytadela was a necessary step in the struggle for power.[1] Bereza, however, was not a nineteenth-century prison but a twentieth-century detention camp, where prisoners were subjected to harsh discipline, slave labor, and other forms of physical punishment.

Days in the camp started at 4:00 a.m. with the morning roll call. With the exception of Sundays, the prisoners worked for eight to ten hours a day at a road construction site. Numbered, uniformed, and divided into large units, they were housed in overcrowded cells. Their daily diet consisted of black bread, coffee, buckwheat, and peas. Solitary confinement and corporal punishment were the penalties for insubordination. At the time of Piasecki's internment in Bereza, the camp housed two hundred prisoners: National Radicals, communists, Ukrainian nationalists, Belorussian left-wing activists, and a few Endeks. The nationalists enjoyed far better treatment than the other inmates, who were often subjected to beatings.[2]

Piasecki devoted his free time to reading. The camp library, though minuscule, included the collected works of Piłsudski. The marshal's critique of parliamentary rule, his early conspiratorial texts from the 1905 revolution, and above all his statism made an impression on Piasecki, convincing him of the regime's strength. He understood that the overthrow of Sanacja required new tactics, a view no doubt reinforced by the tough reality of life in Bereza. In its use of prison regimentation and violence, the system was both efficient and utterly modern. According to Sznarbachowski, Piasecki turned his accumulated reflections on Sanacja into a twelve-year plan for political takeover. By infiltrating various political, social, and cultural institutions, he hoped to conquer Sanacja from within. He envisioned a limited alliance with the regime, which, as Piłsudski grew older and sicker, was already beginning to lose its unity. He confided, allegedly, to Sznarbachowski that the differences between Piłsudski's camp and the young radicals were not substantial and that nationalism could bring the two camps together: "We have to persuade the Legionnaires that by complementing Piłsudski's thought with Dmowski's program they will be able to unite the nation."[3]

Piasecki was released from the camp in September 1934. At this point, little remained of the ONR. Some National Radicals had joined the youth sections of the National Party; others awaited the return of the interned leaders. Soon, Rossman and Piasecki entered into a rivalry over what was left of the organization. Unlike Piasecki, who wanted to create a highly centralized organization held together by a leader, Rossman and his followers favored a collective leadership and conspiratorial structures under the cover of a legal organization.[4] These differences and, above all, their personal disagreements proved impossible to reconcile, and the ONR soon split into two branches: Rossman's ONR ABC (named after its newspaper, *ABC*), and Piasecki's group, which later adopted the name of the National Radical Movement (Ruch Narodowo-Radykalny, RNR). The public often referred to Piasecki's organization simply as "Falanga" after the press organ it launched in 1936, but contrary to the opinion of some Western scholars this was never an official name, nor was it adopted in tribute to the Spanish Falange.[5]

Piasecki consolidated his group by stepping up propaganda and recruiting new followers. Among the most active of these was Zygmunt Przetakiewicz, in whom Piasecki acquired a lifelong collaborator and friend. "A man of a direct action" rather than a strategist, Przetakiewicz organized shock troops and became Piasecki's security expert.[6] Relieved from organizational work, Piasecki could now focus on elaborating a political program. He undertook this task in his first book, *The Spirit of New Times and the Youth Movement* (Duch czasów nowych a Ruch Młodych), published in early 1935.

The Ideological Crystallization

Convoluted and repetitious, *The Spirit of New Times and the Youth Movement* is nonetheless Piasecki's magnum opus, the foundation of his ideology. In Piasecki's view, the epoch was witnessing a clash between traditional and new forces, old and new generations. This conflict also signaled the advent of a new political era in the history of national communities. He proposed that only a clear break with the past could guarantee the development of the modern nation. The gradualist approach had outlived its usefulness, as had parliamentary order, which contaminated the ideals of freedom and equality with moral relativism; party politics, meanwhile, destroyed the spirit of brotherhood by manipulating voters. The ensuing ideological chaos was prompting democratic governments to experiment with new authoritarian methods, creating hybrids, or "democratic dictatorships," exemplified by state interventionism.[7]

There was nothing new about Piasecki's criticism of democracy: this was the premise of his earlier political writings, and not a correct one, considering that authoritarians rarely rise to power in functioning democratic environments. There was innovation, however, in his proposal to redesign nationalist politics. He insisted that young nationalists could achieve unification by convincing the population that work for the nation was a prerequisite for individual happiness and social harmony.[8]

Such a design would require the nationalists to adapt to three dominant trends of the era: the pursuit of absolute values (*pęd do wartości bezwzględnych*), the pursuit of hierarchy (*pęd do hierarchii*), and the pursuit of political participation (*pęd do udziału we władzy publicznej*). The first trend stemmed from an opposition to moral relativism; in its stead, Piasecki favored hierarchy, a principle, he argued, that constituted the only valid test for the evaluation of men and their acts. According to Piasecki, hierarchy could fulfill individuals' pursuit of power by allowing them to occupy the position best suited to their abilities. All citizens would be required to act politically, he claimed, because mandatory political participation fostered the individual's sense of responsibility for the well-being of nation.[9]

In Piasecki's view, three nations in Europe had already adapted to these new trends: Italy, Germany, and the Soviet Union. Piasecki saw the Italian Fascists as pioneers of the new nationalism. Not only had they succeeded in recruiting the entire population to participate in the nationalist project, but they also had demonstrated the pursuit of absolute values. By distributing privileges and obligations equally, the Italian corporatist system provided each citizen with a share of power. Even Mussolini, however, came under Piasecki's criticism for preserving the institutions of monarchy and parliament.

Looking at Germany, Piasecki concluded that Hitler's movement had achieved a nationalist revolution through mass mobilization, anti-Semitism, the eradication of traditional separatist tendencies, and the exaltation of self-sacrifice. But he rejected Nazi secularism as too much grounded in the religious disunity of the German nation and the crisis of the Protestant ethic. In Piasecki's view, the Nazis simply denied that the ultimate goal of mankind did not belong to this world.[10]

Piasecki's inclusion of Soviet Russia among the three most advanced nations deserves sustained attention. He was repelled by communism but attracted by the Soviets' dynamism and their grand vision of a modern state. He acknowledged that the Bolsheviks had launched their revolution as an internationalist project but insisted that Stalin's victory over the internationalists Trotsky and Zinoviev constituted a nationalist revival. The Soviets had proved themselves extremely adaptable to all three dominant currents of the new era by building a hegemonic party, reeducating the population, and achieving mass political mobilization. Piasecki's innovation was to see the Soviet Union not as a Jewish masquerade or an evil empire but as a profoundly modern and pragmatic regime. In this, he differed from the main body of Polish nationalists.[11]

In Piasecki's view, the analogy between Poland and these three countries was strained but not implausible because the National Radicals possessed three great assets that other political players in Poland lacked: an understanding of the Polish character, a modern program, and above all the will to implement it. Unlike their Italian, German, and Russian counterparts, the young Polish nationalists also realized the necessity of combining metaphysics with rationality and religion with secular ideas, particularly statism. Piasecki remarked: "The good of the nation does not constitute the final criterion for what is good and what is bad, because the good of the nation is not the absolute. God is the absolute and the highest end of man. Thus [striving to achieve] the good of the nation is only the means for reaching this absolute goal."[12] This axiomatic construct would remain one of the cornerstones of Piasecki's political doctrine for his entire life.

Piasecki explained that there were two major prerequisites for launching a nationalist revolution: a consistent educational policy and the existence of a strong nation-state. He insisted that because all nations showed distinct traits, no single state could accommodate several nationalities. National minorities simply had no place in Poland.[13]

He concluded with the question of Poland's destiny. Piasecki asserted that the will to influence the fates of other nations was deeply embedded in the Polish psyche. At the moment, Europe was torn by a conflict between its western and eastern halves that in the long run could lead to the destruction of its civilization. Because of its geographical location and history, Poland had the cultural and military capacity to mediate among its neighbors and introduce them to Western values. From this capacity there arose, in turn, an obligation to lead a spiritual revival that would ultimately produce the victory of a new Christian nationalism and the redemption of Europe.[14] Here Piasecki went beyond the National Democrats' earlier *Lebensraum* argument for dominating the backward nationalities of Ukrainians and Belorussians.[15] In his resort to traditional Polish messianism, however, he dropped the notion of suffering in favor of cultural and military expansion.

Piasecki's political manifesto was a mishmash of Dmowski's Endek ideas, Italian Fascism, militant Catholicism, and traditional Polish messianism. It was also representative of a larger political and cultural movement within European thought, namely, a search by young Christian-oriented ethnonationalists for a fourth path alongside liberalism, communism, and secular fascism. To be sure, Piasecki's formulation of the Political Organization of the Nation (OPN) as an all-embracing national front drew on the pseudototalitarian solutions advanced by like-minded contemporaries elsewhere in Europe. The most interesting of its aspects, however, was the entanglement of protofascist nationalism and religion, which bore some resemblance to the doctrines of Ferenc Szálasi of the Hungarian Arrow Cross; Corneliu Zelea Condreanu, the leader of the Legion of the Archangel Michael in Romania; and Léon Degrelle of the Rexist movement in Belgium, who wavered between a Christian and an ethnic basis for his nationalism. Not only did the leader of the Arrow Cross view Christianity, Marxism, and nationalism as the three great ideologies of the twentieth century—a belief Piasecki shared—but he also considered Hungarians to be predestined to bridge East and West and to play a dominant role in central Europe.[16] Yet Szálasi's concept of Christianity as the unifying national religion also admitted to confessional divisions among Magyar Catholics, Calvinists, Lutherans, Greek

Catholics, and others. He aimed to transcend these differences, something Piasecki refused to contemplate. Although a practicing Catholic, Szálasi hoped to reduce churches to mere nationalist instruments, a position that made their autonomous status extremely problematic. That he also went to absurd lengths to prove Christ's non-Jewish ancestry—something Piasecki never bothered to deal with—suggests that the Hungarian partly mimicked the Nazis' stance on religion, whereas the Pole did not.[17]

Far more striking is the comparison to Codreanu of the Iron Guard, who also merged nationalism and religion into a single phenomenon, linked religious salvation to participation in nationalist politics, and preached millenarian struggle for the redemption of the nation and of mankind. In addition to being the educators of the nation, the legionaries were "recipients of the saving force," blending transcendental nationalism and the sacred, fighting the battle of those who strive for the salvation of humankind against the agents of degeneration and decadence, and providing spiritual training for the people.[18] Unlike Piasecki, Codreanu was a religious mystic, paying as much attention to the redemption of the nation as to the expiation of sins and, above all, to the legionaries' self-sacrifice. If the Iron Guard proclaimed that it would fulfill the Romanian people's destiny by promoting virtue and salvation, Piasecki opted for an opposite hierarchy of goals: work for the nation would eventually secure personal salvation. Unlike his Polish contemporary, Codreanu also combined his futurist religion-based utopia with a "regressive" glorification of peasant tradition. Last but not least, he refrained from territorial expansionist schemes.

At first glance, the relevance of Degrelle to Piasecki's case may seem rather marginal.[19] Their similarities included militant Catholicism, youthful dynamism, and leadership in protofascist movements. Degrelle, however, started as a dissident within the Catholic Party, whereas Piasecki was a nationalist who drew more heavily on Catholic inspiration than did his older mentors. Operating in democratic Belgium, the Rexists capitalized on a protest vote and won a respectable 11 percent in the 1936 general election. Such electoral gains were unthinkable in authoritarian Poland. Degrelle's subsequent political defeats, coupled with the outbreak of World War II and Nazi occupation, led him to espouse collaboration and the German cause. Piasecki's marginalization did not overturn his nationalist loyalties, and he remained a resister during World War II.

Yet it is precisely these differences that make this comparison worthwhile, as they reveal a quintessential contrast between the democratic West and authoritarian East, between a liberal, advanced society and a newly born nation-state at Europe's periphery. By the mid-1930s, the fragmentation of political Catholicism in western, and particularly French-speaking, Europe had produced conflict among Catholic intellectuals previously united by their antiliberal and antimaterialist approaches and often influenced by the traditional Right of the Maurrassian or Carlist type. Degrelle became a fascist, whereas Jacques Maritain, initially close to Action Française, endorsed liberal Catholicism. For others, like Emmanuel Mounier, the experience of World War II would prompt a decisive move to the Left.[20] By contrast, the world of Polish Catholic intellectuals, tiny and politically insignificant, exercised little influence on those political groups that, like Endecja or the National Radicals, claimed to act on behalf of Roman Catholics or even to work for the fulfillment of God's will. In Piasecki's circle, only Marian Reutt came close to an actual dialogue with contemporary Catholic or Christian thought. Numerous passages in *The Spirit of New Times* bear a striking resemblance to Reutt's translations of Nikolai Berdyaev, suggesting an influence on Piasecki's rhetoric but not necessarily on the content of the book.

Piasecki's book was yet another example of younger European nationalists emancipating themselves from their patrons. Just as Degrelle's Rexists moved away from the Catholic Party, so Codreanu broke away from A. I. Cuza; Szálasi distanced himself from both Horthy's national conservatives and Gyula Gömbös's protofascist statism; and Piasecki parted ways with Dmowski by merging aggressive ethnonationalism with fascist constructs and religious revival.

The Movement

Piasecki's National Radicals held a founding meeting at the estate of Kąty in June 1935, just weeks after the death of Piłsudski on May 12. For Piasecki and his followers, this was the beginning of the new era. *Sztafeta* marked the occasion with the comment: "Together with Piłsudski departs the Poland of old conflicts, the Poland of pre- and wartime options, the Poland of the National Democrats, the PPS [the Polish Socialist Party], and Sanacja. It is the dawn of social justice and human dignity, the dawn of Poland without Jews and foreign capitalist parasites, the dawn of a free and creative man [who will live] in the free and great fatherland."[21]

The spring of 1935 also marked the end of Piasecki's university education. In September, he left for the ensign school of the Twenty-eighth Infantry Division in Dęblin to begin one year of mandatory military service. Later, he transferred to the elite Training Center of Tank Forces in Modlin. During his service, Piasecki wrote several political articles. One of them, "Our Internal Countenance," was even published in the army monthly *Podchorąży.* Very much like his European authoritarian contemporaries, Piasecki proclaimed the armed forces a model institution for all aspects of public life and declared that the young nationalists fully shared with the military an emphasis on hierarchy, discipline, and patriotism and would not hesitate to obey professional soldiers.[22] Notwithstanding Piasecki's conciliatory tone, it is striking that military censors allowed the publication of an article written by a well-known opposition activist. Clearly, some in the military sympathized with his political reflections.[23] It is noteworthy that in their antigovernment propaganda, the National Radicals always spared the Polish army from criticism.

During Piasecki's absence, the RNR was led by a collective.[24] The structure of the movement, however, still reflected Piasecki's emphasis on hierarchy. At the top stood the leader (*kierownik główny*), who presided over the movement by virtue of his moral superiority. The leader was also the chief exponent of the idea of National Radical Poland, which he received through personal revelation. He led the organization in compliance with the Catholic ethos and National Radical ideology.[25]

The Polish historians Jacek Majchrowski and Andrzej Micewski calculate that RNR membership reached five thousand in 1937. Wasiutyński, however, estimated that the movement never claimed more than a thousand sworn members.[26] The second figure is more realistic, and it corresponds with 1938 police reports. The two sectors of Polish society most attracted to Piasecki's organization were students and middle-class youth.[27] In 1936, the movement's militia was renamed the National Combat Organization "Life and Death for the Nation" (Narodowa Organizacja Bojowa "Życie i Śmierć dla Narodu"). During its three-year existence, the section claimed 250 to 300 men, and constituted the most fanatical element of the National Radical Movement.[28]

The RNR was financed primarily by members' monthly dues, which were insufficient to cover even minor expenses. Piasecki also displayed a considerable gift for fund-raising from nationalist-minded businessmen and industrialists, and he accepted help from Fascist Italy, whose Duce always regarded himself as the protector of European fascists.[29] Yet, as historian Jerzy Borejsza points out, despite Italian sympathy for Polish protofascist and fascist groups, between 1926 and 1939 "Rome always supported those forces that held power in Poland."[30] Actual Italian support for Piasecki's organization amounted to token gestures, such as supplies of propaganda materials and occasional, meager donations from Ambassador Pietro Arone di Valentino.[31]   During the early days of its existence, the RNR proved remarkably adept at propaganda. In October 1935, the group launched the periodical *Ruch młodych,* which targeted young nationalist intellectuals, popularized National Radical ideology, and discussed current trends in politics and society in Poland and Europe. The first issue, for instance, analyzed the Seventh Congress of the Comintern in Moscow and the Nuremberg Laws in Germany. Marian Reutt published a review of Nikolai Berdyaev's *New Middle Ages,* while Wojciech Kwasieborski attacked the political minimalism of Dmowski's generation.[32]

The weekly *Falanga,* published since July 1936, was aimed at a broader readership. In 1938, the peak of its popularity, *Falanga* had a circulation of between ten and twenty-five thousand. The newspaper carried primitive anti-Jewish and anticommunist propaganda but also displayed an aggressive anticapitalism, placing itself at the forefront of the struggle for "daily bread and dignified wages for the Polish workers, peasants, and intelligentsia." It did not hesitate to commemorate May Day in spite of the leftist tradition of the holiday.[33]

In September 1936, Piasecki completed his military service. Meanwhile, the impact of the Great Depression had brought about substantial social unrest, anti-Semitic riots, labor protests, and a mass peasant strike. These dramatic events also reflected the leadership crisis within Sanacja that followed the death of Piłsudski. A new constitution ratified in April 1935, just a month before Piłsudski's death, had increased the powers of the presidency while decreasing those of parliament. This authoritarian system had been designed specifically for the old marshal. Post-Piłsudski Poland, however, had not a single leader, but three strongmen: President Ignacy Mościcki, Marshal Edward Rydz-Śmigły, and the foreign minister, Colonel Józef Beck. After the 1935 general elections, which were boycotted by the main opposition parties and were marked by low voter turnout, the regime dissolved the Nonpartisan Bloc for Cooperation with the Government. The military group around Rydz-Śmigły increasingly took over the government. A group of midlevel officers known as "the Colonels" brutally put down the peasant strike and suppressed anti-Semitic riots that Endecja had tried to transform into regional rebellions.[34]

Though they quelled this outburst of anti-Jewish unrest, the leaders of Sanacja soon began to adopt a limited anti-Semitism as part of a populist platform. In the summer of 1936, the government endorsed the slogan of economic struggle against the Jews, lending its support to a boycott of Jewish enterprises. Among the first effects of this approach were various projects restricting ritual slaughter.[35]

Anti-Semitic frenzy did not bypass the Polish universities. Calls for numerus nullus were followed by the implementation of the so-called bench ghetto, a forcible segregation of Jewish students from Christians in lecture halls.[36] In 1936, student protests against new tuition fees evolved into another anti-Jewish campaign. Having established contact with activists of the youth branch of the National Party, Piasecki began preparations to launch an occupation strike at Warsaw University. Both groups decided to make dealing with the Jewish problem the main agenda of the strike. They also demanded tuition-free enrollment of proletarian students. The strike was to begin in late November 1936.[37]

Other Piasecki initiatives in this period included the launching of the Polish Organization of Cultural Action (Polska Organizacja Akcji Kulturalnej), intended to "rescue Polish culture from the Jews, decadence, and communism," to bridge art and life, and to instill a didactic approach into artists.[38] Piasecki also initiated the creation of the Committee of the Young Press (Komitet Prasy Młodych), a loose coalition of Catholic, nationalist, and right-wing Sanacja newspapers united by anticommunism.[39]

In November 1936, Piasecki and several of his comrades were arrested, charged with creating an illegal and subversive organization, and put on trial at the Warsaw municipal court. The case proved difficult for the prosecution, as crucial evidence had vanished from police files. Piasecki's lawyers praised the defendants' patriotism and recommended *The Spirit of New Times* as an example of "healthy political thought."[40] The judges were lenient with the National Radicals—Piasecki and his comrades were found guilty of participation in a clandestine organization, sentenced to six months in jail, and immediately granted pardons.[41]

After the trial, Piasecki threw himself into organizing the blockade of Warsaw University and eventually took full control over the strike. On November 25, using water cannons and tear gas, police forces crushed the student resistance and arrested dozens of participants.[42] The strike, however, demonstrated the RNR's ability to mobilize nationalist students and influence government policies. By 1938, several institutions of higher learning in Poland had adopted the bench ghetto, often with the blessing of the Ministry of Religion and Public Education.[43] As for the RNR, it rapidly matured into a well-known political grouping.

In December 1936, Piasecki presented the most complete elaboration of his economic policies to date. Reprinted in 1937 as *The Principles of National Radical Economic Thought,* the text departed from the 1932 *Guidelines on the Issues of Jews, Slavic Minorities, German Policy, and the Principles of Economic Policy* published by the academic section of the OWP. Piasecki argued that in the future Poland, employers who did not participate in the process of production would lose their property rights. As long as there was unemployment, no one should be allowed to earn more than the actual cost of living. By adopting a planned economy and launching colonial expansion, Poland would acquire economic self-sufficiency.[44] Piasecki demanded the liquidation of big land estates and their redistribution among the peasants. The purge of Jews from industry and trade would facilitate the migration of ethnic Poles from the overpopulated countryside to urban centers, while expropriated Jewish capital would boost investment. Piasecki also advocated the nationalization of big industry and wholesale trade as well as the creation of small shopkeepers' cooperatives. State acquisition of banks would render the annihilation of the capitalist economy complete.[45]

Piasecki's theses on the economy anticipated the release of the RNR's program, *The Principles of the National Radical Program* (Zasady programu Narodowo-Radykalnego), published on February 7, 1937. Often referred to as the "green program" for the color of its cover, the manifesto consisted of twenty-eight short points. The first three referred to the absolute values invoked by Piasecki in his earlier publications: God was the highest destiny of man, the path to God ran through work for the nation, and man's personal happiness derived from his effort to increase the might of the nation. The remaining points defined National Radical Poland as the total unification of state and society through the OPN. All political parties and secret organizations would be liquidated. The OPN would create a new Poland free of class, religious, and ethnic divisions, with "truly national culture" purged of alien influences. The army, after its merger with OPN political structures, would play a pivotal role as an institution for forging national unity through compulsory military service.[46]

National minorities were to vanish. The Jews would be banned from all Polish institutions, expropriated, and subsequently expelled from Poland. In the modernization of the eastern borderlands, Slavic minorities were expected to fully assimilate.[47] The Catholic State of the Polish Nation would win the European East for Christian civilization and secure the survival of the nations of central Europe against Soviet communism and the German drive for racial supremacy.[48]

The formulation of the RNR program marked the organization's emergence as a new movement separate from the National Democrats. In reviewing *The Principles of the National Radical Program,* the nationalist *Myśl narodowa* commented: "We read about a single-party state, omnipotent, and ruled dictatorially by the OPN and its leader in typical Nazi and Bolshevik manner. . . . In fact, the only thing that distinguishes the National Radical Movement from the Popular Front is the Jewish question."[49] It is not that Piasecki's followers worried about being dubbed "national Bolsheviks." Far from it. "The National Party," *Ruch młodych* explained, "largely supports capitalism and rejects any attempts to reform this system."[50] When both the Endeks and Jerzy Turowicz of the Catholic group Odrodzenie (Revival) declared Piasecki's program totalitarian and thus incompatible with Catholicism, the National Radicals pointed to the absence of any binding Christian political doctrine.[51] Turowicz was referring to the two 1937 encyclicals, the anticommunist *Divini redemptoris* and *Mit brennender Sorge,* which condemned Hitler's regime for the persecution of Catholics, the promotion of neopaganism, and the elevation of state to the position of the absolute. But was denouncing Nazism in Germany equivalent to condemning totalitarianism in Poland? Considering the Vatican's ambiguous relationship with Mussolini's regime, which always claimed to be totalitarian, Turowicz's point was problematic.

With the exception of a few radically chauvinistic priests, the Polish Church hierarchy ignored Piasecki's movement. Anti-Semitic and nationalistic members of the clergy might have sympathized with the National Democrats; but in their determination to "Catholicize" Polish society, they vowed to fence off a secular state and its movements.[52] Cardinal August Hlond also tried to keep the Church on good terms with Sanacja. Fundamentally, the National Radicals paled in comparison to the nominally proclerical Endecja, which made no attempt to influence matters of religious doctrine.

But the RNR did get a sympathetic reception from some of the most authoritarian elements of Sanacja. On February 21, 1937, two weeks after the release of the green program, Colonel Adam Koc announced a new pro-government mass organization, soon known as the Camp of National Unity (Obóz Zjednoczenia Narodowego, OZN). A few months after Koc's dec-laration, Piasecki, as the leader of the RNR, entered an alliance with the very regime he had long opposed.

The OZN Venture

The Camp of National Unity was similar to efforts by other authoritarian, monarchist, and military-based regimes to create government parties or mass organizations in eastern Europe and the Mediterranean. The conserva-tive, yet pragmatic, government politicians of Greece, Romania, Yugoslavia, and the Baltics all advocated organic nationalism, subscribed to fascist ide-ology to a greater or lesser degree, and embraced corporatism and paramili-tarism; but they also competed with domestic fascists and other nationalist radicals.[53] The OZN was a byproduct of the struggles between Piłsudski's heirs, President Mościcki and Marshal Rydz-Śmigły.[54] The marshal pro-moted himself as a new leader capable of continuing Piłsudski's tradition and bridging the gap between the regime and society. His intention was to build a movement beyond Sanacja, which would consolidate power in his hands.[55] On May 24, 1936, in an address to the Union of Polish Legionnaires, the Piłsudskiite veteran organization, Rydz announced that the security of Poland, trapped between the Soviet Union and Nazi Germany, depended on national unity and consolidation, and he called for the creation of a new mass organization.[56]

Rydz entrusted this task to Colonel Adam Koc, chairman of the Legion-naires' union, but he turned out to be a rather unfortunate choice. Koc was an ailing man who lacked both personal charisma and tactical skills. His nationalist and authoritarian views made him extremely unpopular among the Left and Sanacja moderates. Nor could he count on the support of Endeks, who rejected any compromise with the regime.[57] Koc was able to attract to his organization only a few career army officers, Sanacja hardliners, and marginal right-wing groups.

The program of the OZN advocated national unity above party and class divisions and praised the army as a uniting force, while paying nominal re-spect to the Church. Although its declaration promised land reform, it failed to spell out how this redistribution would take place. Koc also declared that state regulation of the economy would increase through closer supervision of private enterprises. More revealing was its muted anti-Semitism: while denouncing anti-Jewish violence, the OZN also emphasized the need for Polish society to defend its culture and seek economic self-sufficiency from the Jews.[58]

It was a populist-nationalist-authoritarian platform meant to impress the public. The OZN did not intend to liquidate opposition parties that refused to cooperate. Instead, it tried to win over the masses, ignoring opposition leaders.[59] Above all, its creation marked the regime's conversion to the vision of a "nationalizing state" already advocated by Endecja, championing the interests of ethnic Poles only, assimilating Slavic minorities, and dissimilating (and eventually purging) Jews and Germans.[60]

The first reactions of the National Radicals to the creation of the OZN were negative. *Falanga* ruled out any possibility of cooperation between the RNR and the OZN.[61] This editorial probably expressed the genuine sentiments of Piasecki's followers and suggests that Piasecki's decision to establish contact with Koc was a personal one.[62] Piasecki's first meetings with members of Koc's entourage took place in the winter and early spring of 1937 but brought no binding agreement.[63] Piasecki agreed to join the OZN youth section only on condition of gaining full control over the organization, a proposal that Sanacja negotiators rejected as too far-reaching.[64] At last, Koc decided to meet Piasecki in person and accepted an invitation to visit the RNR training camp south of Warsaw. Rejuvenated and impressed by the radicals' discipline and unconditional loyalty to their leader, Koc declared that the atmosphere at the camp reminded him of the spirit he had experienced in Piłsudski's legions.[65]

The negotiations continued in the shadow of the RNR's violent campaign against Jews and the Left. On April 29, explosions rocked the editorial offices of the Jewish daily *Nasz przegląd*. On May 1, Przetakiewicz's storm troopers fired on the Bund May Day demonstration in Warsaw, killing a six-year-old girl and wounding several other people.[66] The savagery of this attack was condemned even by the Endek press.[67]

That the attacks took place during negotiations with the OZN suggests that Piasecki intended to impress Koc with a show of strength. At the same time, he must have been aware that most of his supporters opposed any deal with Sanacja. The escalation in violence, therefore, may also have served to pacify the RNR rank and file, to prove that the organization remained un-compromised. Attacks on Jews also helped attract new recruits.

Finally, the terror offensive built on the concept of "breakthrough" (*przełom*), a substitute term for national revolution that Piasecki coined in his pamphlet *Przełom narodowy* (National Breakthrough).[68] Piasecki might have been thinking here of the violent campaign of Mussolini's *squadristi*, who rampaged through Italian towns and countryside, assaulting socialists and anarchists in the months that preceded the March on Rome. These vic-tims of Fascist terror could hardly count on protection from the govern-ment, which deemed them more dangerous than the Duce's movement and which could be easily cowed by a show of force. In Poland, Jews, commu-nists, and even members of non-Catholic religious groups constituted equally vulnerable targets.[69] Could Koc or, by extension, Rydz become Piasecki's Victor Emmanuel? Again, the example of Mussolini, who allied himself with political elites in order to dominate them in the future, was highly seductive.

Piasecki, who was boycotted by the National Democrats and hated by the Left, was an opposition activist who fit the OZN's nationalist and au-thoritarian formula. Yet his personal reputation overshadowed the strength of his organization (or rather the lack thereof). As Wasiutyński put it: "Both of the partners, Koc and Piasecki, tricked themselves. Koc thought that Piasecki commanded the nationalist youth, and Piasecki thought that Koc and Rydz constituted the entire ruling camp."[70]

The agreement was probably concluded after Koc's visit to the RNR training camp. Koc handed over to Piasecki the youth branch of the OZN, the Union of Young Poland (Związek Młodej Polski, ZMP), and agreed to make Jerzy Rutkowski, Piasecki's collaborator, its new boss. In a radio speech on June 22, 1937, Rutkowski outlined the goals of his organization: the implementation of "breakthrough," the mobilization of the people's energy for national creativity, and the struggle against communists, Freemasons, and conservatives. The Jewish problem was to be solved through emigration. In Rutkowski's words, responsibility for Poland was to be taken by soldiers, veterans of the independence movement, and the young nationalist gen-eration. These groups formed a coalition of pro-state nationalist forces (*siły narodowo-państwowe*) determined to crush the Left, which Rutkowski called the *Folksfront*. (The term derived from Yiddish usage and referred to the alleged Jewish character of popular fronts.[71])

The Koc-Piasecki pact faced numerous obstacles from the start. Some OZN officials continued to work behind the scenes to undermine the alliance.[72] Beck and Mościcki, the other two members of the ruling triumvirate, opposed Koc in order to restrain Rydz's appetite for power. After Rutkowski's accession to the leadership of the ZMP, many progovernment youth activists walked out.[73] Equally negative responses came from the centrist faction Naprawa (Restoration), which had intended to use the broad forum of the OZN to cooperate with the socialists and peasants.[74] All these groups criticized the ZMP for its openly fascist tendencies, fearing that the link between the military and the fascists could push the Polish state toward political extremism.

As long as Koc could count on his boss's support, Piasecki's position was safe. At times, Piasecki also rendered services to the Polish political police, the so-called Dwójka (Second Department), by breaking up communist meetings or ransacking the office of the Soviet Intourist travel agency, which was suspected of espionage.[75] The ZMP grew in size, claiming forty thousand members in the fall of 1937.[76] Piasecki also gained control of the Union of Polish Teachers (Związek Nauczycielstwa Polskiego). On September 29, 1937, the authorities suspended the organization's executive committee on charges of financial irregularities and procommunist agitation, appointing Paweł Musioł, a Piasecki follower from Silesia, as the union's government minder.

After the takeover of the ZNP, Piasecki's alliance with Sanacja threatened to dissolve. Musioł's purges of left-wing teachers led to a socialist-backed school strike and galvanized the elements of Sanacja that opposed Rydz and Koc. At a meeting of the Union of Polish Legionnaires, Rydz tried to pacify the unrest by dismissing rumors of a military coup that had permeated liberal circles.[77]

There is little evidence to corroborate the allegation that Rydz and Koc had planned a coup. The story emerged from two sources: Information Communiqué no. 14 of November 22, 1937, produced by Front Morges, a centrist opposition group led by Ignacy Paderewski and Władysław Sikorski, and a Communist Party of Poland report, *Listy z domu* (Letters from home). By these accounts, the coup was to have taken place on the night of October 25 and in the early hours of October 26. Selected army and police units, accompanied by Piasecki's troopers, were to massacre some fifteen hundred people, mostly socialists, peasant leaders, and Sanacja liberals. Twice that number, including Mościcki and Piłsudski's widow, were to be detained. The bloodbath was to coincide with Rydz's and Piasecki's official visit to Bucharest, so that neither of them would be implicated. The coup was understood to have failed, however, because the opposition of Warsaw's garrison and the preventive arrests of Piasecki's followers.[78]

No other documents support this tale, and it seems likely that the rumors of a Polish Night of Long Knives constituted a political provocation launched by Rydz's opponents within Sanacja.[79] The report of the Front Morges contained numerous factual errors—for one thing, Piasecki did not accompany Rydz on the trip to Romania—and the report's author, Colonel Izydor Modelski, was one of the staunchest critics of Rydz.[80] It is highly unlikely that Sikorski would have appointed Koc his treasury minister in the government in exile in 1939 had he believed that Koc had planned to murder his political friends only two years earlier.[81]

During the crisis, Piasecki's followers denounced the rumors of the coup as completely groundless.[82] Years later, Sznarbachowski admitted that although the idea of staging a coup was popular among the National Radicals, no steps in this direction had been taken because Piasecki knew that the army and police would not support him.[83] Proud that people thought him of capable of leading such a bloody purge, however, Piasecki neither admitted nor denied his role in the supposed plot.[84]

The affair carried grave consequences for Piasecki, undermining his successes of the previous months. Even those political commentators who praised Piasecki's political skills were puzzled about the young politician's future. Stanisław Mackiewicz, a prominent journalist and conservative politician, never hid his sympathies for Piasecki, often describing him as an intelligent and charismatic man with a great future ahead of him. Yet Mackiewicz also expressed a growing skepticism about Piasecki's alliance with Koc. Who would dominate this partnership? Was Koc to become Piasecki's Hindenburg? What were Piasecki's chances in a struggle against other Sanacja strongmen? For Mackiewicz, the October crisis had demonstrated that the old political guard was still able to block the young nationalists.[85]

As if in answer to Mackiewicz's questions, Piasecki opted for political boldness. On November 28, between one and three thousand of his followers, dressed in sand-colored shirts, flocked to a mass rally at the circus building in downtown Warsaw.[86] When a handful of socialists disrupted the opening speeches, security guards quickly apprehended, beat, and expelled the troublemakers. Piasecki came to the podium dressed in a long black coat. The audience raised a forest of hands in the fascist salute. He spoke slowly and methodically. "In our organization, we wear uniforms," Piasecki observed. "And I say more: We will dress all Poles in uniforms of spirit. In doing so, we shall not destroy individuality, but we will redirect the moral and ideological course of the nation." He concluded with a tirade: "There is widespread doubt in the national camp—who should be called to attend sick Poland, a doctor or a surgeon? And I say: We will call a surgeon! Evil, stupidity, materialism, failures of the system, and exploitation must be removed by a single cut."[87]

But the November rally did little to improve Piasecki's declining position vis-à-vis the regime. After weeks of internal intrigue, Rydz resolved to end cooperation with the National Radicals and forced Koc to resign.[88] The OZN's new leader, General Stanisław Skwarczyński, advised the National Radicals to abandon their extremism in service of "an ill-defined revolutionary goal" or to leave the camp.[89] On April 22, 1938, Rutkowski and his associates left the ZMP.

Piasecki's political defeat illustrates a broader European trend—that is, the failure of east European fascists to acquire power in an environment dominated by conservative authoritarians. As in Horthy's Hungary of the 1930s and Antonescu's Romania, Sanacja partly emulated the fascists, adopting radical ethnonationalism, aggressive statism, vague corporatism, and mass organizations based on the leadership principle. These regimes, however, still feared the masses and would not support the formation of fascist paramilitaries.[90] Sanacja was a military-based regime, and it would not tolerate any intrusions into this sphere.

The story of Koc also illustrates how little differentiated some officials of the regime from young nationalist militants. The colonel was exceptional in his enthusiasm and readiness to fuse Sanacja authoritarianism with Piasecki's movement. More mainstream leaders of the Camp of National Unity, such as Skwarczyński, cut short Koc's love affair with Piasecki; but at the end of the day, they too would adopt substantial parts of Piasecki's program, especially the idea of modernization at the expense of Jews. By 1938, the OZN openly advocated both economic struggle against the Jews and cleansing Polish culture of Jewish influences. The government also took steps to reduce the Jewish population by encouraging emigration to Palestine and revising citizenship laws.[91] The religious and political persecution of Ukrainians and Belorussians also accelerated in 1938. Did Piasecki contribute to the radicalization of Sanacja? Perhaps. More likely, the Polish regime simply was turning nastier, like others in authoritarian eastern Europe.

The regime clung desperately to power, keeping opponents at bay with the carrot and the stick. But it also feared radical sociopolitical experiments and tried to reduce political violence to a minimum. Unlike the fascists, the Polish authoritarians displayed a lack of will and readiness to expunge political opponents, be they nationalists, peasants, or socialists. The majority of the Sanacja Colonels were authoritarian soldiers but also members of Piłsudski's school: occasionally violent, yet old-fashioned. Some were former socialists. Perhaps Piasecki's short-lived ascent rang enough alarm bells in the Colonels' minds to prevent them from proceeding further in their protofascist journey.

The Fall of the RNR

Following the failure of the OZN venture, Piasecki's previously unchallenged position within the RNR began to wane. Piasecki tried to restore his flagging authority by quelling dissent in the ranks of the organization, uniting other radical nationalist groups with his own, and courting opposition parties. He failed at all three tasks. Przetakiewicz—designated by his boss to enforce discipline within the organization—turned to spying on prominent activists and succeeded only in aggravating their loss of confidence in their leader.[92] By the spring of 1938, the RNR had lost even its earliest bastion of strength—student government at the universities—to the rival ONR ABC.

Having failed to improve the organization's standing through political maneuvers, Piasecki turned to propaganda, advocating Polish territorial expansion, popularizing other eastern European fascist movements, and intensifying agitation among workers and women. His press showered special praise on Codreanu, leader of the Romanian Iron Guard. On March 15, 1938, *Falanga* published an interview with Codreanu that drew analogies between Poland and Romania, between the Iron Guard and the RNR, and finally between Codreanu and Piasecki—two charismatic leaders who had devoted their lives to the struggle against Jews, communists, and liberals and who melded nationalism with Christianity. After Codreanu's arrest in April 1938, *Falanga* even declared, "The enemies of the Iron Guard are our enemies."[93] When the news of Codreanu's execution reached Poland,

Piasecki's followers mourned the leader of the Romanian fascists in public ceremonies.[94]

In the summer of 1938, Piasecki dispatched several female activists
to disrupt the Congress of Citizen Women's Action, organized in Warsaw
by the Left and liberal Sanacja groups.[95] One of them, Jadwiga Kunsteter-
Rutkowska, published a lengthy article in *Falanga* titled "Let Us End the
Women's Ghetto!" Accusing the congress's organizers of a class-based program, internationalism, and aggressive feminism, Kunsteter urged Polish
women to "emancipate themselves from this emancipation."[96] This and other
radical texts on the question of gender projected the old nationalist belief
that motherhood constituted women's primary role in the nation and that
the right place for Polish women, already enfranchised, was at home. On
the other hand, women in National Radical Poland were to enjoy the same
rights to education, employment, payment, and political participation as
men—through their membership in the OPN, of course.[97] Hardly innova-
tive in view of positions advanced by the Left and some pro-Sanacja groups,
the National Radicals did little to introduce women's emancipation into the
discourse of the nationalist Right.

As Piasecki's political position continued to decline, his propagandists
began turning out comforting visions rather than practical proposals. A series of articles published by *Falanga* under the common title "Reports from
the Future" presented fictional accounts from everyday life in a future National Radical Poland. Some of these articles read like fairy tales. The country grew so prosperous that Polish farmers traveled to Denmark to lecture
on the achievements of Polish agriculture. Poland underwent a vast industrialization, as the Labor Front built roads and modern railways, drained
marshes, and dug canals. Modern housing and green neighborhoods changed
the urban landscape. Synagogues were converted into museums where citizens could study the Jewish menace of the past. Poland was a leading European power with no minorities left: the Ukrainians and Belorussians had
assimilated, the Jews had emigrated, and the Germans had been subjected to
population transfers.[98] Compulsory labor service had forged patriotism in
the nation's youth and eradicated class divisions. (*Falanga*'s accounts of labor battalions bore a striking resemblance to Nazi and Stalinist propaganda
pieces detailing the transformation of mothers' boys into a disciplined and
united collective.[99]) People had free access to public libraries, lecture halls,

cinemas, and theaters, where they could watch documentaries about the modernization of the eastern borderlands or plays featuring the National Radicals' past struggles.[100]

All of these stories lacked one important plot element: they did not explain how the RNR came to power. Piasecki failed to capitalize on the Munich crisis and on the subsequent Polish claims to Zaolzie, part of former Austrian Silesia lost to Czechoslovakia in 1919. When he ordered the formation of the Zaolzie Volunteer Corps, however, only two hundred men responded to his call.[101] At the end of the day, the Polish army occupied Zaolzie without the aid of the RNR.

Piasecki saw his movement moving toward rapid collapse. In the highly contested municipal elections of December 1938 and March 1939, the National Radicals did not win a single seat.[102] Police reports from that period testify to the thorough disintegration of Piasecki's group, its internal struggles, and the defection of its members to the National Party, the ONR ABC, and the Camp of National Unity.[103]

As international tensions increased and war loomed on the horizon, Piasecki sought to reestablish relations with the army.[104] In the spring of 1939, he placed a few associates in the army-sponsored Union of Petty Nobility (Związek Szlachty Zagrodowej), intended to Polonize the eastern borderlands.[105] Then, in the summer of that year, came the Brochwicz affair.

Stanisław Brochwicz, born of a Polish father and German mother, served as a correspondent in Vienna and Rome for the Polish army newspaper *Polska zbrojna* and for Polish radio. As his reports became openly pro-Nazi, he lost his job in October 1938. After his return to Warsaw, he contacted Piasecki through Professor Zygmunt Cybichowski, a leading Germanophile and the father of an RNR member.[106] Brochwicz gradually became a regular guest at the National Radicals' organizational meetings and a *Falanga* contributor.[107] He evidently viewed Piasecki and his followers as potential Nazi allies. He found a sympathetic reception from two senior activists, Stanisław Cimoszyński and Olgierd Szpakowski, who advocated a tactical alliance with Germany against the Soviet Union. In case of a major international conflict, however, Poland would switch sides, ally itself with Britain and France, and stab Germany in back. But Piasecki categorically opposed any collaboration with the Nazis.[108] He was especially outraged by remarks Brochwicz made at one of their meetings in May 1939. "You must declare yourself now," Brochwicz said. "Even if [Marshal Rydz] Śmigły goes as far as to declare war on Germany, you can be the man who will sign a peace agreement and save Poland."[109]

Piasecki began to suspect that he was dealing with a German spy, and surveillance of the journalist confirmed these suppositions. Piasecki reported Brochwicz to Polish counterintelligence and arranged for his arrest in early June.[110] After the outbreak of war in September 1939, Brochwicz was transported to the fortress at Brest. Tried by a military court, he was found guilty of espionage and sentenced to death. The capture of the fortress by German troops saved his life, however, and Piasecki and Brochwicz would meet again in occupied Warsaw in December 1939.

In July 1939, Piasecki closed down *Falanga* and soon afterward announced that the organization had suspended its activities because of the prospect of war.[111] On August 31, 1939, following the announcement of general mobilization, Piasecki left for his unit, the Warsaw Tank Motorized Brigade.

The Anti-Semitism of the RNR

Was Piasecki's anti-Semitic platform the main reason for the notoriety that he and his followers acquired in prewar Poland? This seems indeed to have been the case. When Halina Krahelska, a prominent progressive social worker, referred to anti-Semitic remarks made by a Polish peasant whom she encountered during the war, she labeled his tirades as "National Radical."[112] For members of the prewar liberal intelligentsia, this was a common understanding. The adjective "ONR-ic" (*oenerowski*) stood for the most aggressive and violent forms of anti-Semitism in prewar Poland. The term was applied indiscriminately to all forces behind violent anti-Semitic excesses, whether they were Endeks, Rossman's ONR ABC, or Piasecki's RNR.

Prewar Polish anti-Semitism cannot be separated from the country's treatment of national minorities in general. As Antony Polonsky aptly points out, the Poles failed "to adapt themselves to the conditions of independence in a state with large national minorities."[113] The case of the Jewish minority was most significant. Whether Polonized or holding to their ethnoreligious identity, Jews came to be seen as separate from the rest of society. A new Christian middle class considered them an obstacle to national economic advancement.[114] This modernizing anti-Semitism was shared by Endeks, the

Sanacja Colonels, and even nominally democratic peasants. The left-wing activism of some assimilated Jews fueled the Żydokomuna (Jewish communist) myth. The prominence of others in the arts and entertainment disturbed self-styled guardians and advocates of national culture. In fact, one could argue that those who assimilated were regarded with greater suspicion than orthodox, Yiddish-speaking Jews: they were said to contaminate the body of the nation.

Piasecki's National Radicals injected Endecja's anti-Semitism with a greater dose of demagoguery and radicalism. For Maria Rzętkowska, anti-Semitism constituted the core of her nationalist worldview: "He who calls himself an anti-Semite and at the same time supports a liberal parliamentarian system, capitalism and a laissez-faire economy, religious and national indifferentism, is a liar, for he intends only to cut out the branches and leave the roots of Jewish power in Poland untouched."[115] Others compared the struggle against the Jews to the fight for independence against the partitioning powers. Alfred Łaszowski put it bluntly: "Was there the Russian occupation? Yes, there was. Is there a Jewish occupation now? Yes, there is."[116] For Piasecki's movement, Jews constituted a lethal threat to the nation-state. Kazimierz Hałaburda of *Falanga* proposed following the Turkish method of ethnic cleansing and genocide to produce an ethnically homogeneous state.[117] Struggle against the Jews was seen as a prerequisite for the modernization of Poland. An editorial in *Ruch młodych* declared: "The solution to the Jewish problem, or, to be precise, the expulsion of Jews from Poland, constitutes a necessary precondition for the reform of our existence."[118]

It should be emphasized that the RNR did not endorse any racial theories, seeing them as both difficult to prove by scientific means and contrary to Catholic principles. In this sense, the Nazis committed a heresy, since no ideology should worship a man.[119]

Finally, in addition to its redemptive function, anti-Semitism was used to brand and disgrace internal and external enemies, including those who favored the status quo and even those who opposed it from nonnationalist positions. In May 1937, *Falanga* claimed to have unmasked the shameful cooperation of Polish aristocrats and Jewish bankers.[120] Similar connections were made between Jews and capitalists, democrats, communists, and cosmopolitan intellectuals.

In comparison to his associates, Piasecki can be viewed as almost a moderate anti-Semite. Years later, in 1958, at the meeting of the Polish Writers'

Union, Władysław Jan Grabski surprised the audience by proclaiming that Piasecki was never an anti-Semite. Jan Józef Lipski, who had vehemently attacked Piasecki on this ground on numerous occasions, was genuinely shocked: "I was astonished that anybody acting in good faith could defend his friend in such a way, as if ordering or inciting criminal acts should be treated more leniently because it is motivated by cynical calculation, not by genuine convictions. Yet, I cannot rule out that Grabski was telling truth."[121] Lipski hit the nail on the head. As supreme leader of the RNR, Piasecki had ordered or authorized actions by his followers, including the bombing of Jewish stores and houses and firing on Bund demonstrators. But the reputation of being a virulent anti-Semite that Piasecki acquired in the 1930s had two results. On the one hand, it made him extremely unpopular among the liberal intelligentsia. On the other, after World War II, it became an asset when the Polish communists, eager to free themselves from the old Żydokomuna myth, reached out to him.

3 ⫿ The War Years, 1939–44

WAR FORCED PIASECKI TO BECOME a soldier, yet he never ceased to be a politician. At a time when the fate of nations depended on military superiority, he had the ambition to build a *political* army whose strength relied on ideology rather than on numbers of soldiers and the power of weapons. During the war, he took over leadership of a small right-wing resistance group, the Confederation of the Nation (Konfederacja Narodu, KN). Piasecki based his strategy on the belief that the war, especially after the Nazi invasion of the Soviet Union, constituted a clash of ideologies. Piasecki perceived nationalism, communism, and Catholicism as the three great ideologies of the twentieth century, yet he found both Nazism and communism to be faulty as doctrines: the first espoused racism and neopaganism, while the second championed a materialist utopia. His program for Polish national renewal, by contrast, would combine elements of Christianity, nationalism, and radical modernity. Thus, he reasoned, Poland would have to fight both the Nazis and the Soviets. To that end, he propounded a program called "Strike" (*Uderzenie*), a mixed ideological-military offensive against Hitler and Stalin to be accompanied by vehement nationalist agitation among the Polish population, with the eventual goal of building a Polish-led Slavic Christian empire in central Europe on the ruins of the Nazi and Soviet powers.

While pursuing his ideological dreams, Piasecki faced the very real challenges of underground struggle in the resistance movement, which operated in a context of terror and brutality experienced in few other German-occupied countries. As commander of a resistance group, he was responsible for the lives of hundreds of men and women serving under him, a duty that he undertook with mixed results.

This episode in Piasecki's life offers compelling evidence of the complexity and disunity of the Polish resistance movement. Divided into numerous factions, the underground forces fought the occupiers and, occasionally, one another. Like underground groups elsewhere in Europe, the Polish resistance shared two broad goals: the liberation of their country and the implementation of socioeconomic and political changes after the war. There could be no return to the prewar order. It remained only to determine what would replace it. By the end of the conflict, these differences proved to be secondary. The fate of postwar Europe was determined not by indigenous resistance movements—which were unable either to liberate their countries or to change the course of the war—but by the Great Powers.

Defeat, September 1939–May 1940

On September 1, 1939, Piasecki, like hundreds of thousands of his countrymen, joined the struggle against the Nazi invaders. It was a war that the Poles could not win. The modern German army faced what General Tadeusz Kutrzeba, a veteran of the 1939 campaign, described as "poor and archaically equipped, though brave" Polish forces.[1] Poland had secured guarantees of military assistance from Britain and France, but following their declaration of war on Germany on September 3, 1939, these allies engaged in what came to be called the Phony War, with no troops committed to battle on the Continent. The fate of the Second Republic was effectively sealed by the secret Nazi-Soviet pact of August 1939, which partitioned Poland between Germany and the Soviet Union.

Outnumbered and poorly armed, the Poles fought gallantly, yet without much success. The Polish lines of defense were easily pierced, broken, and overrun by massive German blows. The massive Soviet attack on September 17 hastened the destruction of the Polish army, and the Polish government fled to Romania, where it was interned. Warsaw fell on September 27, and the last Polish units capitulated in early October. The German victory was quick and achieved with relatively few casualties: 10,000 killed and 40,000 wounded. On the Polish side, 67,000 were killed, 133,000 wounded, and 579,000 taken prisoner. In addition, 2,000 Polish soldiers were killed in chaotic resistance against the Soviets, who took another 200,000 prisoners.[2]

Piasecki took part in the September campaign as an ensign in the Warsaw Tank Motorized Brigade under Colonel Stefan Rowecki, the future commander of the underground Home Army (Armia Krajowa, AK). On September 17, the day of the Soviet invasion, the brigade moved toward the town of Tomaszów Lubelski, where it participated in one of the last big battles of the defensive campaign.

The Polish units consisted of remnants from the Lublin and Kraków armies. They tried to break through the German lines and move southeast toward Lwów, which was still in Polish hands. (The city surrendered to the Soviets on September 22.) Between September 18 and 20, the Poles first stormed and then resisted the counterattacks of the numerically superior German forces in Tomaszów Lubelski.[3] Piasecki's light tank was hit twice, but he escaped unhurt.[4] Before surrendering, General Tadeusz Piskor instructed his soldiers to break into small groups and move toward Warsaw or Lwów. Overall, the Poles suffered heavy losses during the battle of Tomaszów Lubelski: 3,000 dead or wounded and 11,000 taken prisoner.[5] Among those soldiers who escaped captivity was Piasecki. Initially, he set off toward the Romanian border, but then decided to return to Warsaw. He reached the conquered capital in early October.[6]

The collapse of Poland in 1939 was not only a military defeat but also the traumatic end of the nation's recently regained sovereignty. On September 28, 1939, a new German-Soviet treaty partitioned the country between the two powers. The Germans split their share into lands to be annexed to Germany (Polish Silesia, Pomerania, Poznań province, and the city of Łódź) and the General Gouvernement of the Polish Occupied Territories in the central regions of Poland.[7] The Nazis did not rely on a national government, puppet regime, or collaborators in Poland as they did in other territories under their control but instead installed their own civilian administration headed by Governor-General Hans Frank. The Soviets officially incorporated their territorial gains in October and November.

The September catastrophe also constituted a major revolution in Polish politics: it delegitimized the Sanacja regime, which was widely held responsible for the swift collapse of the armed forces. Interned in Romania, the government was prevented from passing into the West by the French, who forced President Mościcki to transfer power to the opposition. The new government in exile, created on September 30, 1939, had little connection to the prewar regime and consisted of the pre-1939 opposition: the Peasant

Party, the National Party, the Polish Socialist Party, and the Labor Party. The government's underground agency in the occupied territories, the Government Delegacy (Delegatura Rządu), aspired to be the sole source of political authority and guidance to Poles. The delegacy started its operations only in April 1940, however. Meanwhile, the government in exile had not yet secured the loyalty of Polish society, especially the nationalist far Right. Twenty years after the end of the partitions that had divided Poland among its neighbors, factions still recognized the potential for collaborating with one partitioning power against another—as Piłsudski and Dmowski, the fathers of independent Poland, had during World War I.

In October 1939, Andrzej Świetlicki, one of Piasecki's former deputies in the National Radical Movement, contacted the German army command in Warsaw on behalf of several right-wing and pro-German politicians who proposed setting up a collaborationist organization. Other participants included the notorious anti-Semite Rev. Stanisław Trzeciak and Professor Zygmunt Cybichowski, the father of National Radical activist Jerzy Cybichowski.[8] With the approval of the German military, they set up the National Revolutionary Camp (Narodowy Obóz Rewolucji, NOR), which called for a Polish-German alliance against the Soviets. The organization was soon joined by Władysław Studnicki, a colorful maverick politician, nationalist, and staunch Germanophile who, motivated by anticommunism, the history of Polish-German cooperation in World War I, and the desire to preserve the biological existence of the nation, preached the gospel of collaboration throughout the war.[9] After the creation of the General Gouvernement and the transfer of power from the military to Frank's administration, the camp was disbanded, but it continued its activities unopposed by the Germans until the spring of 1940.

This episode of Polish wartime history has not been fully researched and analyzed, partly because detailed evidence is lacking and partly because it challenges the myth of Poland as the only European nation without quislings. The NOR, however, was the only collaborationist project in Nazi-occupied Poland that involved Polish fascists. In his study of anti-Jewish violence in German-occupied Europe, Polish historian Tomasz Szarota also suggests that the Nazis used the Polish National Socialists to stir up anti-Jewish riots in Warsaw during the Easter holiday in 1940.[10] There is little doubt that the initiative had the blessing of some members of Wehrmacht occupation authorities, who, in the words of Joseph Goebbels, displayed "too lackadaisical" an approach toward the Poles and who might have contemplated some kind of Polish-German rapprochement before the ultimate assault on the Soviet Union.[11] They quickly lost out, however, to the advocates of a more repressive course in occupation policy. Hitler rejected any collaborationist arrangements in Poland, mostly on the basis of his racial and historical contempt for Slavic peoples, his perception of the Poles as an obstacle to establishing Lebensraum, and his wish to completely eradicate Polish nationalism.[12] A brief discussion—partly window dressing, partly a peace feeler—about the creation of a Polish rump state (*Reststaat*) died in October 1939.[13]

The brutal treatment of the Poles also reflected the circumstances of the Nazi takeover. The Czechs and Danes surrendered without a fight, and the Slovaks and Croats accepted the dissolution of their multiethnic states as the beginning of their own sovereignty. The French surrendered, leaving England fighting alone, while France's Anglophobic, anti-Semitic, anticommunist, and authoritarian Vichy leaders commanded a vast colonial empire and a navy. The Poles, by contrast, had rejected Germany's demands and offered armed resistance. In return, they could expect only rule by terror and deprivation. The fall of France in June 1940 only consolidated this conviction within the Nazi hierarchy. In that same month, the Gestapo executed Świetlicki, together with several other members of his group.

The participation of some National Radicals in the NOR raises a question about the possibility of Piasecki's involvement in collaboration. As mentioned earlier, Piasecki returned to Warsaw in October 1939, where he tried to revive the National Radical Movement. He probably became aware of Świetlicki's doings at this time, but whether Piasecki played a role in negotiations or participated in the NOR remains shrouded in mystery. According to Sznarbachowski, Piasecki sought contact with the Wehrmacht to create Polish paramilitary units. Inspired by Piłsudski's game with the Central Powers in World War I, he believed that in the event of Germany's defeat on the western front the Soviets would attack German-occupied Poland. If that happened, Piasecki's units would conduct guerrilla warfare against the Soviets and hold out until the arrival of the Allies. Sznarbachowski claims not only that Piasecki supported Świetlicki's organization but also that he planned to set up a collaborationist government: operating alongside the legal NOR, a secret organization commanded by Przetakiewicz would prepare an uprising against the Germans.[14] Przetakiewicz contradicts

Sznarbachowski's version, however, arguing that Piasecki established contact with Świetlicki only to dissuade his former comrade from collaborating with the Nazis.[15]

Piasecki's Polish biographers Antoni Dudek and Grzegorz Pytel credit Przetakiewicz's account. "It is difficult to believe," they argue, "that having been raised in the anti-German spirit of National Democracy and knowing about German atrocities, Piasecki would contemplate any arrangement with the occupiers."[16] Piasecki's anti-German views are certainly a matter of record. What this explanation lacks, however, is an appreciation of the fluidity of the political situation in late 1939. At that point, little was known in Warsaw about Nazi designs for Poland. And even before the fighting concluded, the Gestapo had put out feelers to Peasant Party leader and former prime minister Wincenty Witos about the possibility of his collaborating with the Nazis, an event that NOR activists or Piasecki might have known about.[17] German crimes against the Polish population had not yet intensified, so it is not inconceivable that Piasecki might have endorsed limited collaboration in exchange for the opportunity to rebuild his movement and play a role in the further course of war. The lessons of Piłsudski's cooperation with Germany in World War I were still on people's minds. The higher goal of preparing the nation for future struggles might have outweighed Piasecki's scruples about working with the occupiers. Here, as elsewhere, there was a sliding scale between collaboration and resistance, but there is no conclusive evidence as to Piasecki's real actions and motivations. Still, Piasecki never denounced Świetlicki, whose name appeared on the list of the fallen National Radicals published in 1948 by the weekly *Dziś i jutro*.[18]

Throughout World War II, members of the Left accepted rumors that the NOR was Piasecki's initiative.[19] But intelligence reports of the Government Delegacy were more skeptical, dismissing Piasecki's involvement.[20] That Piasecki lacked immunity from the Nazis was demonstrated by the events of December 13, when he and several of his comrades were arrested by a group of Gestapo agents headed by Stanisław Brochwicz.[21]

Having been responsible for unmasking the German agent before the war, Piasecki could not count on lenience from the Nazis. He soon found another influential protector, however. After Piasecki's arrest, Sznarbachowski contacted Luciana Frassati-Gawrońska, whom he had known since the 1930s. The Frassatis had belonged to the Italian establishment for many years. Luciana's father, Alfredo, was the founder of the prestigious journal

La stampa and a senator, while her brother, Pier Giorgio, was a prominent Catholic activist. (After World War II, he was beatified by the Roman Catholic Church.) From her adolescence, Luciana had moved in diplomatic circles, getting to know political leaders and members of the Catholic hierarchy, including Marshal Paul Hindenburg, Archbishop Giovanni Battista Montini (the future Pope Paul VI), and above all Benito Mussolini. In the 1920s, she married Jan Gawroński, the Polish envoy in Vienna. During one of her visits to Warsaw shortly before the war, she met Piasecki, whom she described as a young man of "exceptional mind and character, vivid intelligence, and prominent personality."[22]

After the German conquest, Frassati made numerous trips to occupied Poland. Using her Italian diplomatic passport, contacts, and the goodwill of some Nazi officials, she began smuggling people out of Poland, including Helena Sikorska, the wife of the new prime minister of the Polish government in exile.[23] Later, Frassati served as a secret courier between the government in exile and the underground, as well as the Holy See and the Polish episcopate.[24]

Alerted by Sznarbachowski about Piasecki's arrest, Frassati immediately inquired about his fate at Gestapo headquarters in Warsaw. Gestapo boss Joseph Meisinger claimed, however, that the fate of the prisoner was unknown to him.[25] One day on her way home, Frassati was approached by a young man who informed her that Piasecki was being held on Rakowiecka Street. She quickly drove to the jail, met the warden, and obtained permission to see Piasecki. He looked physically exhausted but otherwise seemed calm. Frassati assured him that she would do everything in her power to secure his release.[26]

She immediately mobilized Mario di Stefano, the last Italian envoy in Warsaw, to help her protégé. The occasion came during a banquet for German and Italian officials at the Italian embassy. One of the guests was Meisinger. Lulled by alcohol, lavish food, and gypsy music, he gave di Stefano his business card with a notation granting Halina Kopeć, Piasecki's fiancée, permission to see her beloved. The meeting took place in February 1940. The couple spent two hours together, undisturbed by prison guards— an unusual treat in occupied Warsaw.[27] Meanwhile, Frassati begged Mussolini, who considered himself the patron of European fascists, to intervene in Piasecki's case.[28] Mussolini had doubts about Hitler's brutal approach toward Poland, particularly before Italy's entry into the war, when he still hoped for some kind of peace settlement. In January 1940, he even urged Hitler to take a more realistic approach toward Poland, perhaps restoring a rump Polish state.[29] Hitler ignored this counsel, but with the Duce's help Piasecki was released in April 1940.

Momentarily safe, Piasecki did not expect the Italians to protect him forever. He started using the name Sablewski, which remained his pseudonym for the rest of the war. Anticipating another arrest, Piasecki went underground. On May 24, 1940, the German regional court sentenced him to death in absentia for crimes against the German state. These developments coincided with important decisions in his personal life. On December 28, 1940, he married Kopeć. Before the war's end, they had two sons: Bohdan (1941–57) and Jarosław (1943–).

The Heralds of New Poland: Confederation of the Nation, 1940–42

In the late spring of 1940, Piasecki was practically alone. The war had dispersed most of his comrades. Some were dead. Others had either escaped abroad or joined rival underground organizations.[30] Tainted by the notoriety he had gained before the war, suspected of having contacts with the Germans, and hunted by the Nazis, Piasecki had to find an underground organization that would welcome him without demanding that he revise his views.

Fortunately for Piasecki, the persistence of political divisions after the defeat of 1939 had produced a tendency for disparate parties and groups to establish their own private armies. These clandestine organizations differed in their relationships to the government in exile, as well as in their programs, membership, and scale of operations. The first efforts to unify the resistance occurred in September 1939, when General Michał Tokarzewski-Karaszewicz set up the Service for Poland's Victory (Służba Zwycięstwu Polski) shortly before the capitulation of Warsaw. He placed the organization under the command of the Polish government in November 1939. But Sikorski, the new prime minister and commander in chief, considered the group too pro-Sanacja. In December 1939, he replaced it with a new organization, the Union for Armed Struggle (Związek Walki Zbrojnej, ZWZ), first commanded by General Kazimierz Sosnkowski, who was replaced after the collapse of France by General Stefan Rowecki (also known as "Grot"), Piasecki's former commander. The aim of the ZWZ was to build a secret army and launch a national uprising on the arrival of the Allied armies. The union and several other groups ultimately merged into the Home Army (Armia Krajowa, AK) in 1942. The military ZWZ-AK existed alongside the civilian Government Delegacy, which sought to maintain the government's political and moral authority on Polish soil.[31]

The ZWZ failed to secure control over the communists and the far Right, however. The communist cells refrained from acts of resistance until the German attack on the Soviet Union and reemerged only in January 1942 as the Polish Workers' Party (Polska Partia Robotnicza, PPR). The extreme Right acknowledged the government in exile but did not recognize the authority of the delegacy. Among its most prominent formations were the Union of Salamander (Związek Jaszczurczy), which had emerged from the ONR ABC, and the Central Committee of Organizations for Independence (Centralny Komitet Organizacji Niepodległościowych), rooted in Endek circles.[32] The National Military Organization (Narodowa Organizacja Wojskowa), associated with the National Party, posed different problems. As it was about to merge with the ZWZ in 1942, its most radical faction joined the Union of Salamander, and together they formed the second most powerful underground group in wartime Poland: the anti-Semitic and savagely anticommunist National Armed Forces (Narodowe Siły Zbrojne).[33]

In May 1940, the small nationalist organization Pobudka (Reveille) admitted Piasecki into its ranks, and by the summer of 1940, he had entered the leadership of the organization. He supported Pobudka's accession to the Central Committee of Organizations for Independence, which soon became known as the Confederation of the Nation.[34] Fiercely anti-Sanacja and hostile to the Left, the KN comprised nationalist-minded career and reserve officers as well as right-wing political activists led by Major Jan Włodarkiewicz. Although the group pledged to cooperate with the ZWZ, it did not recognize the authority of Sikorski's government.[35] Piasecki was put in charge of propaganda work. In this capacity, he led the editorial team of the confederation's press organ, *Nowa Polska*, and penned the group's political manifesto, *Wielka ideologia narodu polskiego* (Great Ideology of the Polish Nation).

Written after the collapse of France, the pamphlet reiterated Piasecki's earlier ideas: a nationalist-Catholic synthesis, the exaltation of hierarchical political order, anti-Semitism, and the creation of a new Poland. Commenting on the defeat in 1939, he argued that the prewar Polish state had lacked nationalist-minded and progressive elites that could have led the nation in the struggle against two totalitarianisms.[36] Evidently, Nazi victories had forced Piasecki to moderate his earlier fascist rhetoric. He no longer referred to the order of future Poland as "totalitarian." Instead, he advocated a "moral-political system," a nationalist-Catholic community organized on the principles of hierarchy, work, and Christian universalism.[37]

The manifesto's references to a "geographical matrix [*geograficzna baza matka*] of Polishness" free from ethnic minorities and to an "intense demographic policy seeking Polish biological expansion" show, however, that Piasecki had not abandoned fascist constructs but instead had expanded them through racialist discourse.[38] In the section devoted to international developments, he pointed to the formation of three rival "racial-political" blocs: German, Jewish, and Anglo-Saxon.[39] But he also theorized that the German-Jewish conflict, which had caused the war, would ultimately lead to the defeat of Germany and the Soviet Union and to the emergence of a new racial-geographical identity, a Polish-led eastern European bloc consisting of Slavs and the non-Slavic Finns, Hungarians, and Romanians. Allied with the British and the Americans, the bloc would defeat the Nazis and set up a federation with a common government, military, foreign policy, and free trade. Pushed westward to the old Piast borders, Germany would become a marginal power, while the Soviet Union would cease to exist.[40] Instead of lamenting their status as victims of unprovoked aggression, Piasecki urged, the Poles should learn from the Germans and Soviets that powerful nations craft their own destiny.[41]

It is clear that Piasecki believed in the imminence of war between the Soviet Union and the Third Reich. The scenario of regaining independence as a result of global conflict also resonated with Poland's experiences in World War I. Piasecki was not alone in advocating some form of central European integration along nationalist and authoritarian lines. To some extent, his idea of a Polish-led regional bloc stemmed from Beck's concept of the Third Europe. But particularly striking was its similarity to Szálasi's Pax Hungarica in the Danube basin, a Magyar-dominated Carpatho-Danubian Great Fatherland that was to be partly a Great Hungary of historic boundaries and partly an "organic state system" of nationalities dominated by Magyars.[42] Both Piasecki and Szálasi saw their respective nations as uniquely capable of mediating between Eastern and Western civilizations, but they differed in how they explained the origins of this mission. For Szálasi, it was the biological superiority of the Turanian race. Magyars were "the only Turanian people of occidental culture," destined to be one of the three "ruling peoples" of the world along with the Germans and Japanese.[43] Piasecki, on the other hand, based his claims on historical and cultural mandates, as well as religion. Poland would bridge Catholic with Orthodox, Roman with Byzantine, and Western with Eastern, thus reconciling the nations of east central Europe. He made it clear that the process of unification would take place on the basis of Catholicism.[44]

Piasecki's increasing prominence in the confederation hastened its division into the military Armed Confederation (Konfederacja Zbrojna), headed by Włodarkiewicz, and the civilian Confederation of the Nation under the control of Piasecki.[45] The separation also reflected the growing irritation of army officers with Piasecki's political style. Piasecki and Włodarkiewicz differed, moreover, over the question of cooperation with the government in exile and its agencies in the occupied country. In early 1941, Włodarkiewicz began negotiating a merger with the Union for Armed Struggle, which he joined in September of the same year.[46] By May 1941, Piasecki had severed all ties with his former superiors and transformed the civilian confederation into a separate organization.[47]

Piasecki boycotted the government in exile, seeing the London Poles and the delegacy as a coalition of Centrolew supporters, Sanacja liberals, and Freemasons who served Jewish interests.[48] Sikorski's cabinet was not legitimate: "The government in London—let us be clear about it—is able to perform only some of its legal functions not for the reason of the incompetence of its members, but due to the current situation of Poland and the politics of its [British] hosts . . . . Real power belongs to those of us who are in the country."[49]

Piasecki's critique of the government in exile grew even more pronounced after the Sikorski-Maiski treaty of July 30, 1941, which restored relations between Poland and the Soviet Union, provided for the release of hundreds of thousands of Polish deportees and prisoners from Soviet detention, and set out to re-create a Polish army in the Soviet Union. But the agreement did not solve the problem of border changes, leaving the issue open to future negotiations. The treaty drew harsh criticism from numerous Polish politicians, resulting in a government crisis. It also met with a mixed response from the underground, although the delegacy and the ZWZ approved Sikorski's decision.[50]

Piasecki opposed the treaty, viewing it as acquiescence to Moscow's annexation of the Baltic states, East Prussia, and the Polish eastern borderlands. He argued that the treaty bound "only those Polish politicians who signed it" and asserted that in the Soviet-German conflict Poland should remain neutral. He hoped that a Bolshevik defeat would occur a moment before Germany's collapse.[51] Piasecki even concluded that the lack of a border agreement with the Soviets gave Poland a free hand to expand its territory at the Russians' expense.[52] He was sure that the Soviets would seize the first opportunity to subdue Poland. Red or White, Russia would always be a menace to Poland's existence, and as such it ought to be destroyed.[53]

Yet Piasecki was careful not to overstep certain limits. In a secret instruction to his closest associates in April 1942, he acknowledged that the confederation would have to recognize the London government. He also ordered his propagandists to spare the person of Sikorski, but left them free to sling mud at Sikorski's associates and coalition partners.[54] Piasecki sabotaged Rowecki's attempts to unify the resistance movement. When Sikorski ordered all "party armies" to submit to the authority of the recently created Home Army, Piasecki endorsed military cooperation with the AK but refrained from joining its structures.[55]

As the chief commandant (*komendant główny*), Piasecki enjoyed full power over the organization and initially made no distinctions between its military and political functions. But in 1942, Piasecki singled out the military units, designating them Cadre Strike Battalions (Uderzeniowe Bataliony Kadrowe). The territorial structure of the organization consisted of two regions, central-north and south, divided into five districts: Warsaw city, Warsaw metropolitan, Kielce-Lublin-Sokołów, Kraków, and the Central Industrial District south of Warsaw.[56] In reality, functioning networks existed only in Warsaw and east of the capital.[57] In March 1942, the total membership of the organization did not exceed 1,600 men and women.[58] This was an insignificant number in comparison with the National Armed Forces, the Peasant Battalions (Bataliony Chłopskie), or the AK, which in the summer of 1942 had 140,000 members under arms.

The majority of confederates came from the ranks of the young, right-wing urban intelligentsia, and their training reflected the priority of ideology. The mandatory course for junior officers consisted of twelve hours of instruction, only two of which were devoted to military matters.[59] Piasecki expected that only 5 percent of KN soldiers would carry firearms in the initial phase of armed struggle. The remaining 95 percent would attack the

Germans with clubs and brass knuckles—an arsenal more appropriate for street clashes in peacetime than for an armed struggle against occupying forces.[60] Women played an important role in the organization, as they did in other elements of the Polish resistance. They ran the communication network, provided medical care, and tended to arrested members. Some two hundred women passed through the ranks of Piasecki's group.[61]

During the four years of its existence, the confederation issued twenty-three periodicals, a considerable effort for such a small organization.[62] The biweeklies *Nowa Polska* and *Do broni* as well as the monthly *Sztuka i naród* were published throughout the duration of the German occupation. Even political adversaries from the AK praised *Nowa Polska* for its level of sophistication, though they dubbed it "the most militant nationalist organ."[63] *Sztuka i naród* was particularly successful and had a significant impact on underground cultural life. The periodical attracted leading young poets, among them Wacław Bojarski, Andrzej Trzebiński, and Tadeusz Gajcy.[64] *Sztuka i naród* did not confine itself to the nationalist microcosm but opened its pages to people of different political persuasions, including Czesław Miłosz and Jerzy Andrzejewski. It organized literary contests, experimental theater, and a music studio.

The open character of *Sztuka i naród* reflected the strength of personal ties among artists and intellectuals. The nationalist Włodzimierz Pietrzak, Piasecki's chief propagandist, befriended and helped the writer Jan Kott, who was both a Jew and a communist.[65] It must be said, however, that Piasecki's organization remained fiercely anti-Semitic. "The Jew will not return," read one of its slogans. "The Germans and Jews set the world on fire, together they will burn," stated another. Anti-Jewish measures adopted by the Germans were viewed sympathetically: "The picture would not be complete if we did not mention such results of the creation of the ghetto as the decline of organized crime, the improvement of the situation in crafts and trade," read one article.[66]

The confederation maintained that after the war, the Poles should retain Nazi-confiscated Jewish property and keep the ghettos running until the final expulsion of the Jews from Poland.[67] The anti-Semitic propaganda continued in spite of the writers' knowledge of the ongoing genocide. "Nobody has any doubts about the direction of these transports," reported one of Piasecki's periodicals. "There are only two destinations: a mass grave in Treblinka and the gas chamber in Bełżec." Yet this report from the Warsaw Ghetto and similar accounts mixed expressions of horror at the carnage with revulsion for the Jews' alleged cowardice and passivity.[68] Although *Nowa Polska* condemned the German methods as sadistic and barbaric, it also pointed to the "positive" consequence of the destruction of the Jewry: Poland would become Jew-free.[69] Later, Piasecki's propagandists covered the story of the April 1943 Warsaw Ghetto Uprising like play-by-play commentators at a sporting event, favoring neither side.[70]

Yet anti-Semitism was not the cornerstone of the confederation's program. Piasecki's major preoccupation was the implementation of Operation Strike, a blend of guerrilla warfare and agitation, armed uprising and territorial expansion.[71] Piasecki and his officers estimated that the confederation could mobilize some fifteen thousand soldiers, a modest but still unrealistic calculation. The troops would attack northeast toward Wilno and Nowogródek, southeast toward Lwów and the prewar border with Romania, south toward the Carpathians, west toward Łódź, and north toward the Baltic Sea.[72] Propaganda and recruitment teams would follow in the footsteps of the field units. After the defeat of Germany, the conquest of new territories, particularly in the east, would begin.[73] "It is not proper," Piasecki observed, "to . . . leave the issue of new borders to a peace conference."[74] The government in exile, for its part, also looked forward to territorial expansion, but at the expense of Germany rather than the Soviet Union. The ethnic composition of the population in the annexed lands posed no problems, as German residents would face deportation. But this Polonization, or ethnic cleansing, would need the approval of the Allies—something the London Poles never doubted they would get—as part of the peace settlement.[75] By contrast, Piasecki's plans for expansion in the east resembled the post–World War I "open door" strategy embraced by Polish leaders, particularly Piłsudski.

Despite Piasecki's denial of analogies between his Strike plan and Piłsudski's formula in the struggle for independence, the influence of the Piłsudskiite tradition is irrefutable.[76] As in 1918, the Poles would stab the Germans in the back after Germany's defeat in the west and the mutual exhaustion of the Germans and the Russians in the east, repel Soviet advances with the aid of the Allies, and conquer new lands.[77] Also like the Legionnaires, confederation troops were to serve as both soldiers and emissaries, mobilizing Polish society and instilling a new nationalist ethos. This kinship was even evident in the name of Piasecki's units: his Cadre Strike Battalions harked back to the first unit of Piłsudski's Legions, the First Cadre Company.

Piasecki ordered the formation of the first Strike unit in March 1942.[78] He decided to deploy his forces in the region of Podlasie, which lay east of Warsaw and fronted on the eastern borderlands across the Bug River. The Cadre Strike Battalions would cross the Bug, attack both the Germans and Soviet partisans, prevent the spread of communism, and establish a bridgehead for further advances in the east.[79]

From the start, the operation was handicapped by a lack of supplies, manpower, and planning. The confederation started building its network in Podlasie in February and March 1942. Recruitment did not proceed smoothly.[80] Procuring weapons posed an even greater difficulty, due mostly to the shortage of funds.[81] Piasecki did not hesitate to authorize stealing weapons from other organizations' arsenals.[82] There was only one way to add to the organization's coffers: the extortion of money from Volksdeutsche (ethnic German residents on Polish lands) and businesses working for the Germans, a method popular with other resistance groups, including the AK. In July 1942, the Polish police caught a confederation team during the attempted robbery of a Polish industrialist who was untainted by collaboration, an incident that drew sharp responses from the AK command. But Piasecki did not abandon his men, who in the meantime had been handed over to the Gestapo. On the night of July 26, 1942, a small detachment posing as Gestapo agents freed the prisoners. It was one of the first and most daring actions of this kind in occupied Warsaw. Not only did Piasecki rehabilitate the reputation of his organization, but he also won the lifelong gratitude and loyalty of his men.[83]

In August 1942, he dispatched two small teams of scouts to the east to check the conditions for guerrilla warfare. Upon their return, they tried to dissuade Piasecki from launching the operation, pointing to the presence of strong Soviet partisan units in the area.[84] But Piasecki remained unmoved. The confederation needed to perform a heroic deed, a military action, that would test its capacities as well as the enemy's strength.[85] Piasecki resolved to begin guerrilla warfare in the fall.

The Failure of Operation Strike and Merger with the AK

Piasecki issued marching orders on October 15. He designated the Sterdyńskie woods, some fifty miles east of Warsaw, as the site for his troops to gather.[86] The partisans left Warsaw on October 18 and 19, boarding trains to Małkinia, the border station between the General Gouvernement and Białystok Bezirk, part of the Reich. The columns of young men carrying backpacks easily caught the attention of both passengers and railroad guards, but they reached the rendezvous point on October 20. Of the two hundred men gathered under the command of Ignacy Telechun, only 30 percent were armed, mostly with pistols.[87] The rest of the arms were to be delivered by a local confederation cell. While waiting for the shipment to arrive, the partisans spread out in the forest and nearby meadows.

It is not clear how the Germans discovered them.[88] First, German gendarmes intercepted the delayed arms shipment, killing the entire escort. Shortly afterward, they attacked the main Polish forces, killing or wounding some twenty partisans and taking thirty prisoners.[89] Still, the majority of the Polish forces managed to break through the line and escape. The decisive failure was Telechun's, who divided his men into two groups: sixty under his command were to cross the Bug River, while the rest were to return to Warsaw. The Germans hunted down many of the unarmed partisans, and Telechun dissolved the unit after two weeks. The survivors reached Warsaw at the end of October, complaining bitterly about the disastrous organization of the action and the amateurism of their commanders.[90] For more than a few, it was the end of service under Piasecki's command.

Despite this colossal failure, Piasecki did not abandon his plans. In the winter of 1943, he dispatched a small detachment of partisans under the command of Ryszard Reiff to the Białystok district. Meanwhile, Piasecki had to cope with another challenge. Rowecki, who viewed the foray into the Sterdyńskie woods as a senseless massacre, was now pressuring the confederation to accept the authority of the Home Army and the government in exile.[91] The merger talks dragged for months, partly because of Piasecki's insistence on preserving some measure of autonomy but mostly because the AK command had to cope with a far more important issue: the deterioration and eventual breakup of Polish-Soviet relations in the wake of the Katyń affair in April 1943.

The response of the London underground to the discovery of the mass graves of Polish officers was far from unanimous, especially in the context of an aggressive Nazi propaganda campaign and the Allies' unwillingness to recognize the Soviet crime. The government in exile avoided placing unequivocal blame on the Soviets, but Piasecki's press showed no such restraint. *Nowa Polska* declared that the Soviet problem should be solved not by negotiations and compromises but only by armed struggle.[92]

In May and June 1943, Piasecki and 160 of his men joined Reiff's unit in the countryside northeast of Warsaw, and after numerous bloody encounters with both the Nazis and communist detachments reached the heavily forested area east of Białystok.[93] Piasecki had planned to advance to Lithuania, but instead had to return to Warsaw for the concluding round of negotiations with the Home Army command. This time, he would be dealing with different men.

On June 30, 1943, the Gestapo arrested Rowecki, the commander of the AK. Five days later, on July 4, Sikorski died in a plane crash at Gibraltar. The result was a significant shift in Polish politics. The new leadership, which consisted of Prime Minister Stanisław Mikołajczyk; General Kazimierz Sosnkowski, the new commander in chief; and General Tadeusz (Bór) Komorowski, who was in charge of the Home Army, lacked Sikorski's prestige and Rowecki's leadership skills. The three men were also sharply divided in their political visions. Mikołajczyk was a pragmatic democrat from the Peasant Party who did not sit well with the Right and the military. He still believed that Polish-Soviet cooperation was possible. Sosnkowski was a pessimistic realist and an ardent anticommunist, opposed to any agreement with the Soviet Union. Komorowski, finally, was a career cavalry officer from the landed elite, brave and patriotic but inexperienced in commanding a large organization. He lacked his predecessor's sense of self-confidence and easily fell under the influence of his entourage.[94]

The three men took their posts at a time when the prospect of Poland's liberation by the Soviets was increasingly real. The victories of the Red Army at Stalingrad and Kursk had elevated the Soviet Union to a dominant position in the anti-Nazi coalition in Europe. The government in exile believed that liberation by the Soviet Union would most likely result in territorial losses and vassal status for Poland. Soviet claims to the Polish territories east of the 1941 German-Soviet border and the strong presence of Soviet partisans in these lands indicated Moscow's plans for annexation. In addition, such actions as the creation of the Union of Polish Patriots in March 1943, the formation of the Polish division of General Zygmunt Berling, and the increased activities of the Polish Workers' Party in occupied Poland signaled Moscow's intention to set up a pro-Soviet, communist-controlled government.

In this context, the question of the Polish response to the oncoming Soviet advance became particularly urgent. The previous plan of launching an uprising during the (presumed) simultaneous collapse of Germany and the arrival of the Allies had become obsolete. By January 1943, Rowecki already had advised Sikorski that the timing of an uprising should correspond not with the disintegration of the Wehrmacht but with the Soviet advance into the eastern borderlands. But first, the Polish government had to secure military aid from the Allies, obtain Soviet recognition of Poland's sovereignty in these lands, and announce a program of radical social reforms in order to disarm Soviets collaborators.[95] Sikorski had been skeptical: in the event of Soviet hostility, he argued, the insurrection should be canceled and AK units withdrawn into central Poland.[96] In his last dispatch to the prime minister, Rowecki recommended that the AK units stay underground and slow down the Soviet advance by carrying out sabotage activities.[97]

Komorowski shared Rowecki's hostility toward the Soviets. He also faced the question of how the AK should act in the east *before* the Soviet advance. In 1942, the Soviets had boosted their partisan network in the eastern borderlands and regularly attacked AK units.[98] Under these conditions, the AK had to strengthen its own military presence in the area. This was Piasecki's chance, since his Strike doctrine had emphasized armed struggle in the east.

On August 17, 1943, Komorowski issued an order merging Piasecki's military units with the AK. Piasecki received the rank of lieutenant. The Cadre Strike Battalions were transformed into a separate AK unit under Piasecki's command, which would be supervised by the commander of the given AK region in which it operated.[99] Ironically, at the time of the merger Piasecki's battalion was placed under the supervision of Colonel Władysław Liniarski, commander of the AK Białystok district, who had expressed strong opposition to Piasecki's "wild" partisan warfare because it provoked harsh German reprisals against the civilian population.[100] Because of Liniarski's open hostility to his new subordinates, the Home Army command decided to move Piasecki's men to the Nowogródek AK region.[101]

Piasecki left Warsaw in mid-September 1943, joined his unit, and reached the Nowogródek region in late October.[102] Sometime in mid-October, he dispatched three couriers to Lithuania to test the possibility of Polish-Lithuanian cooperation. Eventually, his emissaries made contact with General Stašys Raštikis, a leading member of the Lithuanian underground movement, but the talks conducted in Kaunas in November 1943 yielded no practical results.[103] The initiative also drew harsh criticism from the local delegate to the delegatura, Zygmunt Fedorowicz, who accused Piasecki of acting as a "self-appointed ambassador of the Polish cause."[104] This was hardly an auspicious beginning.

In the *Kresy*, October 1943–July 1944

Divided into southern and northern halves by the Niemen River, the scantly populated and heavily forested Nowogródek AK district was of strategic importance because of its railway links. Its ethnic makeup included Poles, Belorussians, Jews (mostly exterminated by 1943), and Lithuanians. Following the German attack on the Soviet Union, the province became part of the Reichskommissariat Ostland. The Germans held only the urban areas, while the countryside remained under the control of partisans. By the fall of 1943, strong Soviet guerrilla detachments controlled the territory south of the Niemen River, while the AK prevailed on the northern bank. The partisans commanded vast forces: 10,000 to 15,000 from the Soviet side and 5,500 to 8,000 Poles from the AK under Colonel Janusz Prawdzic-Szlaski.[105] By December 1943, Soviet forces had eradicated the AK from the southern bank of the Niemen River and made intrusions into the north.[106] The local Home Army found itself in a dramatic situation: on the one hand, it had to fight German antipartisan expeditions; on the other, it had to defend itself from the Soviets.

Piasecki's unit was incorporated into the Seventy-seventh AK Infantry Regiment. Initially, these Warsaw intelligentsia youths and peasant lads from the Podlasie region did not get along with the locals. They did not speak the *kresy* dialect, which contained many Belorussian words and phrases. Ostentatiously religious and cultivated, they soon acquired the ironic nickname of "Queen Jadwiga's army" (Wojsko Królowej Jadwigi).[107] It was not long before they received their baptism by fire. In late November, Piasecki's unit fought a battle against a large Soviet partisan unit.[108] Less than two weeks later, Piasecki was wounded in the leg in a skirmish with German forces. He took a temporary leave to Warsaw, where he stayed for several weeks.

While in the capital, Piasecki wrote an article about the prospects of Polish-Soviet relations. He had no doubt that the Soviets would enter Polish territory not as allies but as an invading army. Although difficult, the Poles' position was not entirely hopeless, as the bulk of the Soviet forces would be engaged against the Germans. In addition, the Allies, who needed a sovereign Poland as a cordon separating western Europe from the Soviet Union, would force the Soviets to recognize Poland's independence and her prewar borders.[109]

The tone of the article differed greatly from Piasecki's rhetoric of just a year before. Soviet victories in the east had forced Piasecki to abandon his dreams of a Slavic empire and to limit his territorial demands to the preservation of prewar frontiers. This, however, was not the core issue. Piasecki echoed the provisions of the so-called Tempest Plan, which anticipated attacks on the retreating Germans, tactical cooperation with the Red Army, and the disclosure of underground Polish governing institutions in the liberated territories.[110] What he did not know was that the battle for the eastern borderlands had already been lost at the Tehran Conference, where the Allies had recognized the Soviet territorial annexations of 1939 and decided to move Poland's borders westward. Piasecki refused to believe that the British and Americans would abandon the Poles, because such a conclusion undermined the very meaning of the five-year-long struggle.

There is no doubt that after the merger with the AK, Piasecki moderated his program and rhetoric. Announced on the 150th anniversary of the 1794 Kościuszko uprising, the confederation's new manifesto, *The Program Theses of New Poland* (Tezy programowe Nowej Polski), presented a mishmash of Christian universalism and corporatist ideas. Naturally, Piasecki's classic concept of serving God as the highest destiny of man crowned the program. The complementary section that had explicated work for the nation as the path to God was replaced, however, by a general appraisal of the nation-state as being among "the principal forms of social life." This point paled in comparison to Piasecki's endorsement of "social democracy," vaguely defined as "the right of each individual to have equal opportunities." On the other hand, a reference to the "highest socioeconomic representation consisting of the representatives of the labor force and institutions of culture" hinted at Piasecki's enduring corporatism. He also emphasized the need for a strong welfare state, land reform, the nationalization of banks and public services, and a central economic plan regulating both public and private sectors. While small industry would remain private, the ownership of large industry would pass to shareholders recruited from the labor force.[111]

Piasecki's abandonment of his earlier protofascist views is not surprising. In the fifth year of the war against the Nazis and in the context of his total reliance on the AK, such remarks would have been unthinkable. In May 1943, the KN publicist who wrote under the pseudonym Włodzimierz from Halicz concluded that the Polish totalitarians (*totaliści*) had disappeared entirely in concentration camps and Nazi prisons or had revised their views.[112] But Piasecki's radical economic agenda also highlighted a general phenomenon among European anti-Nazi resisters. The war constituted a revolution not only in terms of its brutalizing effect on society but also in the development of postwar socioeconomic designs. In unoccupied England, invaded France, occupied Poland, and divided Italy alike, resisters perceived victory over fascism as a chance for social change. Societies and economies were to move to the Left. Even Piasecki recognized this trend.

Piasecki returned to his unit in February 1944. Shortly afterward, he took part in a court-martial against his former commander Major Józef Świda, who was accused of negotiating a temporary truce with the Germans.[113] When the AK High Command resolved to stop skirmishes with the Soviets and to prepare for military cooperation with the Red Army against the retreating Germans, Świda had objected and concluded a nonaggression agreement with a local German commander.[114] The court, consisting of Major Maciej Kalenkiewicz and Major Jan Piwnik—both representatives of the AK High Command—and Piasecki, condemned the defendant to death. The sentence was commuted, however, and Świda transferred to the Kraków AK district.[115]

The lenient treatment of Świda was not unusual. At the time of the trial, there were other AK leaders who had negotiated one or another form of armistice with the Germans in order to defend themselves against Soviet partisans.[116] The affair demonstrates the peculiar character of guerrilla warfare in the eastern territories, where the Home Army engaged in practices that were unthinkable in other parts of occupied Poland. What was taking place in the kresy resembled the pattern of resistance struggles in Yugoslavia or Greece, where anti-Nazi resistance fragmented into rival factions and ethnic groups, often engaging in various deals with occupying forces.

In May 1944, Piasecki's unit crossed into Wilno province and passed under the command of Colonel Aleksander Krzyżanowski. The new terrain differed substantially from that of Nowogródek. The Soviet military presence was weaker, and the Polish underground stronger. At the same time, the province was the scene of bitter ethnic conflict between Poles and Lithuanians. The Wilno region had been conquered by the Soviets in September 1939, then handed over to the Lithuanian Republic, annexed to the Soviet Union in June 1940, and finally captured by the Germans in 1941. Under the Nazi occupation, Lithuanian collaborators were allowed to set up the quasi-governmental Taryba, or Lithuanian State Council. Both the quislings and the underground Lithuanian Liberation Committee (Vyriausias Lietuvos Islaisvinimo Komitetas) treated the province as an integral part of the Lithuanian state. Talks between the Lithuanian underground and the Polish resistance ended in fiasco, since neither side was ready to abandon its claim to the disputed area.[117] Meanwhile, the collaborationist Sauguna police force waged a terror campaign against the Polish population. The situation became even worse after the creation of the German-sponsored Lithuanian Auxiliary Force (Litauische Sonderverbande) under the command of General Povilas Plechavičius in February 1944. When the Lithuanian Auxiliary Force attacked Polish settlements and AK units in May 1944, the Home Army launched a counteroffensive that destroyed most of the Lithuanian field units. In the same month, the Germans arrested Plechavičius and disbanded his units after the general refused to deploy Lithuanian troops outside Lithuania.[118]

By the time of Piasecki's transfer, the local AK had begun preparations for the Tempest Plan. Under Krzyżanowski's command, Polish forces were to attack the retreating Germans and capture Wilno before the advance of the Red Army. The operation received the codename Ostra Brama (Sharp Gate), a reference to the holy shrine of the Virgin Mary in Wilno. Krzyżanowski proceeded with his plan in spite of alarming signals from the province of Volhynia, where after engaging in initial military cooperation with the Red Army, AK units had been disarmed and incorporated into the Soviet-organized Berling army. The attack on Wilno was supposed to take place on July 7 at 11:00 p.m.[119]

By then, Piasecki's unit was a large, well-armed, and battle-hardened detachment with excellent morale.[120] Throughout his service in the east, Piasecki had gained the respect of his superiors and the commanders of other units, though he hardly resembled a classical military man. He used his free time for reading and political deliberation, often dictating his reflections from bed. In his contacts with soldiers, Piasecki showed a great deal of calm and flexibility, far from the strict military haughtiness typical of career officers.[121] Photographs taken during this period show him slim, with a stubble-covered chin, and he appears good-spirited and amiable with his staff. In their testimonies, other AK officers praised his unit as a well-functioning team fanatically loyal to its commander.[122]

On July 4, Piasecki participated in a staff meeting for the commanders of the AK units that constituted the eastern group of the Polish forces attacking Wilno. The assault from outside would be accompanied by an uprising in the city. The absence of units responsible for the northern and southern flanks meant that Krzyżanowski could throw only four thousand soldiers against the Germans.[123] The German defenders anticipated the Polish attack, and even attempted to win the Poles over to the idea of defending the city against the Soviets.[124] They fortified their positions and received substantial reinforcements, increasing their number to seventeen thousand soldiers supported by heavy artillery, tanks, and planes.[125]

On July 5, Krzyżanowski received a report that units of the Soviet Third Belorussian Front had captured the town of Smorgonie, east of Wilno. This meant that the Soviets were expected at the outskirts of the city within a day or two. AK units stormed Wilno shortly after midnight on July 6, 1944. The advance almost immediately stalled under heavy fire from German artillery, machine guns, and planes. After losing forty killed and eighty wounded, Piasecki's unit had to retreat.[126] In the afternoon, the first Soviet detachments reached the city and joined in the battle. Fighting shoulder to shoulder, the Poles and Soviets destroyed the last pockets of German resistance within a week.[127]

In accordance with the directives of the Tempest Plan, the Polish civilian authorities took over the administration of the city. As a precaution, Krzyżanowski kept the majority of his forces outside Wilno in the Rudnicka forest. On July 15, 1944, he sent an enthusiastic cable to Warsaw reporting on talks with General Ivan Chernyakhovsky, the commander of the Third Belorussian Front. The Soviets had agreed to Krzyżanowski's proposal to form one infantry and one cavalry brigade from the AK forces. The Polish troops would work under Soviet operational command, but independently of Berling's army.[128] The next day, Chernyakhovsky invited Krzyżanowski, his staff, and his commanding officers for another round of negotiations. Upon their arrival, the Polish commanders were apprehended and arrested.[129] Those senior officers who escaped led the AK forces into the Rudnicka forest and ordered the troops to break into small groups and disperse or move out to the west. Within days, most AK soldiers had fallen into Soviet hands. Those who refused to join Berling's army were deported to labor and POW camps.[130]

Piasecki escaped this debacle through sheer luck. Instead of attending the meeting with the Soviets, he sent a deputy who managed to escape and alert his commander.[131] Piasecki gathered his men and marched to the Rudnicka forest to join the other Home Army units. At a meeting with senior officers, he announced the dissolution of his unit. The soldiers from Wilno and Nowogródek provinces were free to go home, while those who had come with him from central Poland would return to their region to continue the struggle. Piasecki's superiors approved the decision.[132]

After the meeting, Piasecki divided the remnants of his unit into three groups, which started marching westward.[133] Reiff's march was the shortest. On July 22, 1944, his group was captured by the Soviets in the vicinity of Grodno. But Stanisław Karolkiewicz's and Piasecki's groups sneaked through Soviet lines and reached the General Gouvernement.

In Hiding, August–November 1944

On August 21, 1944, Piasecki entered the already liberated town of Józefów, east of Warsaw.[134] The Warsaw Uprising had begun three weeks earlier. Because German forces had sealed the capital, Piasecki could not join in the struggle. Among AK soldiers fighting in Warsaw were Piasecki's wife, Halina, and his brother, Zdzisław. Both were killed in August. Piasecki learned of the deaths of his wife and brother in October 1944. At that point, he still did not know that his two sons, Bohdan and Jarosław, had survived the uprising.[135]

Adopting the name Leon Wojcieszkiewicz, Piasecki joined the post-liberation AK underground.[136] It was a new kind of conspiracy, operating in a new environment in which Soviet secret police units (the NKVD) and the Soviet-led Polish security forces hunted down Home Army soldiers. By early September, most of the territories on the right bank of the Vistula River had already been captured by the Soviets and put under the administration of the communist-led Polish Committee of National Liberation, created on July 20, 1944.

There were few alternatives for Home Army soldiers. Some disclosed themselves, hoping that they would be allowed to return to normal life. Many joined Berling's army and went on fighting the Germans. But the majority adopted a wait-and-see approach and remained underground. Trapped in embattled Warsaw, the AK command forbade fighting with the advancing Soviets, seeking to dissolve the Home Army in liberated territories and replace it with a new underground organization. After the defeat of the Warsaw Uprising, these directives were carried out by a new AK commander, General Leopold Okulicki.

Piasecki became involved in the reconstruction of the AK underground shortly after his arrival in central Poland. From late September until early November 1944, he frequently conferred with Colonel Henryk Krajewski, Colonel Szlaski (his former commander), and Witold Bieńkowski from the Government Delegacy.[137] He also began organizing a rescue mission for the Wilno AK survivors, oversaw the launching of underground publications, and maintained radio contact with London.[138]

Among those who joined Piasecki's conspiratorial cell was Ryszard Romanowski, a former National Radical and confederate. It is not clear whether he was already an agent provocateur, but there is no doubt that he denounced Piasecki to the NKVD.[139] Piasecki was arrested by military intelligence officers of the First Polish Army in Józefów on November 12, 1944.[140]

4 ‖ Under the Cross and the Red Flag, 1945–56

PIASECKI'S INCARCERATION BY THE COMMUNISTS and his subsequent release were turning points in his life. The decision of Poland's new rulers to exonerate and support a man whose credentials included chauvinistic nationalism, anti-Semitism, and anticommunism was in fact less paradoxical than it seemed. Elsewhere in Eastern and Western Europe, after the initial wave of purges, numerous former fascists and right-wing radicals reentered postwar politics. In East Germany, Hungary, Italy, and Romania, thousands of them joined the respective national communist parties.

The communists often turned a blind eye to these recruits' fascist pasts. In Italy, where fascism had lasted for two decades, millions of people, including some wartime resisters, had ties to Mussolini's regime. Memories of the civil war that had swept north-central Italy from 1943 to 1945 still loomed large in the minds of the country's postwar leaders. Palmiro Togliatti, the head of the Italian Communist Party and minister of justice in the postwar government, quickly understood that retribution would not facilitate the restoration of order. The fate of Greece, where a civil war brought military intervention from the British, victory for a conservative royalist regime, and a purge of the Left, showed what could have happened to Italy if tensions had continued. In 1946, Togliatti pushed for an amnesty law that allowed the return of many fascists to normal life and politics, often in the ranks of the Italian Communist Party.[1]

While Togliatti's strategy rested on caution, East German, Hungarian, and Romanian communists' relative tolerance for fascist small fry reflected their own initial weakness and unpopularity. To put it bluntly, they had to expand the membership of their parties if they wanted to run local government, control the police, and take hold of the economy. Technocrats and seasoned veterans could facilitate national recovery and, by extension, a communist takeover. In Bulgaria, Kimon Georgiev, the leader of the Zveno group that had instigated two military coups and imitated Mussolini's ruling style in the past, joined the communist-dominated government and remained in high posts until his retirement at the age of eighty in 1962.

Some former fascists switched over to communism out of opportunism or fear of retribution. Yet ideology also played an important role, as both movements aspired to build an omnipresent state and a new society in opposition to liberalism, democracy, and capitalism. The communists' use of the nationalist card, as evidenced in the expulsion of ethnic Germans and the lenient treatment of anti-Semitic excesses, appealed to large segments of societies that still harbored a fear of Germans and a loathing of Jews. In Western Europe, the revolutionary rhetoric of liberation soon gave way to a predominantly conservative mood and programs favored by Christian Democrats and other anticommunist moderates. National consensus often necessitated collective amnesia. All these developments undermine the "hour zero" myth and point to significant political continuities in post–World War II Europe.

Enter Piasecki, who benefited from the communists' readiness to experiment with nationalism and to accept its right-wing adepts. Unlike nationalist elements in Western Europe or in the Balkan countries that had joined the Axis powers, the Polish Right largely escaped the stigma of having collaborated with the Nazis. Because Poland's communists faced strong opposition, they sought supporters from outside their ranks as a way of adjusting to political realities in a hostile country. In addition, Piasecki and the Polish communist leader Władysław Gomułka shared some common ground: both men were nationalistic and believed in a unitary Polish nation-state. Indeed, they would cooperate for many years to come.

For Piasecki, postwar Poland had much to offer. The old classes had vanished from the scene, and few Jews remained. It fell to the communists to execute the Polish nationalists' long-standing goal of transforming Poland into an ethnically homogenous and predominantly Catholic country.

It was clear to Piasecki that the Soviets were there to stay. In a conversation with Ryszard Reiff in 1946, Piasecki stated that the power of the Red Army and the directives of Soviet leaders would shape political reality in Poland. The country could regain its independence only on two conditions: First, it had to rebuild its devastated economy and infrastructure. Second, communism had to be eroded away. Piasecki anticipated that the Soviet

Union gradually would lose its political, ideological, and economic dynamism. "The fall of one superpower is more likely than the simultaneous end of three powers," he continued, recalling the collapse of the partitioning empires in 1918. "[Last time,] we had to wait for this moment for one hundred twenty-three years. This time, it will not take so long." His estimate was fifty years.[2] Very much like Dmowski, who forty years earlier had decided to participate in the 1905 elections to the Russian Duma, Piasecki determined that the nation was more important than state independence, which was a means of national development rather than its final goal. But he also recognized that the state, even in truncated form, was fundamental to the preservation and expansion of national cohesion, spirit, and discipline.[3]

The Pact with the Devil, 1944–45

Piasecki's arrest was part of a major NKVD operation against the Polish resistance. On December 19, 1944, Lavrenty Beria reported to Stalin about the liquidation of the AK network east of Warsaw.[4] By the end of the year, the Soviets had wiped out what might have become the new command center of the Home Army in central Poland.

Following his arrest, Piasecki was moved to General Ivan Serov's headquarters in Lublin. He also spent time in Włochy, a suburb of Warsaw, where the NKVD held a number of detainees.[5] In his confessions to interrogators, Piasecki portrayed himself as a leader in underground conspiracy structures. He gave the impression that not only had he coordinated clandestine operations, but he also had been in charge of building the new resistance network.[6] By magnifying his importance, Piasecki hoped to buy himself more time.

The tactic paid off. He caught the attention of Serov, who conferred with Piasecki, probably in Lublin in late 1944.[7] The atmosphere of Piasecki's conversations with Serov was rather informal—Piasecki's son, Jarosław, later recalled his father's astonishing confession that he and Serov even talked about their erotic conquests.[8] Transcripts of these talks cannot be found in Polish archives, and the absence of this crucial evidence contributed over the years to the proliferation of rumors suggesting that Piasecki had become a Soviet agent.

The harshest accusations against Piasecki came from Colonel Józef Światło, a high official of the Polish security police who defected to the West in December 1953 and who had been part of the team investigating Piasecki's case in 1945. Światło alleged that Serov had recruited Piasecki in the Lublin prison.[9] A ruthless Stalinist henchman himself, Światło tried to rehabilitate himself by discrediting his communist superiors. For this reason, Światło's reports cannot be taken at face value. In an interview with Polish journalist Teresa Torańska, Jakub Berman, the éminence grise of the Stalinist leadership in Poland, mentioned that Piasecki's charm and intelligence were not lost on Serov, who exuberantly praised Piasecki as a "genius boy" (*genial'nyi mal'chik*). In all probability, Berman said, Piasecki had succeeded in presenting himself to Serov as a valuable asset in pacifying Poland.[10]

Gomułka sought to learn about Piasecki's contacts with Serov, yet his opinions on the subject were inconsistent. In his memoirs, Gomułka implied that Piasecki had worked for Soviet intelligence.[11] But on a different occasion, he characterized Piasecki's agreement with Serov as "political cooperation." Essentially, he saw Piasecki as a political opportunist.[12]

Despite the absence of transcripts, Piasecki's memo to the communist leadership, drafted in jail on May 22, 1945, alludes to topics that they may have discussed:

> During my detention, I wrote several reports on issues which were suggested to me by General Ivanov [Serov] and Colonel Becun [Franciszek Bycan, deputy chief of Polish military intelligence]. These issues included an analysis of the situation in the country at the end of 1944; methods of increasing the influence of the Polish Committee for National Liberation; the characteristics of particular Polish political groups; and ideas about my cooperation with the Provisional Government.[13]

Russian-language translations of Piasecki's memoranda to Serov contain specific suggestions that Piasecki offered his Soviet captors. He pointed out that the ongoing persecution of Home Army soldiers by the communist authorities had galvanized former resistance fighters into taking action against the new government. If the communists sought peace, he advised, they had to acknowledge the sacrifices that the AK had made in the struggle against the Nazis and terminate the repression of these former partisans.[14] Piasecki also vowed to cooperate with the Polish Committee of National Liberation. Not only did he endorse the communists' social and economic reforms, but he also supported the struggle against the "reactionary current in Polish society." His own contributions to the reconstruction of the country, he suggested, might range from work in academia—interestingly, Piasecki styled himself a scholar—to the recruitment of former brothers-in-arms for close work with the communist government.[15]

Piasecki's talks with Serov changed the course of the investigation. On April 10, 1945, military intelligence forwarded Piasecki's case to the Polish Ministry of Public Security (Ministerstwo Bezpieczeństwa Publicznego, MBP).[16] On May 22, Piasecki submitted to the communist leadership two draft memoranda, which in all probability ended up on the desk of Gomułka. In the first statement, Piasecki recanted his totalitarian and anti-Semitic prewar views but also emphasized that the National Radicals shared with the communists the goal of social revolution. Nazi ideology had never influenced his anti-German and pro-Catholic doctrine. He also praised the achievements of the Provisional Government, including its land reform program, the establishment of the Oder-Neisse border, and the conduct of foreign policy on the principle of Slavic brotherhood.[17]

In the second document, Piasecki admitted that until 1944, he had viewed the Soviet Union as an enemy. Since then, however, he had realized that Polish society needed to be "reeducated" vis-à-vis its eastern neighbor. The new government could secure the support of noncommunists—with Piasecki's help. "I am deeply convinced," he stated, "that through my influence I can mobilize the reluctant strata of society to active cooperation," particularly the "young generation," which he called "a social and ideological force that matured during the war."[18]

Piasecki reminded the communists that Soviet bayonets and terror alone could not pacify Poland. To secure internal peace, they had to extend a hand to people at the other end of the political-ideological spectrum. Both sides needed to modify their political platforms, the communists by permitting political pluralism and the nationalists—for that matter all non-Marxists—by terminating their support for the London government and the anticommunist underground.

The pact that Piasecki envisioned made sense in the short term. Although the Yalta Conference in February 1945 had cemented Poland in the Soviet sphere of influence, its provisions also called for the reorganization of the Provisional Government through the inclusion of noncommunist politicians and for free elections. The Yalta decisions were accepted by former prime minister Stanisław Mikołajczyk and by Home Army commander General Leopold Okulicki.[19] By the spring of 1945, however, the attitude of the AK loyalists was no longer a factor. Lured by an invitation to talks with Serov, leaders of the underground state were arrested, flown to Moscow, and tried for crimes against the Soviet Union. On June 21, 1945, all but three defendants were found guilty and sentenced to prison.[20] The Trial of Sixteen, as it was called, took place as the Polish communists and democratic politicians were in negotiations for the creation of a government of national unity in Moscow; the talks ended on the day the court rendered its verdict. Intimidated and pushed into a compromise by the Allies, the noncommunists agreed to enter the new government. Two weeks later, on July 2, 1945, Captain Józef Różański signed the order for Piasecki's release. The communists had decided to test his usefulness on the Catholic front.

Commissars and Catholics, 1945–48

The Polish church came out of the war decimated. Some two thousand Polish priests, including six bishops, had perished in Nazi concentration camps, jails, and mass executions. But the combined effects of border shifts, population transfers, and the Holocaust also had transformed Poland into an ethnically homogenous and predominantly Catholic country. Whereas before the war Roman Catholics had constituted 60 percent of the population, in 1945 that figure had risen to 90 percent, facts not taken lightly by the communists.[21] Although they nullified the previous government's concordat with the Vatican on September 12, 1945, they refrained from placing restrictions on the Church's pastoral activities. Monastic orders, clergy-administered schools, and charitable institutions continued to operate freely. High state officials and military officers participated in religious festivities.[22]

Church leaders also tried to avoid antagonistic moves. In general, the bishops pushed for a return to normal life and welcomed the acquisition of the western territories from defeated Germany.[23] In Kraków, Archbishop Adam Sapieha ignored appeals from London and the underground to boycott the new order and arranged for the publication of *Tygodnik powszechny*, a Catholic weekly devoted to social, cultural, and religious issues.[24] Under its editors, Rev. Jan Piwowarczyk and Jerzy Turowicz, *Tygodnik powszechny* quickly became the voice of the liberal Catholic intelligentsia. Kraków also hosted an informal debating club that attracted people of diverse political opinions, including conservatives and young nationalists such as Dominik Horodyński, Wojciech Kętrzyński (both affiliated with Piasecki), and Aleksander Bocheński.

In April of that year, Bocheński came into contact with Major Jerzy Borejsza. Both men were known for their unorthodox political views and pragmatism. A member of an aristocratic family, Bocheński had joined Sanacja's conservative circles.[25] During the war, after a brief flirtation with Piasecki's group, he had withdrawn from resistance activities and worked for the charitable Main Welfare Council (Rada Główna Opiekuńcza).[26] Raised in a Jewish family, Borejsza was the brother of Józef Różański, the security officer who had supervised Piasecki's case. A communist since the 1930s, Borejsza spent the war in the Red Army. After his return to Poland, he quickly became the main organizer of publishing ventures in the liberated territories. Borejsza did not limit his advances to the pursuit of left-wing writers and journalists. "This man lied a lot," wrote journalist Stefan Kisielewski years later. "He fancied the crazy idea of attracting all Endeks and rightists."[27] Borejsza's politics might have been unconventional, but his overtures of goodwill to noncommunist intellectuals reflected a drive by the Polish Workers' Party (PPR) to broaden its support base.

Borejsza's meetings with Bocheński, Kętrzyński, and a group of Catholic activists that included Stanisław Stomma and Turowicz, took place in Kraków in late April and early June. Warning that the country was drifting toward a full-scale civil war, Catholic intellectuals proposed the establishment of an opposition group that, while supportive of the government's foreign policy, would still contest domestic matters. Borejsza, for his part, declared that nothing prevented non-Marxists from reentering politics. But when he tried to extract from his interlocutors a public appeal for social peace and national reconciliation, he left empty-handed.[28]

Though Borejsza's talks were a fiasco, he did succeed in developing a good rapport with Kętrzyński. At one meeting between the two men, Kętrzyński learned that Piasecki was alive and that his release was a foregone conclusion. "We are not going to prosecute your group for wartime activities," stated Borejsza. "Although you were in the camp of our enemies, we recognize you as anti-German resisters."[29]

When Piasecki left the prison, Kętrzyński and others attributed his freedom to Borejsza's goodwill. Indeed, both Borejsza and Różański played prominent roles in Piasecki's release. The brothers acted, however, on orders from the regime, which already had decided Piasecki's fate. On July 4, 1945, two days after his release from prison, Piasecki was received by Władysław Gomułka. The secretary-general sought to learn more about the possibility of dialogue with Catholics and his guest's political program. By the time of their next meeting on July 18, Gomułka had received Piasecki's political theses.

Piasecki pronounced God, mankind, nation, and family to be absolute values. He endorsed land reform and the nationalization of major industries and banks. In reference to national minorities, he observed: "Poland is an ethnically homogenous country. The Germans can stay only as a labor force. All separatist movements [a reference to the Ukrainian Insurgent Army] should be dealt with through the policy of population transfers." Piasecki condemned expressions of anti-Semitism, but with some reservations. "One should pay attention to the fact that the disproportionate number of Jews in the state apparatus nurtures a new anti-Semitism among the population," he stated. The military should be free from party politics, he declared, and open to members of all resistance organizations. Turning to the Catholic issue, Piasecki proposed the basis for a rapprochement: The communists should not view the Catholics as the incarnation of political reaction, whereas the latter would have to relinquish their distrust of Marxists. Dialogue between Marxists and Catholics would benefit both sides and enable Poland to serve as a bridge between the East and the West.[30]

Gomułka might have scorned the idea of enriching Marxism through Catholicism, but otherwise he was probably pleased with Piasecki's observations. Known for his opposition to the dogmatic thinking of many pre-war communists, he hoped to consolidate political power through a coalition model rather than through repression and ideological unanimity.[31] He also repeatedly contested the influence of Soviet experts in the Polish military and security services.[32]

The demand for a one-nation state and a distrust of Jews were elements of the traditional program of the nationalist Right, but they were not necessarily unacceptable to Gomułka. Having excluded the possibility of legalizing the National Party, he nonetheless could not ignore the fact that ethnocentric nationalism commanded considerable support in Polish society, especially in the context of the country's new ethnic and confessional makeup. In this respect, Piasecki had the potential to channel nationalist clientele into the government camp without the attendant risk of rebuilding Endecja. It would be a safety valve, easy to control or shut off when necessary.[33] His partial endorsement of Piasecki's views did not mean, however, that Gomułka trusted the former fascist. The communist security police placed Piasecki under surveillance and set about recruiting agents in his circle—with quite a bit of success, judging from their well-informed reports.

Gomułka gave the green light to Piasecki's initiative of forming an association around a new newspaper called *Dziś i jutro* (Today and Tomorrow). Borejsza and Piasecki hammered out the specifics of launching the Catholic weekly at a café in downtown Warsaw. Piasecki's release and his public appearance at the side of a prominent communist produced a political sensation. The poet Julian Tuwim wrote a short, sarcastic poem commenting on Borejsza's meetings with the former fascist: "Forgetting about their yesterday / With 'Today and Tomorrow' he flirts today."[34]

Piasecki's resurrection was astonishing, but in the course of the summer and autumn, the political scene in Poland became populated with other figures of sundry and diverse persuasions. Stanisław Mikołajczyk arrived in Warsaw on June 27 to take the posts of deputy premier and minister of agriculture. Cardinal August Hlond, the primate of Poland, returned from exile in July 1945. In a homily delivered in Poznań in October of that year, he signaled the possibility of "reconciliation between the healthy revolutionary content of the time and the faith of [the Polish] people."[35] Stanisław Grabski, the nestor of Endecja, even accepted a position in the communist-controlled National Council of the Homeland (Krajowa Rada Narodowa). "The PPR does not have enough people to prevail over the whole administration," Grabski observed. "Therefore, all patriots should enter the state apparatus and sociocultural organizations." His enthusiastic appeals encouraged several former Endek politicians to push for the legalization of the National Party. They soon found themselves behind bars, however.[36]

The communists used numerous methods against the legal opposition: selective arrests, kidnappings, and even murders. Communist agents infiltrated opposition groups and orchestrated party splits.[37] By the end of 1945, however, Poland still had five legal parties: the PPR, the Polish Peasant Party (Polskie Stronnictwo Ludowe, PSL), the Democratic Party, the Labor Party, and the socialists. All shared a desire for radical social and economic reforms, such as the nationalization of heavy industries and banks, land reform, and the introduction of substantial welfare benefits, including free medical care and unrestricted access to education. They were vehemently anti-German and enthusiastic about the acquisition of the western territories. They also deemed military resistance suicidal.

What distinguished Piasecki from opposition politicians was his approach to the communists. Whereas Mikołajczyk complied with the Yalta principles in hope of preventing a complete communist takeover, Piasecki aimed at establishing himself within the PPR-dominated system. He did not command a fully fledged political party, but this limitation also spared him the worries that beset opposition leaders. Parties could be crushed and eliminated, but Catholics were there to stay.

Not only did the communists facilitate Piasecki's initiative to launch the weekly newspaper, but they also allowed him to lease numerous workshops and small factories.[38] These were the beginnings of a financial empire that by the 1950s had grown into two giant commercial companies, INCO and Veritas—possibly the biggest private enterprise to function behind the iron curtain. In the fall of 1945, however, Piasecki had to seek other resources to finance his newspaper. The initial capital of $4,000 came from the remnants of the conspiratorial funds of the Confederation of the Nation. In addition, Piasecki received $500 from Cardinal Hlond.[39]

For any organization that declared itself Catholic, the support of the Church hierarchy was absolutely crucial. The editorial team of *Dziś i jutro*, gathered for the first time on October 12, 1945, consisted of an assortment of odd bedfellows: Piasecki; Aleksander Bocheński; Witold Bieńkowski, formerly in the Government Delegacy; Jan Dobraczyński, a Catholic writer close to Endecja; Konstanty Łubieński, a former AK soldier; and the renowned journalist Ksawery Pruszyński, previously associated with Sanacja. All came from the Right, but only Bieńkowski and Dobraczyński could be described as prewar Catholic activists.[40] When Hlond received Piasecki, he described him as someone who acted "chaotically," explaining, "He can easily become entangled in schemes and be manipulated."[41] Nevertheless, Hlond endorsed Piasecki's group. Apparently, Piasecki's fascist past and virulent anti-Semitism posed no obstacle. In a conversation with Stomma and Kisielewski, the cardinal described Piasecki as "a good Pole, a good Catholic, and a trustworthy person."[42] The same ardent nationalism that characterized the Polish church before the war facilitated the transformation of a former fascist leader into a Catholic activist.

Lay Catholic circles did not shun Piasecki's group, either—initial relations between *Tygodnik powszechny* and *Dziś i jutro* could be described as good. Several journalists from the Kraków weekly also wrote for Piasecki's paper, and the two publications issued a joint statement condemning the

Kielce pogrom of July 1946, in which a Polish mob killed forty Jews.[43] *Tygodnik warszawski,* connected to the Labor Party, was more reserved toward Piasecki's group but still allowed members of the *Dziś i jutro* staff to publish in its pages.[44]

The frequency of contact among circles representing different political persuasions should come as no surprise. The world of Catholic intellectuals in Poland consisted of a few dozen individuals who knew each other well. In the past, they had belonged to tightly interconnected networks, religious congregations, student corporations, and resistance organizations. But unlike Piasecki and *Tygodnik warszawski,* the editors of *Tygodnik powszechny* were more cautious about making political commitments. They pledged to keep the weekly "apolitical and nonpartisan."[45]

Piasecki had no use for such self-restraint. The first issue of *Dziś i jutro,* published on November 25, 1945, carried two articles by Piasecki, "Speaking Plainly" (Po prostu) and "Essential Issues" (Zagadnienia istotne), in which he argued that the war had discredited totalitarianism. Piasecki recanted his fascist past, his rejection of democracy, and his anti-Semitism, but he did not intend to flog himself. "It is impossible to explain the evolution of our views without highlighting the parts of our program that still remain valid," he wrote. "These elements include . . . our belief in the necessity of radical social and economic changes, and our Catholicism."[46] Although the communists led the revolutionary charge, there also was room for those who adhered to nonmaterialist beliefs to effect positive change. "Poland does not lack Christian revolutionaries," stated Piasecki. "However . . . if these forces do not revolutionize themselves they will lose any impact on reality."[47]

Piasecki broadened these theses in a series of articles published in *Dziś i jutro* from January to March 1946 under the common title "Directions" (Kierunki). The war against Nazism had obliterated the traditional division between Right and Left, he argued. Therefore, nationalists could seek accommodation with the communists.[48] And it was now the Soviet Union that protected Poland's western borders, provided the necessary means for the country's economic reconstruction, and constituted the revolutionary avantgarde of a new era.[49] According to Piasecki, the modern world was dominated by three superpowers: the United States, the Soviet Union, and England. They represented two major ideological currents, Marxism and capitalism, the former on the rise and the latter in decline. The Catholic sociopolitical doctrine, which could serve to counterbalance or to enhance the other two, had not yet been fully formulated. But Poland, he was certain, could serve as the bridge between Western and Eastern Europe, between Christianity and Marxism.[50]

In every case, Piasecki killed two birds with one stone. He talked about Polish manifest destiny by linking it to Soviet control of Poland. He legitimized communist rule by declaring Marxists the avant-garde of progress. He also put himself and his followers on an equal ideological footing with the communists. Perhaps his most revolutionary claim was that both Marxism and Catholicism worked for the good of humanity, Marxism on a materialist level and Catholicism on a spiritual plane. Piasecki's appraisal of the nationalists' revolutionary potential, as well as his reading of Catholicism as the cornerstone of Polish national identity, make it clear that he aspired to a Marxist-Catholic-nationalist trinity, which he believed would benefit all participants: The communists would strengthen their popular appeal and legitimize their rule. The Catholics would share power and enrich Marxism spiritually. The nationalists would convert the Marxists into Polish patriots, in all probability under Piasecki's guidance.

Catholic-Marxist dialogue was not unprecedented. The immediate postwar period was the heyday of Left Catholicism in Western Europe. The ideological confrontations of the 1930s—especially the Spanish Civil War—and above all World War II, with its delegitimization of a nationalist-Catholic Right tainted by social reaction and collaboration with fascism as well as Catholic participation in the resistance against the Nazi occupiers, forced numerous Catholic intellectuals to reconsider Marxism. Of particular importance was the role played by the communists in resistance movements, as well as their increasing hold on the working class. Before Cold War politics in the late 1940s and 1950s eliminated the possibility of establishing some third way, French, Italian, and Belgian progressive Catholics had sought to instill a radical spirit in established Christian democratic parties, to organize Catholic workers, and to open the Church to theological innovations. In Italy, some former resisters from the Christian Left merged with the communists.[51]

Was Piasecki part of this drive? On the surface, his program had much in common with the philosophical thought of the French Personalist Emmanuel Mounier.[52] Deeply revolted by capitalist exploitation and sympathetic to the workers' movement, Mounier sincerely considered nonviolent social revolution to be a form of spiritual advancement and believed that the transcendence of the human model, as well as the complete realization of Christian ideals, could occur only in a just social system. While advocating revolution against liberal capitalism, he sought to disentangle it from materialism. Like his collaborator on the journal *Ésprit*, Jacques Maritain, he deemed Marxism a serious intellectual alternative.[53] In fact, he believed that Personalism complemented Marxist thought in its mission of liberating man: while the former articulated the concept of transcendence, the latter mastered social and economic analysis and practical action.[54] Although opposed to bourgeois individualism, Mounier emphasized the primacy of the human being over ideology, political systems, and economics. Piasecki based his premise on quite opposite reasoning: Polish Catholics should join with the communists because Marxism was a dominant ideological paradigm, because the communists were in power, and because the Polish raison d'état dictated such an alliance. Unlike Mounier, Piasecki emphasized historical determinism at the expense of philosophy.

Yet Mounier considered the members of Piasecki's group to be genuine Christian revolutionaries. He traveled to Poland in May 1946 as part of a delegation of twelve French intellectuals, six communists and six Catholics. In Kraków, Mounier witnessed the creation of the intellectual Catholic journal *Znak* (Sign). Turowicz and Stomma sought to propagate Personalism on Polish soil, but Mounier found them "too entrenched in their aggressive nationalism" and stubborn in their opposition to the communist regime. He believed that their inflexibility could derail the entire project. After his visit to the Warsaw headquarters of *Dziś i jutro*, however, he declared Piasecki's young Catholic group the most dynamic in Poland.[55] Above all, Mounier believed the Poles should establish a modus vivendi with the Soviet Union, adopt socialism—which in its Polish version was not anticlerical—and use their unique historical opportunity to reconcile Catholicism with Marxism.[56] This formula matched exactly what Piasecki and his collaborators were declaring needed to be done, and Mounier's *Ésprit* would cooperate with Piasecki's organization until the late 1950s.

In retrospect, Mounier's message to his Polish hosts seems rather naïve, but nonetheless accurate: the fundamental question for Polish Catholic intellectuals was whether to refrain from social and political activism in a communist-dominated environment. Stomma's answer was minimalism. Piasecki opted for full engagement. And the "three-times-yes" referendum of June 30, 1946, left few alternatives.

In a dress rehearsal for upcoming general elections, the government held a referendum on three questions: the abolition of the Senate, the endorsement of land reform, and the recognition of Poland's new western borders.

The opposition recommended voting no on the first question. The communists, however, already had rigged the vote and claimed to have received affirmative majorities on all three questions.[57] The message to the opposition was clear: there was room for dissent, but the opposition had no right to question the supremacy of the PPR.

The lesson of the referendum was not lost on Piasecki, who wrote to Gomułka in August 1946 to encourage "the replacement of the existing conditions by a new political configuration" that included a Catholic party capable of improving church-state relations, moderating the bishops' anticommunist stance, securing Catholic support for the communists, and serving as coalition partner.[58]

Days before submitting his letter to Gomułka, Piasecki notified Hlond about his plans, justifying his initiative on the grounds that the new party would preserve national identity and consolidate the gains of Catholicism.[59] In October 1946, however, unification talks among the several Catholic factions collapsed when Hlond withdrew his support, pointing out that a separate Catholic electoral list would weaken the position of Mikołajczyk's Peasant Party in the upcoming general elections.[60] Most of the Catholic activists who had participated in the talks obeyed Hlond's implied directive. Piasecki did not.

On November 20, 1946, the daily *Rzeczpospolita* published Ksawery Pruszyński's interview with Polish president Bolesław Bierut, who acknowledged that the Catholic Church occupied a vital position in Polish history and argued that the government had no intention of altering this standing. "The Polish Catholics have neither fewer nor more rights than other citizens," Bierut observed. He concluded that the government needed the support of all Catholics for the tasks of rebuilding the country and raising young people.[61]

The communists were acutely aware of the Church hierarchy's support for the opposition.[62] But they also knew that some lay activists continued to lobby for government approval of a Catholic electoral list.[63] This was Piasecki's chance. On December 20, 1946, Bierut received a delegation from *Dziś i jutro* and assured his visitors of the government's support for their electoral lists.[64]

In the rigged elections of January 1947, the communist-led Democratic Bloc secured 80 percent of the vote. Mikołajczyk's Peasant Party got only 10 percent. Piasecki's Catholics obtained 1.4 percent, which was enough to win three seats in the Sejm.[65] Piasecki's other rewards included control of the new Catholic daily newspaper *Słowo powszechne* (Universal Word). Two years later, Piasecki launched the PAX Publishing Institute (Instytut Wydawniczy PAX), which turned out theological, philosophical, and historical books, as well as Western literature, at a time when state publishing companies were flooding the market with socialist-realist junk. Its first two releases were Georges Bernanos's novel *Under Satan's Sun* and a new edition of the New Testament.

Of the possible reasons why the regime turned a blind eye to Piasecki's publishing of authors who were not communists or fellow travelers, perhaps the most plausible is that by doing so the authorities promoted the fiction of freedom of speech. In addition, the profile of the publishing company helped legitimize Piasecki's group as Catholic, both in Poland and abroad. But Piasecki had no intention of confining himself to the role of publisher. He was launching a political movement, "a movement with no name" that would "address the spiritual and material needs of the masses," mobilize Catholics for participation in public life, and dissuade the communists from viewing the Catholic camp as defenders of the bourgeoisie.[66]

Neither the Church nor other Catholic circles shared this vision, however. Bishop Stefan Wyszyński, who had known Piasecki since 1946, urged the *Dziś i jutro* group to withdraw from politics and to channel its energy into culture and education instead.[67] Hlond conveyed similar concerns: "Your newspaper can serve Catholicism on the condition that it will not misrepresent Catholic thought by being reticent about Marxist totalitarianism, abuses of power, and crimes."[68] Church distributors boycotted Piasecki's two newspapers and banned them from the Congress of the Catholic Press in September 1947.

The reactions of other Catholic groups were more nuanced. In *Tygodnik warszawski*, Stefan Kisielewski lambasted "the Fascist survivors" for posing as a Catholic movement.[69] Stanisław Stomma lent a different perspective to the subject of Catholic activism in socialist Poland. He cautioned against "social maximalism," which deployed Catholicism in the political conflict over the future of the nation. "Catholicism," wrote Stomma, "cannot be limited to culture or national identity, because Christianity is universal and concerns the whole of mankind." Instead, he advocated "seeming minimalism," which transformed social formations through cultural revival.[70]

Stomma's minimalism was the exact opposite of what Piasecki was demanding. In retrospect, however, Stomma's concept prepared Catholic intellectuals and the Polish intelligentsia for the approaching realities of Stalinism, and by the end of the 1940s, *Tygodnik powszechny* had largely adopted Stomma's arguments. "We are not socialists or Marxists," wrote Stomma and Turowicz in 1950. "Therefore, we cannot and should not take any responsibility for the implementation of socialism in Poland and elsewhere."[71] Thanks to Stomma's strategy, the weekly was able to survive until 1953, resurface after the end of Stalinism, and continue as an enclave of intellectual Catholicism and autonomous culture throughout the communist period. The defiant *Tygodnik warszawski* was liquidated in September 1948, and its editors thrown into jail.

Piasecki's representatives in parliament witnessed day by day the transition from permissible pluralism to communist monopoly on power. They refrained, however, from participation in the heated debates between the communists and the PSL.[72] Throughout Eastern and Central Europe, the formula of the soft revolution, based on a popular-front strategy with coalition governments at its center, was coming to its end. The meeting of the nine national communist parties in the Polish town of Szklarska Poręba in September 1947 signaled the beginning of Stalinism in Eastern Europe and of Moscow's complete control over national party structures. In Poland, the Stalinist offensive undermined Gomułka's vision of building a new socialist state that would take into account the country's traditions, conditions, and needs. Gomułka, therefore, first opposed and then only hesitantly endorsed the new course.[73] Mikołajczyk fled Poland in October 1947, and his party quickly became a PPR satellite. By the end of the year, the legal opposition in Poland had ceased to exist, and the anticommunist underground was fighting a hopeless battle.

Disbanding the military underground was one of Piasecki's initial priorities. In 1947, he had attempted to convince his former brothers-in-arms from the Wilno region, the partisans of Colonel Zygmunt Szendzielarz, to reveal themselves to the authorities. At a meeting with one of Szendzielarz's deputies, Piasecki claimed that he had made arrangements for negotiations with the government, but mutual distrust prevented any deal. In 1948, the authorities captured Szendzielarz, sentenced him to death, and executed him.[74] During a meeting of the *Dziś i jutro* team in May 1948, Andrzej Micewski, one of Piasecki's recent recruits, admitted gloomily: "We failed to extinguish the underground." Piasecki added, "Both sides regard us as collaborators."[75]

The fiasco did not prevent Piasecki from intervening on behalf of former AK soldiers and members of the anticommunist resistance.[76] In this respect, he benefited from good relations with two high officials from the security services, Minister of Public Administration Władysław Wolski and Julia Brystigier from the Ministry of Public Security. Piasecki's ties to Brystigier led to rumors that that the two of them were lovers.[77] The relationship with Wolski, well-known for his ties to the NKVD, was even more compromising. It was his ministry, however, that coordinated the government's policy toward the Church and Catholic organizations. Piasecki was quick to learn how informal one could be with these people and how much profit this familiarity could bring. Consider the case of Ryszard Reiff, who had escaped from a Soviet camp and secretly returned to Warsaw: Piasecki resolved the matter over a bottle of cognac that he and Reiff shared with Wolski.[78]

Piasecki gradually transformed his group into an extended family, complete with personal friendships and intermarriages.[79] He often intervened on behalf of his associates and their relatives, defending them from harassment by the security police or providing entry into university for their children after an initial denial due to "reactionary class background."[80] Among the young recruits were Andrzej Micewski (1926–2004) and Tadeusz Mazowiecki (1927–). Both joined *Dziś i jutro* motivated by their progressive Catholicism.[81] They were the first of Piasecki's collaborators from the post–World War I generation and would, in the long run, prove to be the least accommodating to their leader.

Piasecki was frankly alarmed by the struggles within the Polish Workers' Party. The Tito-Stalin split endangered Gomułka's position, as it signaled the beginning of a purge of Eastern European communist leaders, especially those suspected of harboring unorthodox views. In September 1948, Gomułka was accused of "right-wing nationalist deviation," removed from the post of secretary-general, and replaced by Bierut. The communists and the socialists were merged into a new organization, the Polish United Workers' Party (Polska Zjednoczona Partia Robotnicza, PZPR), which launched a policy of replicating the Soviet political and socioeconomic model in Poland. Gomułka was expelled from the party in 1949 and arrested two years later.

Piasecki sympathized with Gomułka, whose survival he viewed as crucial to preserving a moderate political course.[82] From this moment on, however, Piasecki and his followers had to present themselves as the Catholic component of the socialist movement. In doing so, they had to take into consideration three important factors: the regime's turn to a more confrontational policy concerning the Church, the Vatican's anticommunist stance, and the new primate of Poland, Cardinal Stefan Wyszyński.

The Broker, 1949–53

The advent of Stalinism brought an assault on the Roman Catholic Church across the Soviet bloc. Determined to eliminate what they considered the last bastion of reaction, ideological competition, and autonomous society, the communists pursued a strategy of intimidation, administrative harassment, and outright terror. In Czechoslovakia, the government had Czech primate Josef Beran detained in a remote monastery in 1951. In Hungary, Cardinal József Mindszenty was arrested in December 1948 and convicted of espionage, currency speculation, and antigovernment conspiracy. He was sentenced to life imprisonment in February 1949.

The lack of similar repression in Poland reflected not only the communists' accommodation to ethnoconfessional realities there but also the pragmatism of the young Polish primate Wyszyński, who became the head of the Polish Church in November 1948 at the age of forty-seven. Mindszenty went to jail believing that persecution was a necessary price for maintaining the Church's identity.[83] Wyszyński's tone was considerably more sober than that of his Hungarian counterpart. "Martyrdom is undoubtedly an honorable thing," the primate observed, "but God leads His Church not only along an extraordinary way, that of martyrdom, but also along an ordinary one, that of apostolic work." In other words, the Church had to preserve its social base and institutional framework, even at the price of limited appeasement of the communists. Wyszyński traveled around the country, animating local and national religious events. He made sure that priests refrained from political involvement and redoubled efforts to create a permanent intermediary body between the episcopate and the government.[84] The Joint Commission of the Government and the Episcopate (Komisja Wspólna Przedstawicieli Rząou Episkopatu), established in July 1949, immediately began working toward a church-state agreement.

Piasecki was pleased with the accession of Wyszyński. He offered the primate his services as a mediator, even while he also was advising government officials.[85] In August 1949, he suggested an agreement with the Vatican. According to Piasecki, the authorities needed to assure the Vatican that they had no intention of forcing the Church in Poland to break away from Rome or of organizing a split between proregime and pro-Rome Catholics.[86]

If Piasecki was working toward closer contact between the Polish government and the Vatican, the circumstances of the moment were highly unpropitious. In March 1948, Pope Pius XII condemned the deportation of

Germans from Eastern Europe and called on Catholics to forgive the Germans for their war crimes.[87] The papal message met with vehement criticism in Poland. Sixty-three Catholic intellectuals, including members of Piasecki's group and the leadership of *Tygodnik powszechny,* publicly defended Poland's right to the western territories and described their incorporation as an act of historical justice.[88] The Holy See also continued to recognize the government in exile and maintained an uncompromising anticommunism. In July 1949, a decree of the Vatican's Holy Office forbade Catholics to join, vote for, or cooperate with communist parties. Violators were to be refused the sacraments and excommunicated as apostates.[89] The Vatican's goal was to dissuade left-wing Catholics, in Italy especially, from voting against the Christian Democrats. In the case of Eastern Europe, full obedience to the edict of the Holy Office was impossible, and Piasecki, whose own deeds matched the transgressions listed in the decree, knew it.

It is important to remember that Piasecki was a devout Catholic, a regular churchgoer, and a religious traditionalist. While hiding in Nazi-occupied Warsaw, he regularly attended masses at the Church of Christ the Savior, even though such visits could have led to his denunciation. After the war, Piasecki belonged to the parish of Saint Michael's Church on Puławska Street in the Mokotów district. He contributed to the rebuilding of the church in the 1950s, a time when the government consistently blocked building permits for churches. He cultivated friendly ties with the parish priest, Rev. Stefan Piotrowski, a prominent member of the Warsaw curia who had spent many years working in student ministry and later served as Wyszyński's man in charge of religious instruction. Piasecki's confessor was Rev. Jan Twardowski, an internationally acclaimed Catholic poet and longtime rector of the Church of the Nuns of the Visitation, one of the most prestigious religious sites in Warsaw and popular among the Catholic intelligentsia.[90] In short, Piasecki would never have broken away from the Holy Church.[91]

The Vatican's decree might or might not have influenced Polish communists' attitude toward the Church, but there is no doubt that in 1949 the regime began implementing a policy of splitting the clergy. On September 2, the government set up a veterans' association, the Union of Fighters for Freedom and Democracy (Związek Bojowników o Wolność i Demokrację, ZBOWiD). Among the delegates who attended the union's founding congress were forty-five priests, mostly former military chaplains in the Soviet-controlled Polish Army. They formed the union's Priests' Commission, which expanded into a thousand-strong association of Patriotic Priests

(Księża Patrioci) in 1950. Some members joined the organization voluntarily. Others were blackmailed into cooperating by the security police, who threatened charges of alcoholism, sexual scandal, or corruption.[92]

Also in September of that year, the government suspended its talks with the bishops, and in January 1950 it seized the Church-run charity Caritas, handing it over to the joint control of the Patriotic Priests and Piasecki's group. Piasecki accepted this assignment with the hope of eventually expelling his rivals, the Patriotic Priests, for whom he had nothing but scorn. He resolved to counterbalance their influence by offering an intellectual alternative, led by *Dziś i jutro* and approved by the episcopate.[93] Caritas became a gold mine for the Patriotic Priests, who stole stocks of penicillin and sold them on the black market. Outraged by the looting, Micewski, who was Piasecki's man at Caritas, resigned from his post after three months.[94] Ultimately, Piasecki's representatives failed to gain control over the organization.

Piasecki's participation in the takeover of Caritas provoked an angry reprimand from Wyszyński.[95] But the primate also recognized Piasecki's efforts to bring the government and the episcopate back to the negotiating table. Piasecki briefed Wyszyński about his conversations with Wolski concerning controversial points in the proposed agreement: condemnation of the anticommunist underground, approval of collective farms, and a special clause defining the role of the pope. He also arranged a meeting between Wyszyński and Wolski to break the deadlock in negotiations.[96] Piasecki's mediation worked. On April 14, 1950, the episcopate signed an accord (*porozumienie*) with the Polish government.

The 1950 accord was the first signed between a Roman Catholic national hierarchy and a communist regime.[97] It was based on a rudimentary premise: that the regime would respect the ecclesiastical rights of the Church, which in exchange would recognize the communist state's secular powers. The agreement required the Church to support the economic policies of the regime, condemn any antistate activities, resist the political use of religion, and recognize the Vatican's authority only within doctrinal and canonical domains. In return, the state guaranteed religious freedom, permitted religious instruction in public schools, allowed the existence of Catholic educational institutions, and vowed to refrain from any interference in the functioning of monastic orders, Catholic publications, and charity work.[98] The communists' arbitrary treatment of law rendered illusory any semblance of a binding contract, and Wyszyński knew it. He was buying time.[99]

Piasecki celebrated the signing of the accord in an article published in *Dziś i jutro* under the weighty title "The Significance of the Event." He also proposed that since the progressive Catholic leaders of *Dziś i jutro* had always propagated a Catholic-Marxist dialogue, they should be given a share of responsibility in the implementation of the agreement.[100] "Our main goal," Piasecki stated on a different occasion, "is the reconstruction of Catholic doctrine ... with respect to the ongoing conflict between Marxism and capitalism. It is our belief that Marxism will win in this confrontation, but that subsequently, it will be conquered by Catholicism."[101] For Piasecki, the first step toward the implementation of this program was the unification of Catholic intellectuals under the tutelage of his own movement. In May 1950, he organized a conference of Catholic activists in Warsaw. Among the participants were the editors of *Tygodnik powszechny*, members of Polish academia, priests, and representatives of the laity. Developments at the meeting, however, dashed Piasecki's hopes. Dominik Horodyński's enthusiastic speech on new possibilities for a Catholic-Marxist dialogue drew a rather cool response. Professor Konrad Górski, affiliated with *Tygodnik powszechny*, replied eloquently and with self-effacing humor. "The Marxists would never consider us equal ideological partners," he declared. "It is my impression that they would take offense if we tried to assert our tolerance [of their views]; they accept other views only out of necessity."[102] The failure of the conference proved to Piasecki that in his efforts to establish a proregime front of Catholic intellectuals, he could rely only on his own circle.

As the tensions of the Cold War mounted, the Soviets and their allied communist regimes intensified the "struggle for peace." They often gained backing from progressive intellectuals who opposed European colonialism, American hegemony, atomic weapons, and rearmament in general. Piasecki quickly joined this front. In November 1950, the government approved his proposal to establish a clerical section of the Polish peace committee. Finally, Piasecki had his own priests. Set up on November 4, 1950, the Commission of Catholic Intellectuals and Activists (Komitet Intelektualistów i Działaczy Katolickich) consisted of two to three hundred clergymen, some of them intellectuals of a high caliber who had no intention of antagonizing the episcopate.[103]

The government, meanwhile, violated the accord systematically. It arrested and tried a number of clergymen, including Bishop Czesław Kaczmarek of Kielce, on charges of Nazi collaboration, espionage, and antistate conspiracy. Using as an excuse the Vatican's ambivalence toward the Oder-Neisse border (Pius XII refused to nominate Polish bishops for the western territories), in January 1951 the government removed church administrators from five northern and western dioceses and replaced them with proregime priests.[104] One year later, the regime removed religious instruction from public schools and closed down dozens of seminaries.

On most of these occasions, Piasecki declined to act as a moderator while he eagerly awaited a decision legalizing his new, expanded organization.[105] On April 9, 1952, the Warsaw People's Council registered the PAX Association (Stowarzyszenie PAX), whose mission was to propagate progressive political ideas among Polish Catholics in the municipality.[106] At its first meeting in May 1952, the PAX assembly elected a high council, which promptly appointed Piasecki chairman. PAX supervised the Commission of Catholic Intellectuals and Activists, and it owned two newspapers, a publishing house, one high school, and two commercial enterprises. By August 1952, approximately a thousand people worked for PAX-run projects and companies.[107]

The Church hierarchy reacted to the creation of PAX with hostility, and the episcopate soon accused PAX of propagating views that violated the teachings and practices of the Church.[108] Admittedly, Piasecki's first acts in his new capacity as PAX leader did little to refute these accusations. He declared that the association combined "the principles of the gospel with the theory and practice of socialism, especially those elements from the ideology of Marx, Engels, Lenin, and Stalin that served the eternal truth of religion."[109] Piasecki was promoting these concepts at a time when the Catholic Church was under attack. In these circumstances, he found himself—perhaps against his own intentions—among the forces that sought to subordinate the Church to the communist regime.

In late 1952, the authorities arrested, tried, and sentenced to harsh prison terms five priests from the Kraków curia on charges of espionage. In January 1953, the government forced Kraków's Archbishop Eugeniusz Baziak to step down from his post and prevented Wyszyński from going to the Vatican to receive his ordination as cardinal. But the worst blow was the government's decree of February 9, 1953, which made all church appointments subject to approval by the authorities and demanded that appointees take an oath of allegiance to the Polish People's Republic.[110] Nothing prevented the regime from simply ousting unreliable chaplains and replacing them with more accommodating or proregime priests. The decree also enhanced the prerogatives of the Office for Religious Affairs, a government institution of ministerial rank created in 1950 to oversee relations with churches and religious communities.

When Wyszyński refused to endorse the government's decree, Piasecki suggested to the primate that the Church accept the necessity of collaboration with the government if it wanted to salvage some of its authority.[111] The problem was that Piasecki's recommendations would turn the Church into the regime's mouthpiece, something Wyszyński could never accept. For Piasecki, capitulation was preferable to schism, though the creation of a communist-controlled national church also would have harmed PAX. As Piasecki remarked on one occasion, "No Marxist would ever speak to us if there was not the powerful institution of the Church."[112]

Having said this in private, Piasecki still publicly insisted on the primate's full cooperation with the communists. He also continued criticizing the Vatican. Appalled by statements that Piasecki made in a 1953 article attacking papal infallibility, Wyszynski refuted Piasecki's charges in an interview granted to Jerzy Turowicz of *Tygodnik powszechny*.[113] The interview was never published, however. On March 5, 1953, Stalin died. Across the Soviet bloc, newspapers competed to publish sycophantic and laudatory articles about the late Soviet leader. Only *Tygodnik powszechny* stepped out of line. Ordered to publish Stalin's obituary on its front page, the weekly refused. The authorities closed down the paper in April and three months later transferred it to PAX. The new publisher had to preserve the newspaper's title, logo, and the numerical order of issues in order to deceive readers into thinking that they were buying the same newspaper.[114] The PAX-owned *Tygodnik powszechny* continued until May 1956, when Piasecki finally abandoned the troublesome title. Control of the Kraków weekly was returned to its founding editors in December of that year.

The primate knew that compliance with the February decree would undermine his entire strategy of maintaining the Church's autonomy. This time, he vowed to resist. In May 1953, he had the episcopate issue a memorandum, *Non possumus* (We Cannot). "We shall follow the apostolic voice of our calling and priestly conscience, with inner peace and the consciousness that we have not given the least reason for our persecution, that suffering will become a part of our share in the affairs of Christ and Christ's Church," read the document. "We cannot place what belongs to God on the altar of Caesar. Non possumus!"[115] Wyszyński's act of personal courage—he was the author of the memorandum—might also have been motivated by the death of Stalin.

Indeed, the government hesitated to punish the defiant primate until it had an opportunity to consult with the new Soviet leadership.[116]

Piasecki's reaction to *Non possumus* was wholly negative. He believed there were only two ways to avoid a split within the Church: either to extend the Polish episcopate's legal powers or to foster the development of a pro-socialist clergy.[117] Referring to a recent meeting with Wyszyński, Piasecki told his collaborators that the primate "had formulated his strategy extremely well by saying that his ultimate goal is to celebrate a Holy Mass in socialist society and to add 'Catholic leaven' to socialist 'flour,' so that the acid will dissolve into the flour." In principle, he shared Wyszyński's goal.[118] But Piasecki poured scorn on other bishops who, in his view, had not risen to the challenge of modernity. One goal of PAX was to expand the number of "honest priests" who would be willing to talk to the communists.[119]

In essence, Piasecki's plan was a contradiction. On the one hand, he hoped to convince the primate to make concessions to the regime; on the other, he sought to politicize the clergy—precisely what Wyszyński had warned him not to do. In making his calculations, however, he had completely ignored the intentions of the regime. On September 14, the show trial of Bishop Kaczmarek of Kielce began. Broken by a long detention, the bishop played his role well: he confessed to all charges and implicated the Vatican, the episcopate, and even the primate. The court sentenced Kaczmarek to twelve years in prison.

The government then insisted on Wyszyński's public condemnation of the bishop. But Wyszyński had become convinced that only firm resistance could preserve his moral authority, and he condemned the trial of Kaczmarek.[120] On the morning of Saturday, September 26, Piasecki learned of Wyszyński's detention.[121] The regime never put Wyszyński on trial, because it did not want to make a martyr of him. Instead, it detained the primate in a remote, defunct monastery. Banished from public life and stripped of his powers, the primate ceased to be an obstacle on the communists' path toward full domination of the Church.[122]

Bitter Honeymoon, 1953–54

The elimination of the primate from the political scene diminished Piasecki's influence, as neither the state nor the Church required a broker. The day after Wyszyński's arrest, Piasecki summoned the Catholic MPs to his office and instructed them to launch a protest at their meeting with Edward Ochab, the top member of the central committee of the PZPR.[123] This could have been Piasecki's finest hour. However, PAX's protests were half-hearted and feeble. Only Łubieński dared to speak on behalf of the primate. He deemed Wyszyński's arrest a grave mistake, likely to harm the prestige of the Polish government abroad. According to Łubieński, the government had lost a valuable partner: Wyszyński was progressive, sensible, and immensely popular. Ochab reprimanded Łubieński and sent Piasecki's men home.

Immediately after this fiasco, Piasecki arranged a meeting between two of his friends, Julia Brystigier from the Ministry of Internal Security and Bishop Michał Klepacz, bishop of Łódź diocese, and they agreed to a plan to pacify the clergy. Piasecki also was involved in the drafting of the declaration that the episcopate issued in response to Wyszyński's arrest.[124] On September 28, the intimidated bishops expressed loyalty to the regime, condemned Kaczmarek, and vowed to work together with the government for a church-state dialogue. The declaration made no reference to Wyszyński's arrest.[125] The Polish bishops were on their knees, and on December 17, 1953, they took an oath of allegiance to the Polish People's Republic.

On October 19, less than a month after Wyszyński's arrest, Piasecki made a stunning observation in an address to his followers. "In Poland," he remarked, "we observe a great paradox: it is the Marxists who express concerns about the intellectual condition of the Church."[126] Catholics, therefore, faced the daunting task of reforming Catholic theology without losing its mystical component. Piasecki admitted that social revolution did not stem from the gospel. Nevertheless, it was still possible to use the universality of Catholic doctrine in revolutionary struggle without involving the institution of the Church. He claimed that PAX could mobilize Catholic support for the revolution both at home and abroad.[127]

At this point, Piasecki had hardly any means at his disposal to achieve such an ambitious goal. Having subdued the bishops, the government began to limit its contacts with PAX. The leader of PAX no longer received invitations from party bigwigs.[128] To avoid marginalization, Piasecki devoted more attention to promoting his movement across the Soviet bloc. By the mid-1950s, PAX had established fraternal ties with the Christian Democratic Union (Ost-CDU) in the German Democratic Republic (GDR). A junior coalition partner of the communists in the GDR government, the Ost-CDU occupied the position Piasecki emphatically advocated for PAX: that of a political party involved in running the state. By burnishing his eminence in the GDR, Piasecki signaled to Polish party leaders that they should modify the status of PAX. Departing from the point he had reached in articles for *Dziś i jutro* in 1945 and 1946, Piasecki developed his political philosophy into the doctrine of "pluralism of worldviews" (*wieloświatopoglądowość*), promoting the convergence of Marxism and Catholicism and the concomitant admission of Catholics to the communist system of power.

New Ideological Synthesis: *Essential Issues*

As Piasecki toured the GDR in 1954, PAX's publishing arm was printing *Essential Issues,* a volume of Piasecki's essays from 1945 to 1954. As Andrzej Micewski has pointed out, had it not been for the introduction, the book would not have amounted to much.[129] But the introduction turned out to be a manifesto of Piasecki's political beliefs comparable only to his prewar opus *The Spirit of New Times and the Youth Movement.*

First of all, he set about reexamining the relation of Catholic theology to earthly concerns. Piasecki declared that up to this point, Catholicism had focused on the act of salvation, pushing aside the act of creation. This emphasis on redemption had led Catholics to adopt the view that social injustice was a natural state of affairs regardless of the dominant political order, be it feudalism, capitalism, or socialism. This blindness to the Promethean character of Christianity derived from an erroneous interpretation of labor, understood by Catholic theologians as a punishment for original sin. Consequently, Catholic theology dissuaded believers from struggling to better the world, earning them a reputation as enemies of progress. Piasecki, in contrast, claimed that the notion of progress was deeply embedded in Christianity. "The act of creation," he wrote, "contained God's plan for the perfection the world, a plan that required people to transform reality around them."[130]

Piasecki distinguished people who praised God "intentionally" from those who praised him in an "ontological" way. "Ontologically," he stated, "God is praised by those who continue God's creation, regardless of whether they believe in God or deny his existence." This distinction allowed Piasecki to declare that Marxists were not the enemies of God, partly because an enemy of God was "a being who acknowledged God's existence but refused to worship him" and partly because their atheism was directed against the use of religion for the exploitation of the masses. The Marxists' struggle for

the betterment of humanity possessed all the attributes of ontological worship: they continued God's activity without knowing it.[131]

What then did Piasecki have to say to Catholics? They should sever
their ties to capitalist exploiters, he urged, purge Catholicism of reactionary
influences, and unite themselves with nonbelievers in working for the good
of humanity. In other words, Piasecki proposed that Catholic participation
in building a socialist society was in agreement with God's plan and in
compliance with the social mandate of Catholicism to support the system
that came closest to the idea of social justice.[132] His message to Marxists
was strikingly similar: "The universality of Marxism and Catholicism deter-
mines that the followers of Promethean currents are obliged to use relevant
aspects of other doctrines in their work for the good of humanity." Thus,
Piasecki called for collaboration between two separate worldviews rather
than for their merger. Neither Marxists nor Catholics should have to give
up their system of beliefs. This was the essence of a pluralism of worldviews.[133] In Piasecki's opinion, Poland was the best environment for the
implementation of this concept because Marxism and Catholicism already
were the two major currents in Polish political thought. In addition, Poland
possessed a political force that had prepared the ground for Catholic-Marxist
cooperation: PAX.[134]

It is tempting to dismiss Piasecki's manifesto as simple opportunism.
Despite its philosophical shallowness and theological misinterpretations,
however, *Essential Issues* demonstrated the continuity and persistence of
Piasecki's earlier concepts and tapped into themes of Personalist discourse,
particularly in the notion of the Promethean character of Marxism and
Christianity. Above all, the idea of Catholic-Marxist reconciliation stemmed
from his prewar nationalist-Catholic synthesis: the cornerstone of his doctrine was the notion that God was the highest destiny of man and that allying
Catholicism to the dominant ideological current—nationalism before the war
and communism afterward—was the path to God. Because he always viewed
Catholicism as the basis of national identity, Piasecki might have concluded
that a modus vivendi between Catholics and communists would serve to en-
trench nationalism. Perhaps PAX and the nominally atheistic party regime
could turn socialist Poland into a nationalizing state. Wyszyński, an ardent
believer in the ethno-Catholic narrative of the Polish nation, had reached opposite conclusions. Catholic intellectuals like Stomma and Turowicz de-
emphasized traditional nationalism and embraced intellectual Catholicism as

the organic work that could build an autonomous sphere and foster a valid cultural alternative to the Marxist state in the long run.

It also seems that Piasecki treated Marxism as a political religion. Indeed, at the peak of Stalinism in Eastern Europe, the communists had claimed to know the meaning of history, universal truth, and the plan for man's perfection. Piasecki had to acknowledge the growing ritualization of the communist system. To paraphrase Philippe Burrin's remarks on Eric Voegelin, the chief advocate of the concept of political religion, Piasecki might have found himself "at the crossroads of a dual process of the sacralization of the political on the one hand and the politicization" of Christianity on the other.[135]

Was Piasecki trying to undo the historical split between nationalists and Marxism? Perhaps. Jacob L. Talmon might be correct in his declaration that nationalism and socialism parted ways in the mid-nineteenth century, when nationalists substituted the term "nation" for the word "proletariat" and thus chose a "nationalist particularity" over a "universal revolutionary creed."[136] But as Brian Porter has argued, in Poland this split took place in the late 1890s and early 1900s, only some fifty years before the publication of Piasecki's *Essential Issues.* For much of the late nineteenth century, the nationalists and the socialists were factions within the same independence movement. Neither group denied the link between the nation and the people. The problem was that the socialists cherished only the working-class component of the people, the proletariat, which they believed eventually would embody the nation after the socialist revolution. The nationalists believed that the making of the modern Polish nation could not wait for the revolution, because the nation and the people already existed in the present. In 1905, when the socialists launched their revolution, the nationalists opted for a loyalist attitude toward the Russian Empire, whose liberalization could benefit the Poles. By that time, the break between the socialists and nationalists was complete.[137]

Forty years later, the revolution did take place, and the communist regime presented People's Poland as the end result of the struggle for independence, if not the very culmination of national history—a claim made perverse by the fact that Poland was once again under Moscow's domination. Nevertheless, it demonstrated the communists' sensitivity toward the national question. The majority of nineteenth-century socialists were hardly internationalists, nor were their successors fifty years later. By then, socialism and nationalism also had common enemies: the conservative status quo, capitalism, ideological heterodoxy, and the Other. Piasecki loathed the Jews, whereas the communists had expelled the Germans and diabolized the West. Piasecki already had pointed out the ideological kinship between Soviet communism and fascist movements before the war. At that time, his political doctrine had combined ethnonationalism with a leftist and revolutionary social-economic program. But a millenarian interpretation of history also underlay Piasecki's program. The introduction to *Essential Issues* brought Piasecki's doctrine full circle. He began his analysis with the presentation of one universalist current (Catholicism) and concluded it with another (socialism), hinting all the while at nationalism. It was a return to universalism and the common front. Of course, this ideological solution was not devoid of pragmatic considerations. By proposing a kind of pluralism, here tightly restricted to Marxism and proregime nationalist Catholicism, Piasecki sought to position himself as a shareholder in power.

But what did Piasecki's doctrine do to the Roman Catholic Church? By attempting to elide the differences between Catholics and communists, Piasecki disregarded the policy of the Holy See as well as the evolution of Catholic theology. The Church no longer interpreted labor as a punishment for original sin and did not hesitate to criticize the abuses of capitalism.[138] What brought matters to a head was the rehabilitation of Marxist atheism. By putting nonbelievers' ontological worship on an equal plane with believers' intentional praise of God, Piasecki undermined, perhaps unwittingly, the very existence of a Christian congregation.[139] To be sure, he did not make religious salvation contingent on participation in the communist movement. But from a Catholic perspective, Piasecki was a heretic. As Stefan Kisielewski remarked on Piasecki's theory, to argue that the communists worked for the good of God and the Holy Spirit was plainly absurd.[140]

On the Vatican Index, 1955–56

That Piasecki's book did not evoke a response—whether critical or approving—from the party seems to confirm Kisielewski's opinion. The communists were profoundly indifferent to Piasecki's reinterpretation of Catholic doctrine, partly because they did not want to encourage pluralism of worldviews. The Church took a similar position, but the Polish bishops' reticence in launching a polemic against *Essential Issues* could be explained only by their fear of retaliation.

Piasecki was eager to learn the opinions of Catholic theologians on his theses. In February 1955, he dispatched his sister-in-law, Janina Kolendo, to Switzerland with a copy of the book to deliver it to Rev. Józef Bocheński (Aleksander Bocheński's brother), a philosopher and theologian who taught at Fribourg University.[141] If Piasecki had hoped to win the theologian over to his side, he miscalculated badly. After reading the introduction to Piasecki's book, Bocheński exploded with fury: this was a betrayal of Christian doctrine and a primitive piece of procommunist propaganda that had to be condemned.[142] Bocheński quickly organized a debate on *Essential Issues* at a radio studio in Berne and sent the tapes to Jan Nowak-Jeziorański, chief of the Polish section of Radio Free Europe (RFE) in Munich. Several of Bocheński's friends translated the introduction to the book into French, prepared a special memorandum on the detrimental nature of Piasecki's theses, and handed both texts over to the chaplain of Polish exiles, Archbishop Józef Gawlina, who immediately forwarded these materials to the Holy Office.[143]

Kolendo returned to Poland in a panic. She told Piasecki that *Essential Issues* would be put on the Vatican's index of forbidden books.[144] Her boss hoped—in vain—that the affair would not have any serious consequences. Keeping a low profile in Church affairs, Piasecki redirected his attention to political matters. To him and to all those who followed the situation in Poland and the Soviet bloc, major political changes seemed inevitable.

The death of Stalin did not have an immediate effect on the regime in Poland, but things began to change in 1954. The elimination of Lavrenty Beria from the Soviet political leadership in the summer of 1953 and the subsequent accession of Nikita Khrushchev fueled the process of de-Stalinization. In response to these developments in the Soviet Union, the regime in Poland adopted a model of collective leadership. Far more significant was the purge of the security apparatus, the major impetus for which also came from abroad. In September 1954, the Polish section of Radio Free Europe began broadcasting the confessions of a Polish defector, Colonel Józef Światło, a protégé of Beria and a prominent operative in the Ministry of Public Security responsible for monitoring the highest party officials. Reporting on the inner life of the communist elite, the broadcasts seriously embarrassed the regime. Scores of dignitaries in the security apparatus lost their jobs. Purged communists began leaving their prison cells. Gomułka was freed on December 13, 1954.[145] The Polish party began relaxing its grip on society, culture, and politics.

For Piasecki, the liberalization at home and abroad seemed to open up new vistas for political action. With the approval of the communist authorities, he dispatched several emissaries to contact exiles from the National Party and the Labor Party in 1954 and 1955.[146] Piasecki intended to put himself in a position to coordinate the government's policy toward Polonia, as the Polish diaspora was called, and to create a special committee for contacts with potential collaborators abroad. Populated by noncommunist personalities connected in the past with Sanacja, Endecja, and the Peasant Party as well as socialists, noncommunist World War II veterans, and well-known artists and writers, the committee would facilitate dialogue between socialist Poland and émigrés.[147] In 1955, however, the exiles were not ready to embrace Piasecki's initiative, and at home the regime abandoned Piasecki's project altogether.[148]

Bocheński's efforts to discredit Piasecki bore fruit, meanwhile, as Cardinal Giuseppe Pizzardo, secretary of the Holy Office, set up a commission of experts to investigate Piasecki's case.[149] In April 1955, the Vatican team found Piasecki guilty of undermining Catholic doctrine and serving the enemies of the Church. The experts recommended that Piasecki's book and his weekly *Dziś i jutro* be placed on the Vatican's index of forbidden publications. Such an action would discipline those Catholics in Poland and elsewhere who had fallen under the spell of Piasecki's propaganda; it also would strengthen the prestige of the Polish episcopate and the imprisoned Cardinal Wyszyński.[150]

On June 8, 1955, the Holy Office issued a decree placing Piasecki's publications on the Vatican index. As *L'Osservatore romano* commented: "At a time when Cardinal Wyszyński and other Polish bishops remain in jail . . . , we are witnessing a despicable initiative, which tries to present the communist regime as fully respectful of the freedom of the Roman Catholic Church. Writer Bolesław Piasecki—a leading personality among Polish progressive Catholics—and the weekly *Dziś i jutro* are among the staunchest advocates of this fallacy, which they also propagate on the western side of the iron curtain."[151]

In Warsaw, Piasecki put on a brave face, concluding that the decree itself did not contain any theological justification.[152] But when he calmed down, he reasoned that he could not face excommunication. In these troubled days, Piasecki often found solace in prayer. The writer and Catholic intellectual Jerzy Zawieyski recalled seeing the solitary figure of Piasecki standing in the Warsaw Carmelite Church. "I prayed for him," Zawieyski wrote, "that he would prove his bond with the Church."[153] On July 5, 1955, Piasecki removed his book from circulation. The closure of *Dziś i jutro* was another matter, since it required the approval of the authorities. And as Franciszek Mazur, member of the Politburo, told Piasecki, the party would expel bishops from Poland rather than have *Dziś i jutro* shut down.[154]

Faced with the inflexibility of his communist patrons, Piasecki approached the Church hierarchy. In a letter to Bishop Wacław Majewski, vicar-general of the Warsaw diocese, Piasecki vowed to increase his efforts "to raise the level of doctrinal and religious discussion in *Dziś i jutro*," informed the bishop of the removal of *Essential Issues* from circulation, and asked him to forward the letter to the Holy Office.[155] The case lay outside the authority of Majewski, however. Bishop Klepacz, the chairman of the Polish episcopate, had a good relationship with Piasecki. He sent Piasecki's recantation to the Vatican but refrained from intervening on behalf of the leader of PAX.[156]

When Piasecki realized that the Polish Church would not help him, he again turned to the party.[157] Although meetings with Bierut and members of the Politburo did not improve Piasecki's position in the eyes of the Vatican, they boosted his morale and emboldened him to deal with opposition emerging from the ranks of his own organization. The origins of the conflict went back to 1952, when Tadeusz Mazowiecki and Jan Zabłocki had confronted Piasecki over the drafting of program theses for PAX. Banned from the Warsaw headquarters of PAX, they gradually had succeeded in forming a group of followers, later known as Fronda. The dissenters lacked a coherent program but were united in their opposition to the dictatorial rule of Piasecki and his cronies. To Mazowiecki and his associates, PAX was a mafialike organization run by "the leader and his old guard." Fronda also detested Piasecki's theological innovations, his anti-Church ventures, and his sycophantic support for the party.[158] Mazowiecki and Zabłocki were quickly recalled to Warsaw and put under surveillance.

Soon, Piasecki learned that Fronda members were conferring secretly with the party and the Church. Apparently, Mazowiecki planned to set up a new organization.[159] Piasecki's reaction was quick and decisive. On September 9, Mazowiecki and the others were officially expelled from PAX.[160] Only days later, however, Piasecki faced another challenge, this time from abroad, as he found himself under attack by Radio Free Europe.

Jan Nowak-Jeziorański of the RFE had been keen to discredit Piasecki as a communist agent for some time. As he prepared his broadcasts about PAX, he consulted a number of Piasecki's former associates.[161] On August 14, 1955, Nowak went on the air. He described Piasecki as a Judas, a fascist whom the communists had used to subdue Catholics and break the Polish Church.[162] On September 1, Nowak broadcast Światło's accusation that Piasecki had been an agent of the Soviet NKVD.[163] The broadcasts tarnished Piasecki's image, making him out to be an archvillain comparable to the most notorious members of the Stalinist elite. Nowak killed two birds with one stone. On the one hand, he discredited Piasecki as a turncoat and chameleon. On the other, he delegitimized the communist regime, which in the march to power had cooperated with former fascists.

In response, Piasecki decided to improve his standing by launching an event of huge scale, the tenth anniversary of his political movement. The congress held by PAX in the fall of 1955 lasted for three days. Among the delegates and guests were members of Catholic organizations from the people's democracies and Western Europe.[164] At one of the private parties, Piasecki disclosed to his foreign guests the fate of Wyszyński, informing them about the primate's transfer to a new location and the improved conditions of his detention. It is not clear whether Piasecki acted with the approval of the authorities in revealing this secret.[165]

The congress did not dispel Piasecki's worries about excommunication. Friends and nearly all the members of his entourage pressed him to intensify his efforts to obtain the government's approval to close down *Dziś i jutro*.[166] Communist leaders remained deaf to Piasecki's arguments, however, and the stalemate continued.

Aid came from elsewhere. On February 25, 1956, at the Twentieth Congress of the Communist Party of the Soviet Union, Khrushchev delivered his "secret speech," in which he condemned Stalin's purges. Apparently, it was too much for Bierut, who died in Moscow on March 12 and was succeeded by Ochab. The news from Moscow sent the Polish communists into disarray and fostered factional struggles. The two opposing camps were the so-called Puławska group, which favored rapid de-Stalinization, and the Natolin faction, which displayed more caution. Finally, there were the centrists, including Ochab and Prime Minister Józef Cyrankiewicz.[167]

As the communists plunged into backroom struggles, Piasecki regained the freedom to maneuver. In spring 1956, he finally obtained approval to replace *Dziś i jutro* with a new weekly.[168] He dispatched his emissaries to Rome to negotiate the lifting of the ban. Once again, Piasecki benefited from the help of Luciana Frassati-Gawrońska, whose husband made the arrangements necessary for a meeting of PAX representatives with Vatican officials.[169] What he learned was that the Holy See expected PAX to demonstrate its allegiance to Catholicism and to distance itself from the party. Once again, Piasecki complied. He immediately ordered PAX MPs to raise the issues of religious freedom and the rehabilitation of former Home Army soldiers.[170] The voices of Łubieński, Horodyński, and Dobraczyński in the usually dull parliament created a small sensation, noticed even by the Western press.[171] On May 25, almost exactly one year after the Vatican had put Piasecki's publications on the index of forbidden books, *L'Osservatore romano* reported that PAX had complied with all the provisions of the Holy Office decree.

Frontispiece of the *Przełom* monthly, September–October 1938. Bolesław Piasecki is in foreground. *(The National Library of Poland, Warsaw)*

Frontispiece of the *Falanga* weekly, November 30, 1937. (*The National Library of Poland, Warsaw*)

Bolesław Piasecki, *second from the left,* and officers of the Third Batallion of the Seventy-Seventh AK Infantry Regiment, 1943. *(Courtesy of Jan Engelgard)*

Mieczysław Moczar greets Władysław Gomułka, 1965. *(Polska Agencja Prasowa [Polish Press Agency], Warsaw)*

Zenon Kliszko, Marian Spychalski, and Władysław Gomułka, 1969. *(Polish Press Agency, Warsaw)*

Bolesław Piasecki in Polish parliament, 1971. *(Polish Press Agency, Warsaw)*

Bolesław Piasecki receives decoration from Edward Gierek, July 1974. *(Polish Press Agency, Warsaw)*

Bolesław Piasecki at his PAX office, 1970s. *(Courtesy of Jan Engelgard)*

5 ||| Years of Hope and Disappointment, 1956–67

THREE YEARS AFTER THE DEATH of Stalin, the Polish People's Republic experienced the gravest crisis of its sociopolitical system to that point. By the end of 1956, the country had experienced a war at the top of the party leadership, a bloody revolt among the workers of Poznań, the specter of Soviet military intervention, and Gomułka's return to power. Historians and journalists often refer to these events under the collective term Polski Październik (Polish October). A reference to the Bolshevik October Revolution in Russia, it accentuated the socialist character of the movement, which sought to democratize the system and to bring about a renewal of the communist party and society. Since it was doubtful whether the term "revolution" applied to the events in Poland, the more oblique "October" proved the most convenient wording.

One of the most frequently reproduced images from the fall of 1956 was that of Gomułka addressing hundreds of thousands of enthusiastic Poles in Warsaw. As Jerzy Giedroyc, the chief editor of the Paris-based monthly *Kultura,* put it, the Polish October was the only time when the communist party could integrate itself with the nation.[1] The return of Gomułka was hailed as a great patriotic victory and the beginning of a new social contract between the rulers and the ruled, transforming the entire system. A number of modifications to the system proved long-lasting and even irreversible: the opening of the country to Western culture and the end of Socialist Realism in the arts; the partial rehabilitation of noncommunist chapters in the nation's history; the twin phenomena of intellectual ferment and open debate, which refused to vanish even after the party belatedly tried to squelch them; and the establishment of outlets for the Catholic intelligentsia and dialogue with the Church. But gradually Gomułka's "Polish road to socialism" also began to show its nasty side: increasing authoritarianism and chauvinism as well as assaults on unorthodox and reformist tendencies within the party. Nevertheless, the regime did abandon Stalinism, replacing it with a mishmash of ethnonationalism, populism, and communist orthodoxy. The growing reliance on nationalism reinforced the party's domestic or indigenous credentials, but it also plunged the regime into a symbolic competition over ownership of national identity with the Church, which was bolstering its efforts to bring about an ethnoconfessional nationalism. Overall, this period was instrumental in developing the processes that eventually led to the ideological demobilization of the regime, the birth of the opposition, and the hegemony of the Church in the sphere of nationalist symbology.

For Piasecki, October 1956 was a traumatizing time. Subjected to vehement attacks by liberal intellectuals and party reformers alike, he fought for his political survival. He also had to confront a revived Polish Catholic Church, which had come out of Stalinism united, strong, and increasingly popular. De-Stalinization ended Piasecki's monopoly on the political representation of lay Catholics. The important question was to what degree Gomułka would support Piasecki's aim of transforming PAX into a junior coalition partner and political party.

The Villain of October

Piasecki had refrained from taking any active stance during the initial stages of de-Stalinization. Instead, he cautiously advocated liberalization within the limits of ideological correctness, criticizing the cult of personality but also cherishing the "great achievements of socialism" in the pre-1953 period.[2] At closed meetings with his collaborators, he was more outspoken, insisting that communism did not fit the Polish national character. He reportedly said, "In future Poland, Marxism will be replaced by national-radical socialism, based on the historical traditions of the Polish nation."[3]

The regime, meanwhile, showed signs of uncharacteristic softness. The amnesty act passed by the Sejm in April 1956 practically emptied the jails of political prisoners. The party purged Bierut's leading associates, including Jakub Berman, while the government arrested a number of high officials in the security apparatus and fired prosecutors who had distinguished themselves in Stalinist trials.[4] The advent of debating societies, political rallies, and

candid news reports were evidence of the ferment of free discussion sweeping through the country. Jazz music was no longer considered subversive, and
abstract art went on display in state galleries. As Polish historian Andrzej
Friszke has observed, by the mid-1950s a significant stratum of Polish society
genuinely believed in socialism. Conversely, the rhetoric of the 1956 reformers was quintessentially Marxist. They did not intend to dismantle the communist system, but to improve it.[5]

This new attitude toward the aspirations of young intellectuals and
party members did not necessarily apply to workers and peasants. On June
28, 1956, workers' protests in Poznań evolved into armed clashes with
the police and army that left seventy-three people dead and five hundred
wounded.[6] The revolt sent shock waves through the country and abroad,
compelling the government to admit that the grievances of Poznań's workers had been justified.

At the Seventh Plenum of the Central Committee in July, the party rehabilitated and readmitted Gomułka to its ranks but did not entrust any political posts to him. In the conflict between the Natolin and Puławska factions,
neither side was able to prevail over its opponents. Initially, Piasecki expected
that the Seventh Plenum would end the thaw.[7] Later, he seemed to be satisfied
with its imperfect results: as long as rival party factions counterbalanced each
other, he did not have to declare his support for either side.

But what were Piasecki's thoughts about the return of Gomułka to
power? Little evidence supports the thesis of Piasecki's Polish biographers
that he opposed Gomułka's leadership.[8] After all, the leader of PAX had
enjoyed a good relationship with the secretary-general. When Mikołaj
Rostworowski, a senior PAX official, predicted that Gomułka would stabilize the political situation and discipline the press, which was stretching
the limits of free discussion, he might have been echoing Piasecki's views.[9]
Piasecki also had tried to reach Gomułka, even before October 1956.[10]

Supporting Gomułka was one thing, but embracing reforms was another
matter. Piasecki opposed "excessive democratization," which in his view undermined state authority and dangerously tested Moscow's patience. In this,
he shared the opinion of the Natolin faction, which while advocating the
rehabilitation of Gomułka also attacked political liberalization as a drift
from communism. Piasecki made no secret of his political sympathies. In a
speech delivered at a PAX conference on September 30, he expressed his
support for Natolin.[11] According to Teresa Englert, one of Piasecki's closest

associates in PAX, Piasecki also sympathized with Natolin because the group opposed "Jewish influence" in the country, intended to purge intellectual malcontents, and supported public order.[12]

Englert's opinion is plausible: the Puławska faction included many Jews. But there were other factors, as well. In all probability, Piasecki viewed the reform movement as a force competing against his proregime Catholics, a Marxist opposition that could upset both political balance and his own plans for the nationalization of the communist system.

On October 16, 1956, *Słowo powszechne* published an article by Piasecki titled "The State Instinct," which issued a stern warning: "If we do not conduct [our] discussion responsibly, instead of democratization, we may cause the brutal realization of the *raison d'état,* possibly under conditions of some kind of a state of emergency." In other words, Piasecki appealed to like-minded Poles to oppose radical de-Stalinization, which he believed could lead to Soviet military intervention or to declaration of martial law by the beleaguered government. According to Piasecki, there were "two principles of state instinct" in modern-day Poland: the continuity of socialism and the unbreakable alliance with the Soviet Union. It was Piasecki's self-professed expertise in the Polish national character that prompted him to declare that sometimes the wishes and actions of citizens had to be opposed by those who possessed greater knowledge of the rules of history and a better sense of judgment.[13]

"The State Instinct" constituted only one part of Piasecki's analysis of the situation in Poland. In "The Conditions of Dialogue," published three days later, he remarked that the only proof that the party still governed the country was the communiqué from its plenary session. Piasecki demanded that the government specify which social demands it found realistic and which ones it did not, because "the state must exercise its rule on the basis of really existing conditions rather than popular delusions."[14]

Piasecki's theses largely foreshadowed Gomułka's political message delivered a few days later. But in the context of the still unresolved struggles within the party and heated public debates, the articles were interpreted as a defense of Stalinism and a call for a coup against the reformers. Overnight, Piasecki became a symbol of the old regime. After "The State Instinct" appeared, the proreform *Express wieczorny* daily asked Piasecki to clarify what he had meant by "a realization of the *raison d'état* under conditions of some kind of a state of emergency" and on whose behalf he had issued these warnings.[15] On October 18, intellectuals from the Warsaw-based Club of the Crooked Circle adopted a resolution calling for Piasecki's expulsion from the presiding committee of the National Front.[16] The students of Warsaw University displayed the text of "The State Instinct" accompanied by the comment "Fascism is raising its head," while Jerzy Zawieyski and the former editors of *Tygodnik powszechny* denounced Piasecki's views as unrepresentative of Catholic circles.[17] This last statement came in the wake of a new political initiative, the formation of the Polish Club of the Catholic Progressive Intelligentsia (Ogólnopolski Klub Postępowej Inteligencji Katolickiej), a loose coalition of Catholic groups that endorsed reform.

The timing of Piasecki's articles could hardly have been worse. Three days after the publication of "The State Instinct," the party met for its eighth plenary session to reinstall Gomułka as its leader. The shocking and uninvited visit of a Soviet delegation headed by an enraged Khrushchev and the march of Soviet troops on the Polish capital only aggravated the tense atmosphere in Warsaw. Khrushchev feared that the Polish party was losing control over the country and that under new leadership, Poland would break away from the Soviet bloc.[18] Eventually, Gomułka convinced Khrushchev that he could restore control and that he had no intention of taking Poland out of the Warsaw Pact. A reshuffling of the Polish leadership, most notably the removal of Marshal Konstantin Rokossovsky and other hardliners from the Central Committee, became necessary to appease the radicalized masses and reformers.[19] On October 20, the Soviet delegation left Warsaw, and Russian troops returned to their bases. Gomułka was reelected as party leader on October 21.

The country saw the retreat of the Russians as a great patriotic victory. Gomułka acquired the aura of a national hero. The Polish events also sent shock waves abroad, fostering the myth of the possibility of "national communism" and triggering demonstrations in Budapest that eventually led to the outbreak of the Hungarian revolution in 1956. In Poland, Gomułka carried out the promises he had made to the Soviets. His speech to a crowd of three hundred thousand people in the center of Warsaw marked the beginning of the end of the Polish October. "Enough rallies and demonstrations," Gomułka called. "It is time to work!"[20]

Piasecki might have been one of a few who had the foresight to understand the implications of Gomułka's return to power, but he was battling for his own political survival. Within PAX, Micewski, Łubieński, Kętrzyński, and Horodyński were demanding the revision of the association's program and the temporary suspension of Piasecki's powers.[21] Fearing attack by a revolutionary mob, Piasecki walked in the company of armed bodyguards, changed his car, and moved temporarily out of his apartment.[22]

The meeting of PAX members to decide Piasecki's future took place on October 28, hours after the news of Wyszyński's release became public.[23] In an act of personal courage, Piasecki asked the delegates for a vote of confidence in his leadership.[24] He won, receiving 116 votes. Only 16 delegates voted against Piasecki, and 12 abstained.[25] The opposition failed to attract the support of local PAX activists, who unanimously supported their leader. By early November, Micewski, Horodyński, and Kętrzyński had no choice but to leave the association.[26] Any initiative to reform PAX was doomed from the start because the democratization of the association could be achieved only through the removal of its leader. PAX would not have survived such an operation, because Piasecki was its reason for existence.

It was time, then, for Piasecki to make peace with the new party leadership. To his relief, Gomułka's secretary, Walery Namiotkiewicz, related that Gomułka had no intention of liquidating PAX.[27] But Piasecki's position was far from secure, as the reformist intelligentsia was seeking to eliminate him from public life. At the center of the campaign against him was the article "Piasecki's Case" by the young writer Leopold Tyrmand. Tyrmand focused on Piasecki's collaboration with the Stalinist leadership following his arrest in November 1944. In reconstructing the encounter between Piasecki and Serov, Tyrmand claimed that the former fascist had allied himself with the communists because "it was a wonderful opportunity to achieve the goal of single-party hegemony that he had so long dreamed of." It was an agreement on the basis of ideological kinship, as both parties adhered to the principles of totalitarianism. Tyrmand also alleged that from that moment on, Piasecki had put himself at the disposal of the security police.[28]

In interpreting Piasecki's case as an illustration of fascist-communist affinities, Tyrmand conveniently failed to mention that it was the Polish communists, above all Gomułka, who had exonerated and supported Piasecki in 1945. Like other journalists and intellectuals who led the reformist crusade in October, Tyrmand held leftist views. Hence, he focused on Piasecki, whose dubious distinction derived from the fact that he was on the Right. A fascist turned Stalinist stooge was a perverse phenomenon, and if the Polish October had sought the perfection of socialism, the Left had to purge its ranks of such characters as Piasecki. But Piasecki was also a paragon of the recently defeated Stalinist faction. Once this connection was established, the distinction between PAX and Natolin presented little more than a matter of names.

Enthusiastically welcomed by reformers, Tyrmand's article had a mixed reception among party bigwigs. Gomułka had doubts about sacrificing Piasecki. To restore the party's authority, Gomułka needed to reestablish working relations with the Church, which enjoyed unwavering support among peasants and the new industrial labor force, members of which often were recruited from the religious countryside. The release of Wyszyński partly legitimized the new leadership. Gomułka also canceled the 1953 decree on ecclesiastical appointments, reintroduced religious instruction in the public schools, and permitted papal administrators to enter dioceses in the western territories. In response to these overtures, in January 1957 the episcopate urged Catholics to cast their votes in the general elections.[29]

Gomułka also provided outlets for noncommunist Catholics from the Polish Club of the Catholic Progressive Intelligentsia. He allowed the old editors of *Tygodnik powszechny* to resume publication of the weekly and gave permission for a small number of Catholics to run in the elections to parliament, where nine of them formed the Znak caucus. The group's three leaders included Stomma, the chief strategist; Jerzy Zawieyski, a member of the Council of State who had access to both Gomułka and Wyszyński; and Stefan Kisielewski, the fierce parliamentary orator and leading writer of *Tygodnik powszechny*. Their political philosophy stemmed from, but also went beyond, Stomma's minimalism of the late 1940s. Politics could not be ignored or left to the communists. Stomma recognized Poland's dependence on the Soviet Union and on communist rule without endorsing its ideological system. Znak advocated democratization, seeking to mediate between communists and noncommunists and to instill civic values in the population.[30]

Unlike Piasecki, Stomma and his associates never aspired to enrich Marxism through Catholicism or to create a Catholic party. "We do not want to rule Poland or to have a majority in parliament," wrote Kisielewski. "But we want to be in parliament and to express the views and tendencies of Catholic society and those people who do not share a Marxist worldview." October held the potential to put this scenario into practice.[31]

Gomułka, who was already meeting with Znak leaders in late October, appreciated their realism.[32] But he had no intention of handing the arena

of Catholic activism to a single political faction. There still was room for
Piasecki. When Stefan Staszewski, a leading party reformer, told him that
the liquidation of PAX would win the Church over to the side of the government, Gomułka retorted: "I know, you would like to leave me alone
with Wyszyński, but I am not going to do that: I am not going to make the
rope to hang myself with."[33]

In his correspondence with Gomułka, Piasecki did everything he could
to regain favor, even pledging unconditional loyalty. Reminding Gomułka
of their conversations in 1945, Piasecki observed that he had fully implemented the political line that they had agreed upon.[34] Gomułka came to the
rescue of his onetime protégé. When they met on January 2, 1957, he expressed his dismay at the press attacks on Piasecki and announced not only
that he had no intention of liquidating PAX but that he would permit its
transformation into a nationwide association with a membership of up to
three thousand.[35] After becoming a political pariah, Piasecki had survived.
Yet as the political turmoil of October began to subside, he experienced
the gravest personal tragedy of his life: the abduction and murder of his
son Bohdan.

On January 22, 1957, Bohdan Piasecki left school and started walking
home with three of his classmates. A few blocks from the school, two men
shoved Bohdan into a cab and drove away.[36] Nearly two years later, on
December 8, 1958, a group of workers renovating the cellar of an apartment
building in downtown Warsaw found Bohdan's mummified body.[37] The cor-
oner concluded that the boy had been killed on the day of his abduction.[38]

Police inefficiency marred the investigation from its start, and crucial
evidence was lost more than once.[39] Special investigating commissions produced little but bureaucratic chaos, despite the fact that from day one the
police had identified the key witness and suspect, Ignacy Ekerling, the driver
of the cab used by Bohdan's abductors and a former police informer and
chauffeur of top-ranking officials.[40] The investigation also revealed the involvement of a police officer who had rented an apartment in the building
where the body was discovered.[41] The suspects were never tried, however,
because of the interference of the government. Fearing that Ekerling's trial
would spark a resurgence of popular anti-Semitism—he and several other
suspects were Jewish—and tarnish the image of Poland abroad, the party
leadership ordered the case withdrawn from court.[42] The prosecution closed
the investigation into Bohdan Piasecki's death in 1982.

The murder took place in the wake of public attacks against Piasecki, a circumstance that supports two possible explanations: either the murder was carried out by Piasecki's personal enemies within the regime, or it was a provocation staged by those who aimed to discredit party reformers of Jewish descent. The apparent unwillingness of the party leadership to allow the investigation to go forward makes both theories plausible. One might even conclude that the perpetrators enjoyed the protection of the security police and that perhaps the government was never keen to solve the mystery of Bohdan's death for fear that it would be forced to disclose too much about the murky world of its secret services.

After his son's abduction, Piasecki never regained his former strength. He turned a number of his associates into amateur detectives, filed dozens of memoranda, and held numerous meetings with party, government, and security officials.[43] Piasecki believed that the kidnapping was the act of his political enemies, blaming variously former PAX dissidents, October liberals who had sought to destroy PAX in 1956, Jewish nationalists, and the anticommunist underground.[44] In January 1959, Piasecki met with Mieczysław Moczar and Antoni Alster, two deputy ministers of internal affairs. He reported on the meeting to his friends: "I told them that I knew that the real circumstances of the murder could not be revealed because the results would be too damaging to the prestige of the state. I think that such a resolution on my part has improved our relations with the country's leadership. I would not call my decision a compromise; it was rather a sacrifice."[45]

The Little Stabilization

The social and political climate in Gomułka's Poland was captured by the literary metaphor of "the little stabilization." Coined by the Polish poet and playwright Tadeusz Różewicz, the term underlined the discrepancy between society's expectations, raised by the Polish October, and the actual outcomes of Gomułka's reforms.[46] It also illustrated Gomułka's emphasis on stability rather than a revolutionary approach toward social change. This strategy implied a shift from coercive Stalinist control over society to social integration based on public compliance with and acceptance of the socialist system.[47]

Gomułka consolidated his authority in several ways. Heavy sentences meted out to a few notorious Stalinist henchmen and the exodus of some

Soviet military advisers and security policemen "solved" the problem of punishing those responsible for the Stalinist terror without going to the root of the system.[48] By halting collectivization and establishing working relations with the Church, Gomułka succeeded in bridging the gap between the regime and the Catholic peasant masses. Cuts in military spending, new housing projects, and moderate pay increases improved living standards. By lifting the requirement of ideological orthodoxy in the sphere of culture, furthermore, Gomułka won the compliance of intellectuals. The late 1950s and early 1960s were the golden years of Polish film, theater, music, and literature. At the same time, the party sought to consolidate its popularity by stressing patriotic consciousness and rehabilitating the AK generation. An important part of this strategy was the involvement of noncommunist veterans in public life by admitting them into the Veterans' Union and other state organizations. Gomułka stabilized his own position within the party by balancing hardliners against revisionists and by absorbing the 1956 radicals into the existing network of political organizations. During the Ninth Plenum of the Central Committee in May 1957, he mocked those who harbored illusions of national communism and reformed Marxism.[49]

Piasecki immediately understood that Gomułka had abandoned the strategy of revolutionary change. On September 30, 1957, he sent the first secretary a detailed memorandum outlining the political situation in Poland. According to Piasecki, the party was torn by a conflict between two extremes: the liberals and the conservatives. The liberals, who had been at the core of the reform movement, favored the social-democratic model and wanted to break away from the Soviet bloc. The conservatives, on the other hand, simply did not understand Gomułka's policy. "These comrades are often perceived as [your] enemies," Piasecki remarked. "This is not the case." As for the Church, he wrote, "The Catholic hierarchy views the current situation as the transition from socialism to bourgeois democracy."[50]

Turning to the populace, he observed: "Our society believes that Poland has finally reached a moment of peace." This increased sense of security produced highly ambivalent feelings, however: On the one hand, the majority of Poles supported social and political stabilization. On the other, more than a few had succumbed to a fascination with Western consumerism and to political indifference. Public support for Gomułka had little to do with popular acceptance of socialism on the whole. "A significant part of society," wrote Piasecki, "views your [Gomułka's] program as freedom from socialism rather than freedom in socialism." PAX could help. With nine thousand full and candidate members (a grossly exaggerated claim on Piasecki's part), the organization could play a vital role in mobilizing public support for Gomułka and his Polish road to socialism.[51]

Gomułka's immediate response to the memorandum is not known. At a meeting in June 1958, Gomułka voiced some objections to Piasecki's political conduct: for instance, the fact that PAX was admitting former members of the anticommunist underground into its ranks. He also pointed out that Piasecki's idea of pluralism of worldviews stood in opposition to the ideological principles of the communist movement. Yet, as Gomułka put it, PAX served socialist Poland well.[52]

Gomułka was aware of Wyszyński's hostility to PAX, and by 1958, the period of good relations between the government and the Church was over.[53] Perhaps he thought that Piasecki could be asset to the government. In the fall of 1956, Wyszyński had launched the Great Novena, a nine-year mass campaign of spiritual preparation for the millennium of Christianity in Poland. Gomułka was frankly alarmed.[54]

Poland's symbolic national baptism and the founding of the Polish state had occurred together in 966, the year of Prince Mieszko's conversion to Christianity, and the country pursued two separate programs of millennial celebrations. Like the Endeks before the war, the party-regime exalted the Piast period: the territory controlled by the Piast monarchy supposedly corresponded with the boundaries of People's Poland, and very much like contemporary Poland, it had blocked the German advance to the east. This contrasted with the era of the Polish-Lithuanian Commonwealth, a multiethnic power that had checked the westward expansion of Muscovite Russia.[55] Wyszyński's mobilization of popular religiosity also had deep political implications. The focus of the celebrations on the Virgin Mary, evidenced by the pilgrimage of a replica of the Holy Icon of the Black Madonna across the country from diocese to diocese, promoted a common discourse and spiritual unity. The primate disentangled himself and his flock from the secular communist state and offered Catholic Poles an alternative community, a repository of ethnoreligious identity.[56] On the one hand, he reincorporated Dmowski's views, embodied in the old slogan "Church, Nation, and State." On the other, he also endorsed the romantic tradition of insurrections, which he viewed as decisive in making the modern Polish nation.[57] Both Wyszyński and Gomułka perceived themselves as great patriots and the unquestioned leaders of the nation: a new confrontation was inevitable. It was a duel between ethnoconfessional and ethnosecular identities.

Instead of subjecting the Church to police terror, Gomułka pursued a strategy of limited harassment. The authorities again removed religious instruction from the public schools (1961), canceled building permits for new churches, and extended the military draft to clerics. In 1962, the new Fourth Department of the Ministry of Internal Affairs was given the task of infiltrating the Church, mostly by expanding the existing network of informers among the clergy and lay Catholics.

Gomułka's change of heart drew various responses from the Catholic community. Church leaders were not prepared to countenance energetic protests. The reaction of Znak was more ambivalent. Speaking to Gomułka shortly after the 1958 clashes between police and religious pilgrims in Częstochowa, Zawieyski criticized both the police and Wyszyński, who in his opinion had behaved as if communism in Poland was on the brink of collapse.[58] Znak activists also shared deep reservations about Wyszyński's focus on the Marian cult, especially the traveling replica of the Black Madonna of Częstochowa, which they considered obscurantist and far from authentic religiosity.[59] Stomma even tried to win the primate over to the idea of "the Church of quiet work," active in pastoral missions in the parishes (rather than in mass celebrations) and free from fundamentalism.[60] In the end, both sides came to distrust Znak: for the party, they were insufficiently procommunist, whereas Wyszyński suspected them of being too much on the Left. "You are trying to sit on two chairs," Gomułka warned Zawieyski. "Sometimes you take the cardinal's chair, sometimes you sit on ours. This is a dirty game."[61]

If Znak was naïve in its insistence on political neutrality, at least it was not opportunistic. On March 7, 1959, Stomma presented Kliszko with a memorandum calling for normalization in church-state relations. Although the authors of the document had struggled to mitigate their criticism of the government, they felt that the party should not expect the Church to endorse and support socialism.[62] Not surprisingly, Gomułka and Kliszko severely reprimanded the Znak leaders for yielding to the pressure of the Vatican and the episcopate.[63]

In private, Piasecki criticized both the Church and the government. "The essence of the problem is that the government treats the sociopolitical role of Catholicism with hostility, whereas the episcopate does not want to support socialism," he observed. Yet it was the Church that held the key to compromise. If the bishops thought that they could stay away from politics, they were mistaken. "The idea of isolating Catholicism from politics is like confining the Catholics to the monastery," Piasecki complained.[64]

But Piasecki misread the signals from the regime. Gomułka would have been more than happy if the Church had decided to stay away from politics. Piasecki also misunderstood Wyszyński, whose focus on popular religious celebrations had diverted the attention of the populace from the secular communist state to the Catholic-national community, influencing the political arena. Like Stomma, he failed to appreciate Wyszyński's genius, but for different reasons. Znak undervalued the primate's appeal to popular religiosity, overestimated the regime's goodwill, and invested itself in intellectual Catholicism. Piasecki, for his part, did not explore the nexus of politics and religion beyond his own doctrinaire thinking. He was, above all, an ambitious man determined to access political power.

PAX was rapidly expanding its membership, admitting veteran nationalists, former members of the National Armed Forces, and AK men.[65] "These groups are not political pensioners but the reserves of future political cadres," Piasecki remarked in 1957.[66] According to statistical data collected on PAX in the mid-1960s, the average PAX member was male, aged between thirty and fifty, and usually a white-collar worker residing in a town or city.[67] During the war, he had served in the AK or in nationalist combat groups. More than a few had been involved in the anticommunist underground.[68]

Piasecki's personal interventions in the cases of former Home Army soldiers had gained him genuine respect among noncommunist veterans. When *L'Osservatore romano* accused Piasecki of collaborating with the Nazis, several former high-ranking AK commanders staunchly defended the leader of PAX and forced the author of the article to admit that he had not verified his sources.[69] Piasecki also won the support of a few influential figures who had returned to Poland from exile in 1956. Zofia Kossak-Szczucka, Stanisław Mackiewicz, and Melchior Wańkowicz commanded significant intellectual and moral prestige. Kossak-Szczucka, a popular Catholic writer and activist, had played an important role in rescuing Jews during the war. Mackiewicz, who had praised Piasecki's political skills in the 1930s, was a conservative politician and journalist whose past assignments included presiding over the government in exile in London. Wańkowicz was praised as the leading Polish storyteller. They were drawn to Piasecki for a number of reasons.

Kossak-Szczucka perceived Piasecki as the only spokesman for political Catholicism in Poland, whereas Mackiewicz considered PAX a noncommunist alternative in otherwise socialist Poland.[70] Wańkowicz simply sought material security in the twilight of his life. Piasecki's publishing house paid well and released books much faster than the state publishers.[71]

But Piasecki's protection had its price. In January 1958, he involved his literary protégés in a propaganda crusade called the Action for Moral Revival (Akcja Odnowy Moralnej), a rather feeble attempt to compete with the Novena campaign. In a meeting with the primate in 1959, Kossak-Szczucka spoke passionately about PAX's merits in the struggle for moral revival. After years in exile, she claimed, she had become convinced that Polish Catholics had to close ranks to oppose the secularization of society and to defend the Catholic identity of the Polish nation. "Each time the government has attacked the Church, PAX always has sided with the former," Wyszyński replied. "You also should remember," he added, "that our society's attitude toward PAX is predominantly negative, and that casts a shadow over you, too."[72]

Wyszyński's rebuttal did not dissuade Piasecki from launching his campaign. The plan had two overlapping purposes: activating PAX's local structures and making the organization a magnet for noncommunist intellectuals.[73] Piasecki also sought to counterbalance the influence of the Polish Writers' Union (Związek Literatów Polskich), which he viewed as a bastion of the October reformers.[74] On March 16, 1958, PAX held the Congress of the Front for Moral Revival. In a keynote speech, Przetakiewicz accused liberal intellectuals of supporting the aggressive secularization of society. By assaulting Catholicism, he argued, revisionists attacked a repository of national identity and paved the way for the "derailment of socialism in Poland."[75] Piasecki and his cronies sought to discredit the reformist movement as both anti-Polish and anticommunist. They also cast doubt on the ethnic background and national identity of these critics: Piasecki privately equated revisionists with the "Jewish comrades."[76]

The Premature Call: The Socialist-Patriotic Avant-Garde

Opposition to revisionism followed naturally from Piasecki's doctrine of pluralism of worldviews. At its heart was the notion of a specifically Polish ideological experiment paving the way for the establishment of an authoritarian state that would operate on the basis of nationalism, Catholicism, socialism, and pro-Soviet loyalism. "One has to realize," he claimed in 1958, "that the whole history of People's Poland has demonstrated that the terms 'people's' and 'national' are fully compatible."[77] Essentially, Piasecki argued that patriotism was socialist and that socialism was patriotic. In consequence, anyone who opposed the incorporation of nationalism into socialism was guilty of antisocialist aberration.

Gomułka's frequent diatribes against revisionists and intellectuals gave a boost to Piasecki's confidence. Addressing his followers in March 1959, Piasecki was jubilant. "Let me quote to you a recent joke, which illustrates the course of the Third Congress [of the party]," he began. "The delegates convened under the slogan: 'October? Never again!'" But then Piasecki adopted a serious tone: "God forbid that there will be another situation when we have to go ahead of the party." Now the association could even act as a catalyst for ideological discussions within the party, which had to retain its ideological vitality.[78]

Piasecki believed that communist Poland stood at a crossroads. On the one hand, there was no return to Stalinism. On the other, the revisionist alternative could lead to a national catastrophe because the Soviets would never allow Poland to experiment with democracy without their consent. To overcome the reformist danger, Piasecki argued, the party had no choice but to redefine its ideology by incorporating a pluralism of worldviews into its political program.[79] He believed that Gomułka shared his vision and that together they formed the core of "a patriotic-socialist formation" (*formacja patriotyczno-socjalistyczna*) that combined socialism with the principle of "national dignity" (read: nationalism), a Marxist worldview with a patriotic (nationalist) ethos.[80]

Piasecki had little doubt that nationalist tendencies would blossom within the party. At the same time, he regarded ideology as the Achilles' heel of Gomułka's faction. "Instinctively they feel that socialism and patriotism are one and the same, but at the same time they have difficulties in formulating this thesis."[81] He also claimed to know the remedy: under Piasecki's ideological tutelage and Gomułka's political command, "socialist patriots" would block the advancement of anti-Polish and antisocialist revisionism. The next logical step would be the transformation of PAX into a political party. "We want to become a genuine coalition partner," he exclaimed to his followers in February 1960, "a real movement, the party's ally of authentic strength, not an ornamental institution."[82]

Although Piasecki never had made a secret of his political ambitions, Znak Catholics were alarmed. Julian Eska declared Piasecki's pluralism of worldviews a masquerade for communist-nationalist dualism embodied in the joint rule of "two consuls," one communist and one Catholic, but both loyal to the Soviets.[83] His two colleagues, Micewski and Mazowiecki, both former PAX insiders, viewed Piasecki's organization as "the neo-Endek movement."[84] Zawieyski stated perceptively that Piasecki's increasing self-confidence reflected the growing appeal of anti-Semitism within the PZPR.[85]

Indeed, Zawieyski's observations were well founded. In February 1960, Piasecki's second-in-command, Przetakiewicz, put his boss in an embarrassing situation. While dining at the club of the Polish Journalists' Association, Przetakiewicz got seriously drunk. In the presence of numerous foreign press correspondents, he made derogatory and anti-Semitic comments about Roman Zambrowski.[86] Western media publicized the incident, and in May the association expelled Przetakiewicz from its ranks. But when Piasecki met Kliszko, the number two man in the Polish party, he learned that the affair would have no serious consequences for PAX. Piasecki sent Przetakiewicz to the provinces until the scandal died down. Within less than a year, Przetakiewicz had returned to Warsaw and resumed his work at PAX headquarters.[87] More important, the way in which the party leadership had handled Przetakiewicz's case might have convinced Piasecki that anti-Semitism was no longer a serious offense, but a misdemeanor.

The resolution of the affair boosted Piasecki's optimism about his own political advancement. In December 1960, more than seven hundred guests, including foreign visitors, attended the PAX congress in Warsaw to celebrate the fifteenth anniversary of the launching of *Dziś i jutro*.[88] On this occasion, however, Piasecki received alarming signs of disapproval from Gomułka. While hosting a dinner at his house, Piasecki learned from Wolfgang Heyl, the head of the East German delegation, that the Polish government had prevented Gerald Götting, secretary-general of the East CDU, from attending the PAX convention. It was clear, Heyl claimed, that Gomułka did not want to see the congress turn into a significant political event.[89] Yet Piasecki was determined to fight on. At the close of the congress, he communicated to Gomułka that PAX "would continue its efforts to increase the socialist involvement of the Poles on the basis of the creative doctrine of pluralism of worldviews."[90]

Gomułka would not have it. When he finally received the PAX delegation on January 25, 1961, he blasted Piasecki. "These are absurd demands,"

Gomułka snapped, referring to Piasecki's political aims. "If your theory was correct," Gomułka told Piasecki, "we would have to launch the revolution for a second time." He also demanded to know why Piasecki claimed that the secularization of society harmed the socialist state. He was particularly irritated by Piasecki's attempts to lecture the party on ideology. "PAX intends to reform Marxism," Gomułka observed, "but only Marxists can perfect Marxism, and in this they do not need anybody's help." He added: "The party will take care of its errors . . . without the help of revisionists, because what you are doing is revisionism." Gomułka also accused Piasecki of building an economic empire and bureaucratic structures on a grand scale. This had to end. PAX was going in the wrong direction, and it was up to Piasecki to rectify its mistakes.[91]

Gomułka talked for seventy-five minutes. Piasecki was shocked. He was particularly offended by the charge of clericalism. He also pointed out that PAX had criticized not just secularization but the de-ideologization of society. He pursued his doctrine of two worldviews because he did not trust those who participated in implementing socialism without ideological conviction.

"People build socialism out of true convictions and material concerns," Gomułka cut him off. "In the end, what really matters to them are their material aspirations. The political system is good when it does not repress people and allows them to say what they want. We pay less and less attention to what people are actually saying. In the end we will pay no attention at all." The party let Catholics practice their religion because that was the best form of coexistence and cooperation between Catholics and communists: the former were free to practice, and the latter were free to rule.[92]

Gomułka's remarks left Piasecki speechless. Reiff asked why the two worldviews could not coexist in the final stage of socialism. "The problem with you is not [your] worldview but your aspirations to build a Catholic party. We would have to fight against such a party," Gomułka replied. Jerzy Hagmajer wanted to smooth things over: "We have made mistakes, and today we have been punished." "Not punished, but corrected," Gomułka clarified. "You were patronizing the party like some kind of mentors." He concluded: "I am not here to hit you, but to share some reflections. I just want you to understand that what you have propagated does not serve the interest of socialism."[93]

For Piasecki, the meeting with Gomułka was a huge blow. At the meeting of PAX's high council on February 10, 1961, he admitted that Gomułka had dismissed his pluralism of worldviews as revisionism, favored the process of secularization, and rejected the transformation of PAX into a political party. He announced: "For a while, our ideological role is over. I believe that the current line of the party will be in force for some time."[94]

In private, Piasecki was completely devastated. "All these communists," he told Bocheński, "are saying that you, I, and others of our kind belong to the dying world, that Catholicism in Poland is ending."[95] But contrary to his threats, Gomułka never issued sanctions against Piasecki's organization.[96] As tensions between the Church and the regime escalated, Gomułka had no intention of sacrificing Piasecki. With or without his ideological obsessions, the leader of PAX was a faithful ally whose zeal and energy could be exploited to the benefit of the regime.

In April 1961, to his surprise, Piasecki learned from Antoni Alster that his penance was over. Apparently, the government planned to dissolve the group formerly known as the Patriotic Priests and to put them under the tutelage of PAX. Alster also wanted to know whether PAX had closed down any of its newspapers. The answer was no. "That's good," Alster said. "Do not liquidate anything." Piasecki regained his mood.[97] Even when he learned in December 1961 that the security police had bugged his office, he did not despair. During a "vodka and herring party" before Christmas, he told his alcohol-clouded friends: "I have just learned that our people's power has planted a bug in my office." While calming his alarmed associates, he declared with characteristic cockiness: "So they are learning 99 percent of what is said here, but they will never get the 1 percent that interests them most."[98]

Piasecki had lost faith in Gomułka, or to be precise, he had ceased to believe in the possibility of his own political advancement under the Gomułka regime. In a private conversation with Reiff, he remarked, "We are, in fact, against Khrushchev and Gomułka."[99] He knew that Gomułka's rule would not last forever.

Foreign Contacts: Piasecki's Network in the Soviet Bloc

During the late fifties and early sixties, Piasecki put special emphasis on developing foreign contacts. His top priority was the Soviet Union. He thought that Moscow should recognize his unconditional loyalty, especially in comparison with the wavering Gomułka, revisionist schismatics, and inflexible hard-liners. Piasecki had resumed his contacts with the Soviets in the spring of 1957. At a meeting with V. A. Karpov, the counselor of the Soviet embassy in Warsaw, on April 5, Piasecki declared that he was willing to establish "permanent contacts with the Soviet representatives in order to exchange opinions on matters interesting to the Soviet Union." In his broad assessment of the political situation in Poland, Piasecki described Gomułka as an ardent and honest communist. He also indicated, however, that the party was a hotbed of factional struggles. He provided brief characterizations of party leaders, shared some political gossip, and extolled the ideological correctness of PAX.[100]

Piasecki's revelations were of little value to the Soviets. But they listened, comparing his observations with the opinions of other Polish politicians. They also catered to Piasecki's ego by giving him politically insignificant and selectively filtered information about the plenary sessions in Moscow. On several occasions, they promised to arrange an official visit to the Soviet Union.[101]

Piasecki tried to befriend Soviet ambassador Peter Abrasimov and his successor, Panteleimon Ponomarenko.[102] Soviet diplomats and press correspondents often were invited to dinner parties at Piasecki's house. Piasecki even believed that Abrasimov consistently lobbied for his visit to the Soviet Union.[103]

But it was Boris Zhirnov, the chief editor of the Polish-language Soviet periodical *Kraj rad* (Land of the Soviets), with whom Piasecki enjoyed the most cordial relations. The two men were on a first-name basis. Piasecki thought that Zhirnov had excellent political and personal connections within the Soviet political elite. "I need your help," Piasecki confided to Zhirnov on one occasion, "because you know the right people. . . . What I want you to do is to introduce me to some politicians, so that I can offer them my opinions about the situation in Poland." What for? Zhirnov asked. After all, the Soviet government could not complain of a lack of information about Poland. "Of course, it is true," Piasecki observed, "that they receive information from you, the Polish government, and the party, but I can assure you that they will find my opinions very interesting." PAX needed Soviet support against the influence of liberal party officials and revisionists. "These people hate us because we have always been pro-Soviet, procommunist, and patriotic."[104]

Through its police surveillance of Piasecki, Gomułka's team knew the content of his talks with Zhirnov. But Piasecki was never reprimanded for intriguing with the Soviets. The reason for this leniency is unknown. Was it the positive evaluation of Gomułka that Piasecki passed along to the Soviets? Or was he considered a Soviet agent? The government consistently rejected his requests for an official trip to the Soviet Union, however. Piasecki succeeded in sending Przetakiewicz to Moscow in 1965, but he did not know that Przetakiewicz's assistant was a police informant. In Moscow, Przetakiewicz met mostly journalists and second-rate party officials. No one even raised the issue of Piasecki's trip to the Soviet Union.[105]

As noted earlier, Piasecki had succeeded in establishing a particularly warm relationship with Gerald Götting, secretary-general of the East CDU. The men met on a number of occasions, Piasecki visiting the CDU congresses and Götting attending the PAX conventions. The leader of PAX and his family even spent vacations at the government-owned recreation center near Erfurt.[106]

Eight years younger than Piasecki, Götting represented the new generation of East CDU activists who dominated the party after the 1947 and 1948 purges of the old leadership that had refused to collaborate with the communists. By 1949, Götting had attained the post of party secretary-general. He was also a member of the GDR's parliament (in 1969, he was named president of the Volkskammer) and the deputy chairman of the Council of State from 1960.[107] Unlike Piasecki, Götting was an opportunistic nonentity, a communist puppet.[108] A Lutheran Christian and philosopher by training, he published a number of quasi-theological studies about ideological affinities between Christianity and Marxism, a subject that accorded well with Piasecki's theological experiments of the 1950s.[109] Nominally a noncommunist politician from a country whose only reasons for existence were foreign occupation and ideology, Götting actively proselytized the "progressive" half of the German nation and crusaded against West Germany.[110]

Götting's political career, as well as the position of his party in the GDR, might have made Piasecki's head spin. While talking to Wolfgang Heyl, Götting's deputy, Piasecki did not hide his envy: "In Poland, PAX still has to struggle to establish its position, whereas you have been a political party participating in the government for years."[111] But the leader of PAX either ignored or failed to note the differences between the GDR and Poland. Having established firm control over the Church, the East German communists could afford the luxury of a Christian coalition partner. Also important was the traditional subservience of the Lutheran Church to the state in Germany. In Poland, however, the existence of the powerful Catholic Church obviated the possibility of the German model. The East CDU was a satellite party, a politically insignificant member of the bogus ruling coalition. Furthermore, in the GDR, the class-based formula of the alliance of communists, peasants, and the petite bourgeoisie was slightly modified because of the initial mirroring of political systems in the Western and Soviet occupation zones. If the Christian Democrats were an integral part of postwar political culture in West Germany, then the GDR had to have its own CDU.[112]

When Piasecki celebrated the twentieth anniversary of his movement in 1965, he received plaudits from numerous foreign delegations: Götting's Christian Democrats, members of Rev. Josef Plojhar's Czechoslovak People's Party, activists of Monsignor Gyula Der's Ecclesia group from Hungary, and others. They came to Warsaw to celebrate the "Catholic pioneers of peace and progress" from Poland, to quote Béla Kézai, chief editor of the Hungarian periodical *Katolikus szó*.[113] In the end, these "progressive" Christians amounted to little more than ornaments on the gray edifice of the Soviet bloc.

Pitched Battles with the Church, 1961–66

Although the millennium celebrations were scheduled for 1966, tension between the Church and the party-state built steadily throughout the early 1960s. Neither side intended to be unprepared for the symbolic competition. Consequently, church-state relations in Gomułka's Poland evolved into a series of veritable wars of slogans, administrative skirmishes, and media campaigns.

As noted earlier, in 1961, the regime had decided to use Piasecki to help reorganize the proregime clergy. Established in June 1959, the Central Circle of Priests "Caritas" (Centralne Koło Księży "Caritas") was a continuation of the Patriotic Priests, which had been dissolved after Wyszyński's release in 1956. But the government's plans for the new organization were unclear. Discredited by their previous political involvement and boycotted by the episcopate, the Caritas priests had few valuable contacts with the laity.[114] The decision to keep them afloat reflected the authorities' will to mobilize all available resources against Wyszyński, but it also suggested the ongoing ossification of the communist system in Poland. Like many other institutions and mechanisms put into motion under Stalinism, the proregime priests lingered for years after they had ceased to be useful.

Despite the apparent enthusiasm that he showed to Alster, Piasecki opposed the new organization, believing that there was nothing to be gained from it.[115] Indeed, by the end of 1960s, the movement of the Caritas priests was practically dead. Yet Piasecki continued to support the party on other issues, such as the abolition of religious instruction in public schools. On July 15, 1961, PAX voted in favor of the bill, whereas Znak abstained.[116]

On other occasions, Piasecki acted more cautiously. He refused to get involved in the bitter controversy over the construction of a church in Nowa Huta, for instance. Built as a socialist model town and home to the giant Lenin Steelworks, Nowa Huta had a population of two hundred thousand, but not a single church. In November 1956, the residents successfully requested permission to build a church and later marked the allocated site with a twelve-meter-high cross. In October 1959, however, the government withdrew the building permit and ordered the removal of the cross. In the spring of the following year, Nowa Huta became the scene of violent clashes between members of the Catholic laity and the police.[117] In the autumn of 1961, the regime tried to persuade PAX to accept the building permit and to remove the troublesome cross, but Piasecki did not need this thorn in his side.[118] In September 1965, the government finally granted the building permit to the Catholic Church.[119]

Piasecki postured as a loyal son of the Catholic Church. But in private, he and other PAX leaders vehemently criticized the bishops. "Personally, I think that the episcopate is really stupid," Jerzy Rutkowski told Piasecki. "If only we could replace our bishops with these Italian cardinals, things would be much better."[120]

Indeed, Piasecki and his cronies might well have concluded the "Italian cardinals" would sympathize with their ostensibly progressive Catholicism. From the beginning of the Second Vatican Council, which opened in September 1962, Piasecki had attempted to present PAX as the leading advocate of Catholic emancipation in Poland.[121] Following the announcement of the encyclical *Pacem in terris* (Peace on Earth) in April 1963, *Słowo powszechne* underlined the unity of goals between PAX and Pope John XXIII. "We, lay Catholics, interpret *Pacem in terris* as an appeal for activism," Dobraczyński wrote. "In fact, John XXIII clearly stated that Christians could not and should not live in isolation from political and social developments shaping the modern world."[122] Witold Jankowski, the newspaper's chief editor, went even further, declaring that the pope set an example for those members of the Polish church hierarchy who still insisted on condemning "the socialist involvement of numerous Polish Catholics."[123] Such statements accorded fully with the tone of official propaganda, which contrasted the "progressive" John XXIII with the "reactionary" Wyszyński.[124]

John XXIII did not share the social-political conservatism of Pius XII, and he championed the notion of a dialogue between the Church and the rest of the world. He viewed communism as a product of modernity deserving an approach more complex than unanimous condemnation.[125] The pope never absolved the communist system of its crimes, however, nor did he embrace the Catholic-Marxist alliance.[126] In declaring that the pope's views corresponded with Piasecki's theological innovations of the 1950s, however, the PAX press crossed the line.[127]

The leader of PAX tried to establish contacts with the pope's entourage while traveling in Italy in December 1962. While in Rome, Piasecki sought to secure an audience with Cardinal Giovanni Battista Montini (the future Pope Paul VI), but despite the mediation of the always helpful Luciana Frassati-Gawrońska, the meeting did not take place.[128] Nevertheless, Piasecki continued to express his support for the Vatican Council.

But on what grounds? True, PAX correspondents provided the readers of *Słowo powszechne* with detailed reports about the council's sessions. But the "spirit of the council" (duch soborowy), which had a profound intellectual and religious impact on Catholic intellectuals in Poland and elsewhere, seemed to have little effect on Piasecki. Piasecki's ideal of political Catholicism mixed with nationalism and his contempt for individual rights hardly corresponded with the open Catholicism, ecumenism, and religious tolerance championed by the Second Vatican Council. The council largely dismantled the authoritarian, monarchical structure of the Church, replacing it with collegiality through the collective council of bishops and through greater recognition of the contributions of bishops, clergy, and laity to the Church. One consequence of this "liberation of laity" was the end of clerical control over Catholic political groups, which may have pleased Piasecki.[129] But in addition to engaging the Church with contemporary realities, ecumenism and the new pluralistic political Catholicism also undermined both Catholic distinctiveness and the homogeneity of Catholic communities.[130] This shift was hardly likely to win Piasecki's heart. Dialogue with communist rulers was one thing. The possible erosion of the homogeneity of the Polish-Catholic community and, by extension, of ethnoconfessional identity was another. In that aspect, Piasecki may have been closer to Wyszyński's "theology of the nation" than he suspected.[131]

Such nuances, however, were hardly to be grasped by uninformed foreign constituencies. Shortly after the pontiff's death in 1963, Piasecki found himself at the center of a bitter confrontation between opponents and advocates of Vatican II. In 1961 and 1962, two French Catholic newspapers, the left-wing *Informations catholiques internationales* published by the Dominican monks and the conservative *La Croix*, published a series of conflicting reports about the condition of the Church in Poland. Some of these articles dealt with Piasecki's organization.[132] To complicate matters further, in 1963 the Polish primate responded to these publications by submitting to the Vatican his own report, which accused Piasecki of collaborating with the security police and infiltrating Western Catholic groups, including the publishers of *Informations catholiques internationales*.[133] By January 1964, the report had reached French conservative Catholics, who used it in their campaign against supporters of Vatican II. In Paris and Lyon, Catholic fundamentalists broke into meetings of their progressive coreligionists, accusing them of being agents of PAX and Moscow. Some of these incidents escalated into clashes that had to be put down by the police.[134]

There was something surreal in this situation: French Catholics in a fratricidal battle over a small Polish organization that they knew scarcely anything about. Piasecki did not enjoy this publicity.[135] In Poland, the PAX-controlled newspapers published an open letter to Wyszyński. PAX was not a religious association, the letter read, but a political organization of lay Catholics. Although the ideological antagonism between Marxism and Catholicism had deep historical roots, the pontificate of John XXIII had showed that this conflict was anachronistic and solvable. Arguing along the lines of the Second Vatican Council, PAX proclaimed that though the Polish bishops had authority in matters of faith, they had no control over believers' political involvement.[136]

Even people who could not possibly sympathize with Piasecki viewed Wyszyński's actions as mistakes. Stomma considered the tone of Piasecki's open letter to the primate unacceptable, but he also thought that by starting the campaign against PAX abroad, Wyszyński had improved the position of Piasecki's organization at home and benefited the enemies of Vatican II.[137] Wyszyński did not try to refute these opinions. "It does not concern me," he observed.[138]

The ambivalence of responses to Wyszyński's actions in Poland and abroad proved that the primate was vulnerable. Piasecki also knew that the controversy had improved his standing vis-à-vis the communist party. In May 1965, Piasecki finally achieved his longtime goal of becoming a member of parliament. The months that followed saw further improvement in Piasecki's position, as he found himself at the center of another controversy.

In September 1965, the PAX weekly *WTK* published a special German-language edition devoted to the conference of the Polish episcopate celebrating the twentieth anniversary of the acquisition of new dioceses in the western territories. In Hamburg, bundles of *WTK* were confiscated by the local police on the ground that the newspaper contained anti-German propaganda. In Poland, even Znak admitted that PAX had succeeded in exposing anti-Polish prejudices within the West German government.[139]

Gomułka was impressed. In November 1965, he received Piasecki and agreed to increase the number of PAX regional offices.[140] More important, he used Piasecki's West German venture as a counterweight to recent acts of the Polish church. On November 18, 1965, the Polish episcopate sent an official letter inviting the German bishops to the millennium celebrations in 1966. More important, the letter offered pardon for the atrocities inflicted by the Germans on the Polish nation during World War II. At its heart stood an offer of Christian reconciliation and mutual forgiveness: "We forgive and ask for forgiveness."[141]

The bishops' letter was one of the riskiest decisions of the Polish church in its postwar history. In 1965, Poland and West Germany were divided not only by the iron curtain but also by a wall of historical antagonism and mutual suspicion. In Poland, the official policy of rooting out traditional anti-Russian and anti-Soviet resentments accompanied a parallel strategy of escalating Germanophobia. As Polish scholar Marcin Zaremba observes, "One may well conclude that during the 1960s anti-Germanism, camouflaged as the struggle against West German territorial revanchism, became the only allowable manifestation of popular nationalism."[142]

The Polish bishops challenged this formula as well as the prevailing mood of the laity and clergy.[143] At the time, the majority of Poles could not see any reason why they should seek pardon from their western neighbors. The author of the letter, the Archbishop Bolesław Kominek of Wrocław, believed that if the Polish and German bishops built bridges between the two nations, the problem of the Oder-Neisse border would disappear.[144] One may only speculate as to how Kominek convinced the nationalist Wyszyński to approve the letter. Perhaps the primate believed that the initiative would strengthen the prestige of the Polish church abroad, prompting the Vatican to recognize Poland's western territories and weakening the communists' hold on Polish society.

The regime was furious. According to Gomułka, the Church had "openly acted against the policy of People's Poland on issues fundamental to our nation's future."[145] Zawieyski criticized the bishops for not consulting the government on their initiative and blamed them for making some unfortunate statements badly received by society.[146] By the end of the year, the Polish episcopate found itself the subject of a massive propaganda campaign, which also involved Piasecki's organization.[147] Piasecki based PAX's response to the bishops' appeal on three major principles. First, the initiative had sought undermine the place of Poland in the Soviet bloc. Second, while the letter did not question the western borders, it did propagate pro-Western attitudes. Finally, the bishops' statement was technically consonant with Bonn's aims of demobilizing the Polish public, destroying the GDR, and obtaining a border with Poland in order to subdue it in the future.[148]

The controversy over the Polish bishops' letter was a direct prelude to the battle over the millennium anniversary. Between April and June 1966, the country undertook two separate programs of celebrations. In Gniezno, Poznań, and Kraków, Wyszyński conducted religious services a few streets away from the state rallies attended by Gomułka, Cyrankiewicz, and other state officials.[149] With the exception of Warsaw, however, which saw clashes between the faithful and government-sponsored counterdemonstrators supported by the police, the celebrations proceeded peacefully.[150]

For Piasecki, the millennium jubilee symbolized the unity of Polishness and Catholicism. He objected to the separation of church and state festivities. "What unites these celebrations is their common emphasis on patriotism," Piasecki remarked on one occasion. However, he complained, the rival ceremonies demonstrated that neither the party nor the Church understood the unity of Polishness and Catholicism.[151] He was mistaken. By blending national and religious identity in the Nowenna campaign, Wyszyński moved closer toward the appropriation of nationalist discourse than did his communist adversaries. State-sponsored rallies paled in comparison to the Church's celebrations. The government confiscation of the traveling icon of Our Lady of Częstochowa only fueled the Marian cult and the mass pilgrim movement. The slogan "A Thousand Schools for a Thousand Years of the Polish State" might have captured the imagination of local bureaucrats, but it did not win the hearts of masses as "Mary the Queen of Poland" did. Gomułka's regime lost the millennium battle.

Polish-Vatican Talks, 1966–67

One of the most vivid examples of the confrontation over the millennium was Gomułka's ultimate refusal to invite Pope Paul VI to religious ceremonies at the shrine of Jasna Góra in May 1966. Wyszyński had to be punished. The very existence of talks about a papal visit, however, signaled a major shift in relations between Poland and the Holy See. In fact, both sides were willing to conduct a more open relationship. Gomułka may have perceived an agreement with the Vatican, bypassing the episcopate, as a great opportunity to weaken the position of Wyszyński and to improve his own standing at home.[152] The Vatican's motives were more mixed. Like his predecessor John XXIII, Paul VI believed that communism required an approach more complex than outright condemnation. A former diplomat, the pope treated the establishment of relations with the communist states as one of his top priorities, believing that a policy of opening up to Eastern Europe had a better chance of persuading the communists to exercise religious tolerance toward their Catholic subjects. Monsignor Agostino Casaroli, the pope's foreign policy adviser, fully shared this vision. In 1963, he traveled to Prague and Budapest to establish contacts with communist rulers. Now it was Poland's turn.[153]

Piasecki played an important role in the Polish-Vatican talks. In March 1966, he used his relations with the Italian ambassador to Poland, Enrico Aillaud, to establish contact with Casaroli. On March 24, 1966, Piasecki reported to Kliszko that the Vatican sought regular relations with the Polish government. "Even if the current negotiations [about the papal visit] do not bring any results," he wrote to Kliszko, "the Vatican is determined to maintain these contacts."[154] After Gomułka refused to invite the pope, Piasecki, with Kliszko's approval, continued his contact with Casaroli. In the early summer of 1966, he reported to Kliszko that the Vatican would not inform Wyszyński of the planned talks. The Holy See viewed the current communication channels as the most reliable.[155]

This was information that the government had sought for a long time. From then on, the regime took everything into its own hands, passing all contacts with Casaroli to Andrzej Werblan, Gomułka's ideological watch-dog.[156] Piasecki was given an auxiliary role. In November 1966, he met Archbishop Franco La Costa, whom Paul VI had sent discreetly to Poland to test the ground before making further commitments to negotiate with the Poles. La Costa declared that Paul VI viewed an agreement with Poland as absolutely crucial. Contrary to Casaroli's earlier assurances, however, he said that no agreement could be reached without the approval of the Polish hierarchy.[157]

Casaroli visited Poland on three occasions: in February, March, and April 1967. By failing to inform Wyszyński about his first visit, Casaroli signaled to the Polish government that he intended to keep the Polish episcopate out of the negotiations. More important, following his inspection of the Polish dioceses and his talks with bishops and party officials, Casaroli confided to Werblan that he found no evidence that the Church was being persecuted at all.[158] He displayed less optimism in his conversation with Piasecki on March 5, 1967, however. Casaroli argued the Polish leaders mistakenly believed that they had enough power to limit the influence of the Church, whereas Wyszyński still acted as if Stalinism had never ended. It was a vicious circle. Casaroli also suspected that the government had resolved to sign the agreement in order to defuse growing opposition to its policies.[159] Before his return to Italy on April 7, he proposed the exchange of quasi-official representatives between Poland and the Holy See. But the mercurial Vatican diplomat failed to entice the Poles with his enthusiasm. Werblan, the chief Polish negotiator, indicated that the Polish government needed more time to consider this option.[160] A few weeks later, the Gomułka regime faced priorities other than a treaty with the Vatican. It was about to launch a decisive battle against revisionists, intellectuals, rebellious youth, and last but not least, Jews. Negotiations between the Polish government and the Vatican resumed only in the 1970s, after the fall of Gomułka.

The ten years of Gomułka's rule had taught Piasecki several important lessons. First, he discovered that Gomułka's Polish road to socialism was in reality a process of authoritarian retrenchment to stabilize the absolute authority of the party. Gomułka had no use for Piasecki's ideological experiments, since they implied an end to the party's monopoly on power. He had no intention of delegating the buildup of a nationalist-communist alliance to Piasecki. It was critical that any initiatives of this kind come from the party. Thus, Piasecki's second lesson was that he should never go out ahead of Gomułka to make public demands for ideological innovations. The party had to appear united, and Piasecki had no business revealing factional struggles and ideological deviations.

Finally, Piasecki learned that he could still benefit from meddling in church affairs. But he failed to comprehend fully the importance of Wyszyński's "re-Catholicization" of Polish national identity. His adversaries from Znak made a similar mistake. By putting too much trust in Gomułka's goodwill; by investing in intellectual Catholicism, which did not resonate well with the Church and laity in Poland; and above all, by taking too seriously the promises of October, they failed to arrogate to themselves coresponsibility for national affairs and could not mitigate the conflict between Poland's two leaders, Gomułka and Wyszyński. But while Stomma and Kisielewski eventually would reform their positions, Piasecki remained a prisoner of his doctrine.

6 ⫿ The Last Crusade, 1967–68

JÓZEF PIŁSUDSKI ONCE REMARKED THAT he had alighted from the socialist streetcar at the stop called nationalism. Years later, Gomułka and his comrades decided to merge the communist and nationalist tracks, thus accelerating the metamorphosis of Polish communism. One of the outcomes of this process was the nationalization, or Polonization, of the communist party. The purge of Jewish members and veteran activists reached its climax during the 1967–68 anti-Semitic campaign, as Polish communists committed themselves to creating a nationalist alternative with anti-Semitism as "its main ideological principle," to borrow a phrase from Leszek Kołakowski.[1] By openly embracing chauvinism and authoritarianism at home and military aggression abroad—the Polish Army played a significant role in the invasion of Aleksander Dubček's Czechoslovakia—Gomułka and his cronies built the "Polish road to communism" in a nightmarish fashion. This last offensive ultimately led to the de-ideologization of communist Poland and to its transformation into a nationalist-populist regime that failed to take its own ideological credo seriously.

Piasecki's fusion of nationalism with socialism made him the spiritual father to many of those communists who were calling for a system that was communist in form and nationalist in content. Piasecki joined in and to a degree instigated the witch hunt in 1968 with a fervor reminiscent of his youthful pursuits in the 1930s. After years of imposed conformity, humiliation, and insignificance, his time seemed to have come at last. But his appearance of strength was deceptive, his success short-lived. A turning point in the history of Polish communism, 1968 was also Piasecki's swan song as a politician of real ambition.

The Road to 1968

At a speech to PAX activists in June 1965, Piasecki described his election to the Sejm as a signal to "his political friends" that the "patriotic-socialist forces" were on the offensive.[2] But who were Piasecki's political friends? Did he mean the Partisans of Mieczysław Moczar—the ultranationalist faction within the party and the security apparatus—or the broad antireformist front that united Moczar's men and Gomułka's entourage? In fact, he may have been referring to both.

By the mid-1960s, Gomułka's regime had grown increasingly authoritarian and sclerotic. Gone from the establishment were the radicals of 1956 and the party reformers. Having lost their influence on the party leadership, the revisionists confined themselves to the circles of the progressive intelligentsia. One consequence of this withdrawal was the emergence of a strong anti-intellectual bias among Gomułka and his entourage. Gomułka's regime also tolerated and at times approved of anti-Semitism.

A complete treatment of anti-Semitism among Polish party leaders is beyond the scope of this study. Nevertheless, there is no doubt that the roots of the phenomenon reach far back into the history of the Polish communist movement. Gomułka, Zenon Kliszko, and other Polish leaders of the 1960s represented the second generation of Polish communists (the first having been liquidated by Stalin during the great purges). Plebeian, little educated, and ethnically Polish, they had made their way into the party elite during the war, which they spent in occupied Poland. Accused of "nationalist errors," they had been purged from the party in 1948 and were reinstated only in 1956. They often blamed the "Jewish comrades" for their misery.[3] When Gomułka returned to power in 1956, some of the activists whom the first secretary might have considered his tormentors had become party reformers. Soon, Gomułka perceived them as part of the revisionist opposition.

There was also an element of ordinary anti-Semitism and chauvinism. Kliszko lambasted journalists who "cannot write in Polish," and Ignacy Loga-Sowiński accused the Jews of national nihilism—charges that echoed old anti-Semitic slogans.[4] Unlike the activists of the old school, Gomułka and his collaborators were not internationalists. In fact, their belief system combined the nationalist credo with the communist formula. Thus, Piasecki was quite correct when he described Gomułka's camp as "patriotic-socialist." In all likelihood, Gomułka, Kliszko, and the others were sincere in their attempts to redefine the party as genuinely "Polish" and as the culmination of historical processes that promoted the idea of the nation-state. They were not alone, however, in their endorsement of ethnonationalism. Wyszyński's church was doing it, too. The communists did not have the option of using ethnoconfessional identity to their advantage, but they could try to outbid the Church in the use of nationalist discourse. Distancing themselves from the Jews and offering to chase the Żydokomuna bogeyman from secular, socialist, state-sponsored nationalism promised to do the trick.

Gomułka's party was no monolith, however. Moczar's Partisans represented an even more aggressive brand of red nationalism.[5] The Partisans were high-ranking security and military officers who during the war had served in the People's Army (Armia Ludowa), a major communist resistance group. After the communist takeover, they had languished in second-rate positions in the military and the police. After Gomułka's return to power, their status improved, but it still did not rise to their expectations. By the 1960s, they were joined by power-hungry middle-aged party apparatchiks whose careers had stagnated under the geriatric regime of Gomułka. The Partisans were not a clear-cut political group, but a loose coalition under the patronage of the charismatic Moczar. To some extent, they were a product of mass media, a mental construct that, according to Marcin Zaremba, "simplified the existing relationships and configurations within the elite of power."[6]

Moczar started building his camp shortly after 1956, when he became deputy minister of internal affairs. As the head of the Union of Fighters for Freedom and Democracy (ZBOWiD), he also worked to bring together former resistance fighters from both the People's Army and the Home Army. By the late 1960s, Moczar's union claimed almost three hundred thousand members, including sixty thousand Home Army veterans.[7] The mass influx of noncommunist veterans of the resistance reflected both the partial rehabilitation of the AK after 1956 and the ostensible unity of the nation in its struggle against the Nazi occupiers—a unity constantly invoked by Gomułka's regime.[8] Moczar's own contribution to the myth of unified resistance was the publication of his war memoirs, *Barwy walki* (known in the English film version as *Scenes of Battle*), in 1961. Praised by the party press and lavished with numerous state prizes, the book glorified the communist partisans but also acknowledged military cooperation with the AK on the battlefield, projecting an image of patriotic "boys from the forest."[9]

The Partisans never produced a coherent political program or ideology. Their worldview consisted of fanatical nationalism, anti-Semitism, authoritarianism, a military ethos, and overt opposition to liberalism of all kinds. They had no tolerance for those who questioned the dominant interpretation of national history based on heroism and martyrdom. The mythology of resistance was particularly popular in Moczar's circle. Bound by loyalty to their leader, who adopted the image of a "good chap and partisan," and linked by a strong sense of military camaraderie rather than any organizational structure, the Partisans somewhat resembled Piłsudski's Colonels.[10] They portrayed themselves in sharp contrast to the "Muscovites" and Jews who were bent on subverting the institutions of the Polish national state.[11] Although they combined an emphasis on domesticity—their "Polishness" —with a plebeian appeal, the Partisans were also capable of courting intellectuals and artists, including several popular writers and filmmakers.[12]

The position of the Partisans improved dramatically after Moczar was promoted to minister of internal affairs in 1964. By 1965, several men in his circle had taken important posts in the military and the police. Moczar himself enjoyed the trust of Gomułka, who is said to have declared of Moczar and his collaborators, "Those comrades and I are one and the same."[13] In a manner similar to the spread of Titoist partisan mythology in Yugoslavia, the promotion of the Partisans and their ethos reinterpreted history, magnifying the role of the "home communists" in the liberation of Poland against that of the Soviet-controlled Polish army.[14] There is little to suggest that Moczar intended to seize Gomułka's post. Rather, he tried to influence the Polish leader and the regime by placing himself and his men in high government posts.

Piasecki had been aware of Moczar's growing prominence since the late 1950s. Over the course of the investigation into his son's death, Piasecki frequently had encountered Moczar and Antoni Alster, then deputy ministers and political rivals. Moczar, a Pole and a home communist, and Alster, a Jew and leading member of the Puławska faction, symbolized the two party groups that Gomułka played one against another in the aftermath of the Polish October.[15] In Piasecki's view, both men represented mafialike factions fighting for control over the security apparatus.[16] By 1962, he believed that Moczar was at the forefront of the struggle against the revisionists. He very much hoped for the victory of Partisans, whom he referred to as "patriots."

Yet he also knew that the key figure in the resolution of the conflict was Gomułka. Here, Piasecki showed considerable prescience, believing that the first secretary eventually would side with Moczar.[17]

As for anti-Semitism, Piasecki instinctively detected in Gomułka's struggle against Marxist revisionists an offensive against Jewish communists. When Alfred Łaszowski warned him in January 1962 that numerous people interpreted PAX's opposition to revisionism as ordinary anti-Semitism, Piasecki did not show any sign of discomfort. "When people say 'revisionists' they mean 'Jews,'" Łaszowski pointed out. "PAX does not speak like that," Piasecki replied cheerfully, "but the whole party does. . . . Don't you know that they [the party] accuse us of not being anti-Semitic enough?"[18] Łaszowski thought Piasecki should stay away from any anti-Semitic activities because of his past. "You know that there is a group in the party that is fed up with the Jews, a group that is trying to recruit you, saying: 'You will crystallize these ideas into a plan; you will lead the future revolution.'" But Piasecki ignored Łaszowski's pleas.[19]

For Piasecki, Gomułka's Poland was a socialist state, but it was also the "Polish state," integrated on the basis of an ethnically homogenous community. Did Piasecki believe a Jew could become a Pole? In all probability, no. He doubted the possibility of assimilation, even within the communist movement. When referring to people like Alster and Roman Zambrowski, he used the term "Jewish comrades" (*towarzysze żydowscy*). Of course, he never would have called Gomułka, Kliszko, or Moczar "Polish comrades." They were communists, but above all they were Poles, and this fact went without saying. "During the twenty years that have passed since the end of the war, the Poles have made socialism their own 'home' system," Piasecki proclaimed in 1967.[20] But to conclude this process, the patriotic-socialist forces had to eliminate Jewish Stalinists-turned-revisionists who had gained a foothold among the intelligentsia and now monopolized intellectual discourse in Poland.[21]

The plebeian roots and appeal of Moczar's faction stood in contrast to Piasecki's elitist background, gentility, and ideological obsessions. Yet a shared cultural discourse facilitated a potential alliance between them, as both men rejected artistic revisionism in the treatment of Polish history and national heritage. Jerzy Wójcik of PAX praised Moczar's war memoirs as a protest against those "who would like to negate and mock the sense of the nation's struggle for freedom."[22] This was a clear reference to the Polish School, a generation of filmmakers who raised Polish cinema to international prominence but also questioned the Polish patriotic canon and its glorification of romantic heroism and martyrdom.

Piasecki believed in Moczar's success. "My man advances" (*Mój dochodzi*), he was said to have commented on one occasion.[23] But this does not mean that the two men acted together or formed a close bond. It is not that Piasecki did not try. The ZBOWiD was one of several associations that the leader of PAX hoped to infiltrate.[24] He repeatedly sent emissaries to make contact with Moczar's entourage and to meet the general at official rallies.[25] The results of these efforts did not match Piasecki's expectations. In the end, it did not matter whether Moczar and Piasecki consulted each other. Piasecki's ideas and rhetoric harmonized well enough with Moczar's authoritarianism and primitive nationalism to link them.

Given his ideological pretensions, however, the leader of PAX stood closer to Gomułka's chief ideologues, such as Kliszko and Andrzej Werblan, than to ambitious generals. According to Mieczysław Rakowski, chief editor of the weekly *Polityka*, Piasecki was held in high esteem, particularly by Kliszko. "ZK [Zenon Kliszko] likes to listen to Piasecki, and, as I have been told, he is fascinated by Piasecki and the power of his arguments."[26] Number two in the party, Kliszko was one of the leading advocates of nationalist-communist fusion. As for Piasecki, he had propagated the alliance of patriotic-socialist forces since the end of the war. By 1965–66, Kliszko and Piasecki were smoothing the way for the advance of the nationalist tide.

In this respect, their reactions to the publication of Adam Schaff's book *Marxism and the Human Being* (Marksizm i jednostka ludzka) had much in common. Schaff, a leading party ideologue and member of the Central Committee, published his study in 1965. At the heart of the book stood the thesis that in its daily practice, socialism had moved away from the theory of internationalism to nationalism. According to Schaff, one of the consequences of this trend was a lack of deterrence to anti-Semitism, which he identified as a popular form of racism in Eastern Europe. He recommended a return to an internationalist ethos as a way of containing manifestations of xenophobia.[27]

Schaff's book met with a cool, even hostile reception from Gomułka's circle. Kliszko and Werblan were at the forefront of these attacks. Both of them lambasted Schaff during a meeting at the editorial office of the party periodical *Nowe drogi* (New roads) in October 1965. While trivializing the rise in anti-Semitism as a marginal phenomenon, Werblan complained that Schaff had gone overboard in emphasizing the "threat of nationalism looming over communism." Kliszko went even further, contrasting the nationalism of oppressed nations to the nationalism of their oppressors. The former constituted "progressive nationalism, patriotism stemming from passionate love for a nation." Kliszko added that the successful struggle against colonialism was a precondition for the victory of Marxist internationalism. Until then, the "nationalism of the oppressed" ought not be equated with "traditional nationalism of the old European states."[28]

Kliszko's diatribes obviously fit with the communists' affirmation of anticolonialism. But his response had a deeper meaning: Kliszko broke a taboo against the use of nationalism in official Marxist discourse. As Marcin Zaremba notes, "Only eight years earlier, Gomułka had stated that socialism stood in opposition to nationalism of all kinds." But now Kliszko "signaled that nationalism could be positive."[29]

The message was not lost on Piasecki. In 1966, exactly one year after the debate in *Nowe drogi*, he presented his own critique of Schaff's book at the PAX leadership meeting. According to Piasecki, Schaff ignored the evolution of Marxism and the existence of other ideological currents on the Left, such as PAX's pluralism of worldviews. The concept of a "classless, nation-free individual" demonstrated the heavy influence of "bourgeois existentialism." It was Schaff's emphasis on the estrangement of internationalism and nationalism that most fueled Piasecki's criticism, however. For Piasecki, socialism restored to the proletarians a sense of participation in the national community that had long been denied to them by the privileged classes. "Hence," he continued, "the alliance of socialism and patriotism—which we observe in our country—does not stand in any opposition to the founders of Marxism."[30]

Considering anti-Semitism, Piasecki argued that prewar Polish anti-Semitism had economic roots. The war and subsequent sociopolitical transformation had terminated this specific cause of Polish-Jewish tension along with social inequality. (Characteristically, Piasecki did not mention the destruction of Polish Jewry.) But anti-Jewish resentment continued due to a disproportionate share of Jews in government and to nepotism practiced by people of Jewish ancestry. Resentment of these processes was incorrectly labeled anti-Semitic. "In fact," Piasecki insisted, "the opposition to such practices stemmed from the patriotic understanding of Polish interests and was a duty of all citizens." Piasecki accused Schaff of moving in the sphere of the abstract while ignoring the actual conditions in Poland. It could not have been otherwise, because "Professor Adam Schaff cited in his book only foreign scholars of Marxism, always of Jewish origin," as well as the "theoreticians of Zionism and cosmopolitanism."[31]

Piasecki's indictment of Schaff was notable both for its content and its context. The leader of a nominally Catholic association dared to lecture a senior Marxist on the basics of communist doctrine. True, the book had already been discredited by Kliszko and Werblan. It is clear, however, that for Piasecki, Schaff was a paragon of Jewish revisionists in the party leadership. The case provided a good and, in Piasecki's view, valid excuse to attack the alleged overrepresentation of Jews in the Polish government. Kliszko and Gomułka might have shared the same opinion, but they did not voice it in public. Nor did they reprimand Piasecki for doing so, however. He sensed the political climate at Gomułka's court. In December 1966, he uttered a line that little more than a year later would encapsulate the message of state propaganda. "Zionism," Piasecki noted, "is a political doctrine interwoven with the actions of the state of Israel [and] the Federal Republic of Germany; it opposes the interests of the Polish state and the nation."[32]

Piasecki systematized his views on the patriotic-socialist (read: nationalist-communist) synthesis in a manuscript distributed to PAX training and recruiting teams in February 1967 under the title "For the Creative Continuation of People's Poland." It was a manifesto supplemented by some analysis of political trends in Poland. Piasecki anticipated social-political turmoil leading to the confrontation between the party and the enemies of the patriotic-socialist alliance. By alarming the public about the alleged rise of anti-Semitism in Poland, the opposition aimed to discredit the convergence of patriotism and socialism from the position of a cosmopolitan worldview. They claimed that "attaching patriotism to socialism leads to Polish nationalism, which fights and discriminates against citizens of Jewish origin."[33]

His use of the term "cosmopolitan" here suggested people who alienated themselves from the nation, who did not share community values, and who sold out or looked to foreign cultures. In Piasecki's view, the Jews and Westernized intellectuals fit this category perfectly. He no longer considered "revisionist" an appropriate idiom: "We should not use this term for two reasons: first, he who declares his struggle against revisionists can be suspected of dogmatism; secondly, there are no revisionists in Poland in the classic meaning of this term." Those who contested the socialist system and supported a political pluralism of the bourgeois kind were mere "social democrats." In the end, he coined a new term, "opposition to the system" (*opozycja ustrojowa*).[34] Such a construct provided Piasecki with an opportunity to lump together various groups and circles: revisionists, Catholics from Znak, advocates of Polish-German reconciliation, and unpatriotic cosmopolitans. Not only did they all wish to destabilize the country, but by being pro-Jewish, pro-German, and pro-Western, they were anti-Polish. At this point, Piasecki could not have known he was setting up the rhetorical standards for the future witch hunt.

How did Piasecki envision the "creative continuation," or rather, the modification of government in Poland? He pushed for an ideological offensive propagating the union of patriotism and socialism, the reconstruction of the party regime through a greater involvement of the "authentic allies of the party"—a clear reference to PAX—and the enrichment of state doctrine by other worldviews. More radical were his calls for genuinely free elections and separation of the government from the party, which ought not double the functions of the government. Piasecki described his program as "the critical continuation of the system and power" (*krytyczna kontynuacja ustroju i władzy*).[35]

Critical perhaps, but hardly a continuation, Piasecki's alternative constituted a communist-nationalist hybrid, an authoritarian model based on the coalition of the communists and their patriotic allies. Given Gomułka's earlier opposition a pluralism of worldviews, it is not clear how Piasecki envisioned the implementation of his program. But there is no doubt that in May 1967 he anticipated a political earthquake, which would increase authoritarianism and bring about a government capable of containing the coalition of "the Zionist international and capitalism," fighting social apathy, and reclaiming young people from the influence of Western decadence.[36]

In all probability, Piasecki's calls for discipline and strong rule did not make any particular impression at the time. But within a few weeks, these proposals had acquired a new meaning. What followed was a state-sponsored anti-Semitic pogrom that shook the foundations of the communist system in Poland.

Pogrom, 1967–68

The Six-Day War between Israel and the Arab states of Egypt, Jordan, and Syria started on June 5, 1967. By June 11, the Israeli forces had won a stunning victory. Although the war took place in the Middle East, it had serious repercussions for Poland and the rest of the Soviet bloc: the Arab armies had been trained and equipped by the Soviets. On June 9, during a meeting of the Warsaw Pact in Moscow, leaders of the member states, with the exception of Romania, officially condemned Israel. The next day, the Soviet Union and Czechoslovakia broke off diplomatic relations with Israel. Poland and Hungary followed suit on June 12.[37]

The Polish public generally sympathized with the Israelis, not so much because of solidarity with the Jews but because the Arabs were supported by Moscow. "The prevailing mood in our society is satisfaction that 'our' Jews are beating 'Russian' Arabs," Rakowski noted in his diaries.[38] On June 7, Rakowski attended a meeting at a club of students and young intelligentsia affiliated with the Warsaw branch of the Jewish Social-Cultural Association. He noted "the fighting spirit" among participants, who "accused the Soviet Union of supporting fascist [Gamal Abdel] Nasser" and criticized Polish leaders. "I am afraid," Rakowski commented, "that this meeting will have sad consequences."[39]

After Gomułka's return from Moscow, Moczar rushed to inform the first secretary about these enthusiastic reactions to the Israeli victory. Gomułka was furious. During his meeting with regional party bosses and Central Committee officials on June 12, he compared the Israeli soldiers to SS men. But at the heart of his speech was an evaluation of the situation in Poland. "We will not ignore such events as drunken orgies that took place in some institutions to celebrate the victory of Israel," he thundered.[40] On June 19, in his address to the congress of trade unions, Gomułka condemned "Zionist circles among Polish citizens" and compared them to a fifth column.[41] He stated that although the Polish state treated all citizens equally regardless of their nationality, it would not tolerate those who supported enemies of peace and agents of imperialism. "Let those people to whom I address my words [...] draw appropriate conclusions," he warned. "It is our stance that each Polish citizen should have only one fatherland—People's Poland."[42]

Gomułka's two-hour-long speech was broadcast by radio and TV and published by the press. It divided the Polish public. The liberal intelligentsia reacted to Gomułka's tirades with disbelief and shock.[43] Others did not hide their enthusiasm. Numerous party activists, security officials, and ordinary anti-Semites were jubilant. The press reported on many "spontaneous" rallies taking place across the whole country. More significant events were taking place behind the doors of government offices, however. On June 28, 1967, the leadership of the Ministry of Internal Affairs gathered to analyze the situation in the country in connection with the conflict in the Middle East. The real purpose of the meeting was the preparation of anti-Semitic purges. The security police produced a list of 382 journalists, writers, state officials, and economic managers suspected of supporting Israel. In addition, Moczar instructed his henchmen to collect information on people of Jewish origin employed in government, scientific institutions, and mass media. "We will use it," he said. "If not today, then tomorrow."[44]

Moczar enjoyed the full support of Gomułka—though in all probability, the Polish leader did not believe in the existence of the Zionist conspiracy. But if Gomułka did not credit Moczar's theories about the Jewish plot, why then did he nevertheless approve Moczar's actions and the anti-Israeli propaganda campaign? Although the anti-Zionist campaign followed the Soviet anti-Israeli line, it is incorrect to see the purge as the result only of Moscow's pressure.[45] It was an indigenous affair. The comments made by Kazimierz Witaszewski, the head of the administration department of the Central Committee, during the infamous meeting in the Ministry of Internal Affairs in June 1967 are of particular relevance: "After twenty-three years of people's power, it is time to solve this delicate problem," he said, referring to the Jews in the party. "[At last] our party will cleanse itself of an undesirable element."[46]

The Polish leader might have vowed to free the party from the legacy of the Żydokomuna myth. Gomułka's ideological watchdog, Andrzej Werblan, argued that the Jewish-dominated Communist Party of Poland had ignored the nationalist aspirations of the Poles. Thus, the Jewish communists were antipatriotic and quintessentially anti-Polish.[47] By making his party ethnically Polish and tapping into latent chauvinism, Gomułka could also mobilize the public. If the Church managed to rally hundreds of thousands to its ethnoconfessional vision of national identity during the millennium campaign, perhaps the party-state could try to do the same through anti-Semitism, which still held wide appeal in Poland. Also important were Gomułka's hatred of those activists of Jewish origins, who like Zambrowski had "stabbed him in back" in 1948, and his distrust of the liberal intelligentsia. The model enemy figure was a revisionist intellectual, more often than not of Jewish background.

The initial purge of Jews was carried out selectively, affecting mostly the army and local party organizations.[48] Although limited, it created an atmosphere of uncertainty and confusion. The removal of Jews from public institutions, a state of ferment among liberal intellectuals and students, an aggressive mood in the party and security apparatus, and the impact of democratization in Czechoslovakia: all these factors produced a situation in which a little spark could set off a major political crisis. As often happens in history, the final eruption was caused by a seemingly marginal event.

On November 27, 1967, the National Theater in Warsaw staged a production of *The Forefathers* (*Dziady*) by the great nineteenth-century Polish romantic poet Adam Mickiewicz. The play contained strong anti-Russian scenes, which drew enthusiastic applause among some members of the audience. Soon, Politburo members accused the producers of the play of stirring up anti-Soviet feelings and decided to close down the production. The last performance was to take place on January 30, 1968.[49] That same evening, a group of three hundred university students marched to the site of Mickiewicz's monument to protest the ban on performances. They were assaulted and dispersed by police units. Several demonstrators were detained. But protests continued. On February 29, 1968, the Warsaw branch of the Polish Writers' Union expressed solidarity with the students, condemned censorship and anti-Semitism, hailed Dubček's reforms in Czechoslovakia, and demanded the democratization of cultural policy.[50]

The organizers of the demonstration on January 30, later to be called "commandos" (*komandosi*) by the government, were not political beginners.[51] Born in the 1940s, they were mostly students and young instructors from Warsaw University who had been strongly influenced by revisionist intellectuals. Some of them were the children of prominent communists. Some came from assimilated Jewish families. They were leftist, and hostile toward nationalism. The commandos never formed any organization with a coherent political program. Instead, they operated through clusters of friends and acquaintances. Their leaders included Adam Michnik, Jan Lityński, Józef Dajczgewand, and Henryk Szlajfer.[52]

For the writers who joined in the student protests, the ban on *The Forefathers* was the last straw. After establishing initial expectations of greater artistic freedom, Gomułka had brought back censorship, arbitrariness in cultural policy, and harassment of those who did not want to play by the rules. The regime did not hesitate to sentence people for possessing forbidden books, publishing in exile periodicals, or writing satirical pamphlets. Gestures such as the 1964 open letter to the government against censorship, commonly known as the "Letter of Thirty-four," had little impact. The outbreak of the anti-Semitic campaign only deepened the rift between Gomułka and the intellectuals. At the meeting of the writers' union in Warsaw on February 29, Stefan Kisielewski denounced Gomułka's cultural policy as the dictatorship of ignoramuses (*dyktatura ciemniaków*).[53]

After the expulsion of Michnik and Szlajfer from the university, the commandos called for a demonstration in defense of their leaders. The rally took place at the university on March 8. Instantly, the demonstrators came under brutal attack from police and party thugs armed with clubs. Despite beatings and arrests, the demonstrations continued, spreading to other academic centers across Poland. In late March, the government broke the back of the student protests by detaining thousands and arresting hundreds. The universities expelled fifteen hundred students, some of whom subsequently were conscripted. The authorities also fired a number of university professors.[54]

Only a few public figures found sufficient courage to defend the persecuted students. The emergence of the Partisans and the assault on revisionists had divided Znak activists. While Stomma sympathized with the revisionist intellectuals, Janusz Zabłocki seemed to prefer some kind of agreement with Moczar's patriots.[55] But faced with the police brutality, members of the Znak parliamentary club temporary suspended their feuds and appealed to the government to stop repression of students and discuss the crisis in the Sejm. When parliament met on April 10, Prime Minister Cyrankiewicz refuted Znak's charges. Other speakers defamed the Catholic MPs by calling them reactionaries and Zionist allies. Zawieyski resigned from the Council of State.[56]

The episcopate defended the demonstrators and pleaded for restraint by the police. Neither the primate nor the other bishops condemned anti-Semitic propaganda, however. Apparently, Wyszyński had no sympathy for Marxist revisionists and purged Jews. In fact, he probably viewed the campaign as an inner struggle of the party. While meeting Znak MPs in May, he advised them to "act in the spirit of good nationalism, not chauvinism, but healthy nationalism that embodied love of the nation."[57]

The work of Moczar's henchmen, who had been collecting evidence against the Jews, did not go to waste. The fact that many commandos were the children of state officials of Jewish ancestry enabled the authorities to present student protests as a Zionist plot. But the regime's propagandists lacked appropriate chauvinistic "training." Their language was dull; their rhetoric did not appeal to the masses. In addition, the party had to remain free from the odor of anti-Semitism. The chauvinistic message could be supplied, however, by old noncommunist nationalists. There was no shortage of such people in Poland, but only a few of them occupied prominent positions. Piasecki, the only heir to Endecja in communist Poland, was the best candidate for this task.

The Drum Major: Piasecki in 1968

During the first months of the anti-Zionist campaign, Piasecki kept a low profile. In all probability, he did not intend to break the rules set by Gomułka, who had criticized the leader of PAX for mingling in party affairs in the past. All the same, Piasecki thought that the anti-Zionist campaign was a step in the right direction.[58]

After the outbreak of student demonstrations in March, Piasecki came in from the cold. He probably benefited from his contact with Moczar's circle, because only hours after the protests on March 8, he knew the names of the leading commandos. Piasecki called on the chief editor of *Słowo powszechne,* Witold Jankowski, ordered him to write an article about the organizers of the demonstration, and instructed him as to the content that he wished to see in the piece. Przetakiewicz provided some last-minute editing. The final result undoubtedly reflected Piasecki's opinion about the March events.[59]

The unsigned article, "To the Students of Warsaw University" (Do studentów Uniwersytetu Warszawskiego), was published on March 11, 1968. It presented the student protests in Warsaw as part of an Israeli–West German plot to overthrow the Polish government. The majority of the students were innocent. It was the Zionists under "political orders from the Federal

Republic" who sought to destabilize the situation in Poland by infiltrating and inciting intellectuals and students against the people's power. The notion of a Israeli-German conspiracy ran through about a quarter of the article. While the West German revanchists were trying to shift responsibility for the murder of six million Jews onto the Poles, the Zionists could not forgive Gomułka for condemning the Israeli aggression against the Arab states.[60]

Having identified the instigators of the unrest, the article established the identity of their Polish agents. They were Jewish Stalinists who had tried to derail the patriotic-socialist course after 1956 and later exchanged socialism for Zionist nationalism. Finally, there were the organizers of the student protests, the children of Jewish Stalinists, whose names and family connections the article listed. "It was these people," it read, "who by exploiting our youth's devotion to national culture and democratic tradition tried to cut the link between society and the people's power."[61]

The decision to publish names of the commandos and their relatives was particularly perfidious, since it exposed them to attacks by party officials and individual anti-Semites. But the real purpose of the move was to discredit Jewish communists. Whether already ousted or still politically active, they were doomed. The portrayal of student protesters and their intellectual allies as Jews and Israeli-German agents isolated them from other segments of society.

Jankowski's article was a blueprint for the escalation of the anti-Semitic campaign. The classic opposition of "them" versus "us," the Jews versus the Poles, legitimized communist rule as purely Polish. It was a return to the old myth of Jewish conspiracy propagated by nationalists before the war. That the Jews corrupted the Polish intelligentsia was a classic argument of prewar anti-Semitism. Another element typical of Endek discourse was the presentation of the Jews and the Germans as the mortal enemies of the Polish nation. Before the war, nationalist propaganda had described them as working separately to the detriment of the Poles; in March 1968, the two nations were depicted as having closed ranks. This was the legacy of Stalinist propaganda, which pieced together all enemies. Indeed, the article in *Słowo powszechne* combined the old nationalist constructs with the rhetoric of communist propagandists.

Usually, publication of a text of this kind required the approval of the press department of the Central Committee. It is inconceivable, however, that the head of the department, Artur Starewicz, a party bigwig of Jewish ancestry who opposed the anti-Semitic campaign, would have allowed the release of the article. In fact, Starewicz later told Gomułka he had never seen the text before its publication. Instead, he pointed to one of his deputies, Stefan Olszowski, a rising star in the hardliners' circles.[62] But Olszowski's could not have acted alone. The decision to publish "To the Students of Warsaw University" must have been made by someone in the highest leadership of the party. Kliszko is the most probable candidate.[63]

Twenty-four hours after the publication of the piece, Prime Minister Cyrankiewicz dismissed three deputy ministers whose children's names had appeared in the article: Jan Grudziński, Jan Górecki, and Fryderyk Topolski. A few days later, the Sejm voted Roman Zambrowski out of his post as deputy chairman of the Main Control Office (Najwyższa Izba Kontroli). He was also expelled from the party. The elimination of Zambrowski, whom many perceived as the leader of the revisionists, marked the culmination of the purges. In that sense, March 1968 led to a major shift in the party elite, toppling the remnants of the KPP (Communist Party of Poland) generation.

The article in *Słowo powszechne* extended the anti-Semitic campaign beyond the initial attacks against Zionists. Characteristically, the party press —with the exception of *Trybuna ludu*—did not play a dominant role in this chauvinistic spectacle. At the forefront of the campaign were PAX's *Słowo powszechne*, the Democratic Party's *Kurier polski*, the army's *Żołnierz wolności*, and *Głos pracy*, the press organ of the trade unions. Various nationalist veterans took the lead in producing anti-Jewish articles.[64] Rallies and public lectures accompanied attacks in the media. Some of these gatherings produced genuine enthusiasm among their participants, especially when speakers blamed the Jews for Stalinism, repression of the AK, and economic shortages.

Naturally, none of this could have happened without Gomułka's consent. There is not a shred of evidence suggesting that March was a political provocation paving the way for a takeover by Moczar.[65] To quote historian Dariusz Stola, Gomułka and his collaborators "utilized the crisis to pursue their goals." They did not "manage the crisis" but "ruled through the crisis."[66] It was Gomułka who legitimized the purge of Jews. While addressing a crowd of party activists in Warsaw on March 19, he divided the Polish Jews into three categories: the Jewish nationalists, the cosmopolitans devoid of national identity, and the assimilated Jews for whom Poland was the only fatherland. The nationalists had to leave Poland. Members of the second group would be purged from all public institutions. Those who were Polish patriots had nothing to fear.[67] Gomułka tried to mitigate the anti-Semitic hysteria with his defense of assimilated Jews, but this hardly mitigates his responsibility.[68]

Among the few members of the party establishment who contested the purges was the chairman the Council of State, Edward Ochab. He resigned his post days after Gomułka's speech. "As a Pole and a communist," Ochab wrote in his final note, "it is with the greatest outrage that I protest against the anti-Semitic campaign organized . . . by various dark forces: yesterday's ONR-men and their [current] protectors."[69] It is clear that Ochab was referring to Piasecki and Moczar. He refused to accept the idea that the party leaders could have orchestrated the pogrom—as if Piasecki had enough power to launch a mass campaign on his own! Nevertheless, the role played by Piasecki's newspapers, his well-known aversion to the Jews, and his never-ending mantra about the patriotic-socialist coalition made him one of the symbols of March 1968. Piasecki did nothing to alter this image. On the contrary, he and his PAX cronies threw themselves into the chauvinistic carnival with revolutionary fervor.

On April 6, 1968, while addressing PAX activists in Bydgoszcz, Przetakiewicz delivered one of the most hateful speeches of the campaign. Przetakiewicz's remarks appeared to be almost verbatim quotes from pre-war fascist leaflets and rallies. The Zionists, he accused, had prepared their plot under the guidance of some "supreme rabbi" at their congress in New York. Their Polish allies included Znak, whose "program bridged Zionism with political clericalism"; Archbishop Bolesław Kominek, the author of the Polish bishops' letter to the German episcopate in 1965; and the "self-styled jester" Kisielewski, the leading advocate of cooperation with West Germany. Nor did he spare Cardinal Wyszyński, who in his opinion wished for the disintegration of the communist bloc.[70]

According to Przetakiewicz, the Zionist plot was well-planned, involving the departure of Gomułka from power, aid from the Federal Republic of Germany, and ultimately the ascent of "the Jew-liberals" to power. Fortunately, PAX stood like a bunker in the way of the scheme's success. After numerous grotesque remarks on the topic of the Zionists and recollections of his own days as a street fighter aimed at rehabilitating the National Radicals' reputation, Przetakiewicz even dared to criticize Gomułka. "Indeed," he said in reference to Gomułka's televised address, "he did not look good on TV and felt uncomfortable." The content of Gomułka's speech was typical of the spirit of "the little stabilization," the plague of the 1960s that had demobilized the population. Przetakiewicz professed his loyalty to the first secretary, but without much enthusiasm. He repeatedly praised Edward Gierek, the party boss in Silesia, who "prevented attempts to install a Polish Dubček." Anyone who watched Gomułka's March speech could not ignore the fact that the crowd's chants were "Gomułka! Gierek!"[71]

Rakowski was completely flabbergasted. "Gomułka knows [of Przetakiewicz's speech,] and in spite of that he does not hit PAX," he observed. "It means that the current situation is very bad indeed."[72] But was not PAX following the example that Gomułka had set in his crucial addresses in 1967 and 1968, albeit a bit excessively? It appears that Rakowski and other party reformers who remained staunch supporters of Gomułka refused to believe that the first secretary was behind the anti-Jewish and anti-intellectual witch hunt. Instead, they blamed others, including Piasecki, who admittedly did his best to uphold such judgments.

Przetakiewicz's speech in Bydgoszcz was emotional, rambling, and primitive. Piasecki unveiled his views in a much more coherent fashion during the parliamentary debate on Znak's petition to Cyrankiewicz in April 1968. To begin with, he harshly criticized Znak, though admittedly less severely than did the communist MPs. "I do not address the private intentions that guide Znak activists, but I must say that we are in conflict," stated Piasecki. He would do everything to "immunize Polish society against the reactionary views" of Znak MPs.[73] But lambasting Znak was not the most important aspect of Piasecki's speech. He reminded his audience that after 1956–57, the "slogans of progress and democracy had been captured by antipatriotic forces," Zionists and cosmopolitans who had infiltrated the artistic intelligentsia, contaminating it with the ideas of bourgeois democracy. "If these Zionists who currently reside in Poland were ordinary citizens lacking any social influence characteristic of those who have power," Piasecki observed, "then, knowing our national and historical tradition of tolerance, there would be no problem at all." Because of their presence in the state apparatus, however, the Zionists facilitated anti-Polish activism in the West.[74]

Yet equally important was the introduction of changes to the ruling system in Poland. "It seems necessary," he said, "that social activism and civil initiatives must find better venues to express themselves." In its present state, the Front of National Unity was an ossified institution. Therefore, Piasecki demanded the implementation of "particular decisions on the state level" to facilitate the development of democracy, which should operate on the basis of a plurality of worldviews.[75] One can easily guess what sort of "particular decisions" he required: the elevation of PAX to the status of a fully fledged political party. The PAX propaganda machine spread a fantastic interpretation of Piasecki's speech. *Słowo powszechne* described his parliamentary address as "the program of patriotic and socialist forces." The weekly *Kierunki* went even further, presenting Piasecki's theses as "the program of the nation."[76]

When Piasecki addressed senior PAX activists in Warsaw, his tone was even more biting: "Today we are hearing here and there, from the party and from nonparty groups alike, the following question addressed for the rulers: did you not know that the Zionists co-ruled Poland?" According to Piasecki, those who now tried to mitigate public outrage still adhered to the cowardly and half-hearted spirit of "the little stabilization."[77]

Piasecki offered faint praise of Gomułka: "We must talk about his achievements on *other* fronts: skilled foreign policy, economic development, and victory over Stalinism and its distortions." It was Gomułka who had alerted the public to the danger of Zionism at the congress of trade unions. Yet according to Piasecki, the popular slogan "We Are with Comrade Wiesław" was too vague. Instead, he proposed a new chant: "With Comrade Wiesław against the Little Stabilization."[78] The clear meaning of Piasecki's new slogan was that Gomułka could redeem himself only by eliminating the evils that he had helped foster. But how should the reform of the system progress? Piasecki perceived the purge of Jewish communists as a precondition for further changes. Yet he did not seem to like those upstarts who had jumped into the shoes of the deposed Jews; he called them "mediocrities and opportunists." He hoped that the purge of the ruling elite would lead to the advancement of "competent and disciplined people, unhesitant in expressing their opinions," unconditionally devoted to the alliance of patriotism and socialism, and capable of elaborating a new ideological platform. PAX could provide people who fit all these criteria.[79]

Poland's political system needed to undergo major changes. Though adequate in the immediate postwar period, the ruling coalition consisting of the dominant communists and two satellite parties, the Peasants and the Democrats, had become anachronistic. The solution, again, was for PAX to become a political party. Piasecki advised his impatient underlings to wait for the results of the party congress in November.[80]

It was Piasecki's boldest public speech in many years. Especially striking was his patronizing tone toward party leaders, including Gomułka. It seems that Piasecki was counting on major changes within the party leadership. In all probability, he did not believe that Moczar's faction would succeed. The fact that his faithful lieutenant Przetakiewicz so openly praised Gierek—and it should be noted that Przetakiewicz usually echoed Piasecki's opinions—suggests the leader of PAX understood that it was not Moczar, but the party boss of Silesia, who would be a new key player, perhaps even Gomułka's successor.[81]

Indeed, in July 1968, Gomułka transferred Moczar from the Ministry of Internal Affairs to the party center. As a deputy member of the Politburo, the ambitious general became just one of many figures on the Central Committee.[82] First feared, then outmaneuvered, Moczar accepted his demise. "How could Wiesław suspect that I wanted to step into his place?" he complained to friends.[83] This elimination of old enemies and the pacification of the Partisans secured Gomułka's position. By the end of June, he was instructing propagandists to halt the anti-Semitic campaign.[84] It took months to silence the anti-Semitic frenzy in the mass media and the party apparatus, but the political crisis in Czechoslovakia and the subsequent invasion by armies of the Warsaw Pact nations, including a contingent from Poland, helped Gomułka bring the unruly elements within the party under control.

The March events in Poland paralleled the early stages of the Prague Spring in Czechoslovakia. But the two crises had relatively little in common. In Czechoslovakia, Marxist revisionism and democratization of the communist system from within had been the battle cry of reformers and—after Antonin Novotny's demotion from power in January 1968 and the adoption of an action program in April of that year—of the party leadership and government. In Poland, party revisionists had been pushed out of the center of power by the early 1960s. In 1968, they were confined to segments of the intelligentsia: rebel students and professors, and the writers' association. The Polish revisionists were vocal but politically insignificant; yet they became a convenient bogeyman for the regime's propaganda. The March explosion constituted the climax of the long processes described earlier in this chapter: Gomułka's nationalist drive to legitimize and Polonize the party, and the Partisans' communist-fascist blend of authoritarianism. In

Prague, there was a movement for democratic change, whereas in Warsaw, it was an offensive by hardliners.

Of course, the Poles observed the Czechs, and the Czechs observed the Poles. Dubček's example emboldened Polish students and intellectuals, but above all, it pinpointed their frustration with the regime's policies. While meeting with Dubček in February 1968, Gomułka cautioned him and his party to remain strong and in control. "If things went wrong in [Czechoslovakia], our internal enemy forces would raise their head," he said. "Right now, we have a problem with writers and students."[85] Later, at the July meeting of the Warsaw Pact leaders in Warsaw, he was among the foremost advocates of military intervention in Czechoslovakia, describing the situation in Prague as counterrevolution. But in the summer of 1968, Gomułka's major concern was not the crushing of the opposition—this already had happened months before—but bringing into line the increasingly aggressive party and police apparatus buoyed up by the anti-Semitic campaign. The Czechoslovak government did not take any official stance on the events in Poland. Students, writers, journalists, and filmmakers did express solidarity with their Polish counterparts, however, through public protests, open letters, and critical reports, much to the annoyance of Gomułka's officials, but with little effect on the repression in Poland.[86] More notably, the later purges in Czechoslovakia, which followed the August invasion, also contained anti-Semitic elements.

If Piasecki counted on the replacement of Gomułka and a major political earthquake that would allow him to enter the government, he lost his bet. The Fifth Congress of the party sanctioned the influx of new faces. These were not Moczar's men but the generation of younger apparatchiks whose careers had begun in the communist youth organization.[87] Gomułka was still number one.

But there was no return to the situation before the pogrom. It has been estimated that between 1967 and 1969, some thirteen thousand Polish Jews left the country.[88] The exodus robbed Poland of hundreds of scientists, intellectuals, artists, and students. The anti-Semitic campaign also tarnished the image of Poland in the world. Piasecki belonged to the group of Poles who did not regret these developments. "We are an ethnically homogeneous country," he said in November 1969. "This is an achievement that our society sees and fully accepts."[89]

Communism in Poland would never be the same after 1968. To quote Marcin Zaremba, "Gomułka's decade brought the collapse of Marxism in its previous form. The authorities filled this void with aggressive nationalism."[90] Piasecki himself might have hailed the second phase of this process. The nationalist-communist alliance did not take place on his terms, however. Ironically, by instigating and contributing to the March crisis, the nationalist Piasecki contributed to the ideological demobilization of the system. The combined effects of the anti-Semitic frenzy in Poland and the brutal pacification of the Prague Spring exposed the moral bankruptcy of communism. As Leszek Kołakowski proposes, communism "ceased . . . to be an intellectual problem."[91] The elimination of the revisionist alternative also proved the system's inability to democratize itself from within.[92] The emperor had no clothes: in Poland and elsewhere in the Soviet bloc, the communist parties withdrew from the millenarian struggle for totalitarian utopia and limited their goals to maintaining their hold on power. As Andrzej Walicki has observed, the Polish party "retained its monopoly on political power but paid for it by abandoning the 'Communist offensive' and reducing to a minimum its totalitarian ambitions."[93] To that end, March 1968 concluded the transformation of communist Poland into an authoritarian-nationalist regime with weak ideological credentials.

In the future, the party regime would fall hostage to its flirtation with nationalism; its recurring use of authoritarian nationalism at moments of crisis—for instance during the martial law period—would not go unchallenged. The emancipation of the opposition from the revisionist mindset, the growing appeal of ethnoconfessional identity instilled by the Church, and the ideological demobilization of state socialism would force the Polish communists to walk a tightrope between being "patriotic" and not being able to distance themselves from foreign control.

The events of March 1968 had a negative effect on Polish society, as well. They reinforced popular anti-Semitism and conspiracy theories in public discourse, strengthened ethnonationalism, delayed the moment of coming to terms with the legacy of the chauvinistic demons in Polish history, and apparently instilled a kind of collective amnesia: the absence of the March experience from Polish collective memory is remarkable.

7 ||| The Exit of the Crusader, 1970–79

IN 1972, WHILE SPEAKING TO his collaborators, Piasecki acknowledged: "This is the best leadership of the party and the state we have ever had in the history of People's Poland. But then the question is: if such a leadership does not esteem PAX and its role, then which one will?"[1]

Three years later, Józef Tejchma observed: "Piasecki concentrates on reforming socialism in the spirit of Catholicism rather than Catholicism in the spirit of socialism."[2] These two comments, one by Piasecki and the other by Gierek's minister of culture, hold the key to understanding how Piasecki's position deteriorated in the 1970s. Piasecki viewed Gierek's government as the most PAX-friendly with which he had dealt since the end of the war. Gradually, however, he became aware that the regime did not take him seriously. As the era of ideology declined, Piasecki's doctrinaire obsessions made him a political fossil. Józef Tejchma, one of Gierek's most pragmatic officials, certainly viewed him this way. Piasecki had not changed: under the mask of a politician was the old militant, a revolutionary who still believed in the power of ideology.

As the 1970s progressed, however, Polish communists ceased to be ideology-driven zealots. Downplaying the gospel of Marxism, opening the country to the West, and focusing on the economy, the Gierek government led society away from austerity and ideological discourse and toward a consumerist paradise. Ultimately, Gierek's ambitious modernization exposed the weakness of the Polish economy, the corruption of the ruling elite, and the inadequacy of the sociopolitical system. But before this happened, the complex legacies of World War II, the communist takeover, and Stalinism—all historical factors that determined the course of Gomułka's period—had faded.

The ideological decadence of communism was not the only factor in Piasecki's transformation into a museum piece. Equally important was the birth of the democratic opposition. Although the new opposition did not pose any serious threat to the communist system in Piasecki's lifetime, its advent signaled a new intellectual and political alternative, neither nationalist-Catholic nor Marxist. Unlike Piasecki, the dissidents did not carry ideological ballast from the old era. The inception of dialogue between the Church and the noncommunist Left (which formed the backbone of the dissident movement in the 1970s) obliterated the raison d'être of PAX, the simple idea that the Church would never make peace with the Left. This paradigm had proved adequate for almost thirty years of communist rule, but in the 1970s both the Church and the party-state abandoned the tactic of confrontation. By the time Piasecki died in 1979, both he and PAX had lost all political and ideological relevance.

The Fall of Gomułka

In post-March Poland, Piasecki eagerly awaited Gomułka's replacement by Edward Gierek, the powerful political boss of Silesia. Between the summer of 1968 and December 1970, the two men met several times. These conversations convinced Piasecki that the removal of Gomułka was a matter of time, but meanwhile, he still had to cope with Gomułka's actions.[3] In April 1970, for instance, Gomułka blocked Piasecki's official visit to the Soviet Union. Piasecki also had serious doubts about the mutual recognition treaty signed between Poland and West Germany in Warsaw on December 7, 1970, which accepted Poland's western borders and established formal diplomatic relations between Warsaw and Bonn.

Piasecki's first worry was that the Germans would manipulate the treaty in the future: the agreement bound the Federal Republic, but what would be its value in the event of German reunification? Piasecki was also afraid that West Germany intended to weaken the Polish-Soviet alliance: he warned that the Germans planned to use their normalization agreement with the Soviet Union as a "return to the old pattern of Russian-Prussian relations, symbolized by [the anti-Polish] policy of Bismarck." He also feared that by opening its doors to the German economy, Poland could find itself in the position of Yugoslavia, a nominally socialist country that was completely dependent on Western credit.[4]

As a man educated in Dmowski's school, Piasecki was a Germanophobe: better with Russia against Germany than the other way around was the belief that stood at the heart of Endek doctrine under tsarist rule. In all probability, Piasecki also understood that in the absence of any revanchist threat by West Germany, the communist regime in Poland amounted to little more than a government of Soviet collaborators. The ghosts of World War II, which had benefited the regime and served as a tool for mobilization in the past, no longer held their power. But Piasecki failed to understand that it was the communists themselves who posed the gravest danger to communist rule in Poland. On December 13, 1970, only a week after the signing of the Polish-German treaty, the Polish government announced a 30 percent increase in food prices. It did so without warning, just eleven days before Christmas—and the public reaction proved that the regime had completely misjudged the mood of the country.[5]

During Gomułka's rule, the economy had been characterized by bureaucratic inertia and a lack of any coherent strategy for economic growth. Food prices had been practically frozen at low levels for a decade. In 1970, the regime understood this situation could not continue, and it acted precipitously to resolve it. Although the price increases provoked public outrage across the whole country, the most volatile protests erupted on the Baltic coast in Gdańsk, Gdynia, and Szczecin. Thousands of shipyard workers went on strike and led street demonstrations that evolved into brutal clashes with riot police. Gomułka ordered the army to crush what he considered a counterrevolution. By December 18, at least forty-four people had been killed and a thousand wounded. Although the army suppressed the workers' revolt, it could not save Gomułka.[6]

Gomułka's tactic of violent confrontation alarmed the Soviets, who communicated their concerns to Deputy Prime Minister Piotr Jaroszewicz. The reaction of the Kremlin galvanized the opposition to Gomułka within the regime. At the center of a plot to remove the party leader were two young secretaries, Józef Tejchma and Stanisław Kania. They received the support of Gierek, Piotr Jaroszewicz, Moczar, and Minister of Defense Wojciech Jaruzelski. Leonid Brezhnev himself suggested the removal of Gomułka. On December 19, the Politburo of the PZPR, convening in the absence of the ailing Gomułka, decided to dismiss him. On December 20, the Central Committee elected Gierek first secretary and purged Gomułka, Kliszko, and Spychalski from the Politburo.

That evening, the new leader of the party addressed the nation. Gierek promised to reveal the whole truth about the events in the coastal cities.[7] He never did. But he did prove capable of pacifying social unrest by means other than guns and tanks. On January 24, 1971, Gierek turned up at the gates of the Warski shipyard in Szczecin, where he spent nine hours talking to the strikers. In the end, his show of humility and frankness won over the workers. When Gierek asked them, "Will you help me?" they answered "We will." The next day, he repeated the performance in Gdańsk.[8] The government withdrew the price increases in February 1971, using Soviet loans to stabilize wages. Gierek succeeded in restoring calm to the country.

Courting Gierek

The news of Gomułka's downfall was met with jubilation in Piasecki's headquarters. Piasecki believed that with the elimination of Gomułka, his organization could finally become a fully fledged political party.[9] By the end of the year, he had drafted for Gierek a memorandum advocating the transformation of PAX into the Socially Progressive Movement, whose status would be comparable to that of the CDU in the GDR. By supporting PAX, the party also would clarify its attitude toward lay Catholics, since the existence of three rival Catholic associations—PAX, Znak, and the Christian Social Association—had a confusing effect on the populace. Finally, he argued, PAX could play an important role in the ideological mobilization of the nonparty intelligentsia and petite bourgeoisie, which so far had remained under the political tutelage of the Democratic Party.[10] This comment, as well as his complaints about the disunity of lay Catholics in Poland, revealed Piasecki's two hidden goals: to take over the Democratic Party and to liquidate the other Catholic associations.

Piasecki never submitted this set of proposals, however. Perhaps he concluded that it was too early to advance such bold demands, especially while Gierek's position was not fully secure. In the end, Piasecki filed a brief report that focused on the economy, called for better communication between the regime and the populace, and urged Gierek to bring new faces into the government.[11] Piasecki's personal papers reveal that he favored a more thorough reconstruction of the economy and the country. He advocated the modernization of the countryside and agriculture. He also envisioned cuts in military spending and the reform of education. He believed that shifting the national curriculum from humanistic training to hard sciences and engineering would produce cadres of skilled managers instead of flooding the job market with intellectuals who had the potential to turn into radicals leading a mob, as had happened in France in 1968. Keeping in mind the recent massacre on the coast, Piasecki recommended sophisticated propaganda rather than coercion.[12]

This strategy of authoritarian modernization might have appealed to the pragmatic Gierek. But for it to have any influence, Piasecki needed to talk to Gierek in person. He asked the new minister of the interior, Franciszek Szlachcic, to mediate. The men had known each other since the 1960s, when Szlachcic supervised the investigation into Bohdan Piasecki's death.[13] Gierek agreed to receive the leader of PAX and invited Piasecki to his house for a dinner on January 16, 1971.

Although the meeting proceeded in a friendly atmosphere, the two men did not reach any agreement on the future of PAX. They also held different views on the pace of reform. Gierek announced his intention to carry out the changeover of ruling cadres in a gradual manner, whereas Piasecki favored a thorough purge of government and party officials. They also disagreed about how best to reinvigorate the private sector of the economy.[14]

Piasecki did not reveal his disappointment. In fact, he still believed in Gierek's goodwill and anticipated another meeting with more far-reaching results.[15] Speaking in parliament on February 13, he urged the party leadership not to limit the scope of reforms to the sphere of the economy. "It is important to remember that *homo economicus*, a man who has only material concerns, is a fiction typical of the bourgeois economy," said Piasecki. Striking a familiar tone, he continued to advance his political vision of a pluralism of worldviews. "Unlike ideology, which reflects class struggle, a worldview is a philosophical category," Piasecki observed. "Therefore the same ideology can attract the followers of different philosophical currents." Polish Catholics, he concluded, greatly contributed to the achievements of People's Poland: "The fact that they are Christian does not make them less progressive and politically conscious [than other citizens]."[16]

Piasecki's speech did not receive an enthusiastic response, but he consoled himself with the fact that Gierek was among the few who had applauded.[17] Gierek's courtesy did not amount to much, however, and Piasecki began to grow uneasy. The situation was strangely familiar to him: after the party had managed to defuse the political crisis, it showed no interest in Piasecki's proposals.

The Gierek leadership played a double game with Piasecki. In a conversation with Rakowski in the spring of 1971, Szlachcic complained that Piasecki showed too much interest in the internal affairs of the party and that something should be done to satisfy his political appetite in order to silence him. "But how?" Rakowski asked. "Will he become a deputy prime minister as Werblan has suggested?" To which Szlachcic replied, "No. Perhaps he can be named to the Council of State."[18]

On June 22, 1971, parliament nominated Piasecki to become a member of the Council of State. The news shocked many observers, particularly those without ties to the party leadership. The church, in particular, showed signs of increased nervousness. The episcopate warned PAX to refrain from any political actions that targeted the Catholic clergy and emphasized that the Church did not need any intermediaries in its contacts with the government.[19] Stefan Kisielewski was clearly surprised, but less perplexed. "Bolesław Piasecki is in the Council of State. That's a good one!" he wrote in his diary. "It is a slap in the face for Stanisław Stomma, the Cardinal [Wyszyński], and many others." Kisielewski was genuinely amused by how the official press communiqué had tried to diminish Piasecki's fascist past. He also observed: "His [Piasecki's] anti-Semitism does not offend anymore, even though he puts God into it, but that does not seem to bother the communists. After all, God does not exist."[20] Kisielewski was right: the party leaders hardly cared about their protégé's past, ideological credentials, or innovations.

Piasecki wanted to seal his political success with some concrete benefits, but a year later he was in exactly the same place he had been before. In June 1972, the first secretary finally agreed to meet with him in private to discuss the status of PAX. When Piasecki showed up at the doorstep of a government-owned villa in Warsaw on June 15, he found Gierek, Kania, and Szlachcic. Despite attempts to conduct a friendly conversation, the meeting did not go well. Gierek informed Piasecki that some prominent party officials had complained about the nomination to the Council of State; apparently, his fascist past still bothered some comrades. Piasecki was not to be bullied. He tried to talk Gierek into transforming PAX into a political party and accepting the organization into the government.[21] Gierek's response could not have been more precise: He stated that he respected Piasecki's cooperation and hoped that he would continue to work toward

Catholics' participation in reforming Poland. However, the party had no intention of giving up its materialist credo or terminating the propagation of atheism. Therefore, PAX never would be promoted to the position of coalition partner, nor would it ever acquire the status of a political party.[22]

Piasecki returned to his headquarters completely shattered. When one associate commented that Gierek did not understand PAX, Piasecki replied with a mixture of anger and resignation: "Yes, Gierek did not understand us. PAX is right, but it lacks strength."[23] Indeed, Gierek's vision of how to rebuild communist Poland and Piasecki's sweeping projects had very little in common.

Nothing demonstrated more clearly the difference between the two men than Piasecki's emphasis on ideology and Gierek's escape from it. Gierek was never a member of the Communist Party of Poland, nor did his political baptism take place in Sanacja prisons, a war-ravaged Poland, or the Soviet Union. Born in 1913, he moved to France in 1923. He joined the French Communist Party in 1931 and eight years later enlisted in the Communist Party of Belgium. As he put it, "The period of emigration shaped my political personality."[24] Reminiscing about his politics in exile, Gierek contrasted them to the experience of former members of the Communist Party of Poland. He admitted that he had viewed their factional conflicts as completely absurd. His involvement in the French party was a lesson in legality and pragmatism. "Although [the French party] advocated the liquidation of capitalism, it had to follow the rules of parliamentary democracy," wrote Gierek. "Its candidates could not limit their agitation to abstract revolutionary slogans about a better future. They needed a concrete political program addressing specific elements of reality."[25]

After the war, which he spent fighting in the Belgian resistance, Gierek became active in the communist circles of Polish emigrants, joining the Polish Workers' Party in 1946. Two years later, he was recalled to Poland. He returned reluctantly.[26] Likable and uninvolved in the old factional struggles, Gierek did not make a lot of enemies. By 1954, he was the secretary of the Central Committee, and two years later he became the party boss of Upper Silesia. He proved to be a good administrator, capable of communicating with people of different political leanings. "I was never an ideologue," he admitted. "I did not treat ideology as dogma, but as an instrument—a way of solving problems. If the instrument did not work, I tried to find other solutions, beyond or without it."[27]

Piasecki's memoranda were the products of a profoundly ideological mind operating on the verge of obsession. In all probability, Gierek viewed Piasecki's slogans about the pluralism of worldviews and the ideological reinvigoration of Marxism on the basis of Catholicism as completely abstract. Piasecki urged Gierek not to fall into the trap of thinking that the economy was the key to solving Poland's problems. But Gierek reached exactly the opposite conclusion: he believed in *homo economicus*. He knew that communist ideology could no longer legitimize the party-state. He also ruled out the tactics of open confrontation. "The axiom of my policy was 'Never again December,' that is, no more shooting at people," he remarked years later, referring to the 1970 massacre.[28] Gierek based his ambitious and ill-fated program of making a new Poland on raising standards of living, providing more consumer goods, increasing wages and investment, and moderating political discourse. Piasecki recommended budget cuts, moderation in public spending, and ideological mobilization. In this respect, he was much closer to Gomułka's austere national communism than Gierek's economic modernization and consumerist populism.

Piasecki and Gierek also had different views on church-state relations. Gierek's religious policies could be described as "pragmatism without vision."[29] On the one hand, he viewed Gomułka's anticlericalism as adventurist, dogmatic, and counterproductive. He knew that church-state relations required Cardinal Wyszyński's involvement (something Piasecki tried to bypass).[30] On the other hand, Gierek's officials in charge of religious affairs never gave up the strategy of weakening the clergy and dividing the bishops. Secularization was always the goal of the party-state, but its shape and progress were a different matter. The arbitrary measures of the Stalinist and Gomułka years had failed to instill atheism in the masses. The Gierek regime limited atheist agitation, partly lifted discriminatory measures against the employment of the faithful in state institutions, and refrained from interfering with religious instruction conducted in the parishes.[31] In the 1970s, the secularization drive took less direct forms, such as hijacking TV audiences on weekends in the hope that a generous dose of Western movies, variety shows, and programs for children could make people skip Sunday mass.

In the Gierek years, the regime did not set any serious tasks for Catholic lay associations, including PAX.[32] It needed no mediators in its contacts with the Church, nor did it support any intellectual constructs bridging Catholicism and Marxism. Whether cryptonationalist like PAX or genuine like Znak, organizations of progressive Catholics that sought to facilitate Catholic-communist dialogue were fading. While conferring with Bishop Bronisław Dąbrowski, Tejchma expressed his hope that both the Church and the government could recognize the achievements of People's Poland, regardless of their differing worldviews and philosophical beliefs.[33] In this way was Piasecki's doctrine of a pluralism of worldviews finally put to rest.

The appeals of Polish bishops for social calm in December 1970 and January 1971 had a good effect on the new party leadership, which in return bestowed upon the Church buildings and lands that it had leased in the western territories and granted more permits for the construction of places of worship.[34] Gierek did not meet with Wyszyński until 1977, but his close collaborators had been in contact with the primate since early 1971. Wyszyński hoped to negotiate another agreement that would codify and recognize the position of the Church. To that end, he was unsuccessful. But Wyszyński's declaration of goodwill was significant: "The nation is our common good. State and Church serve the same nation, [and] these spiritual and secular agencies should avoid confrontation."[35]

Gierek also opened new talks with the Vatican in the spring of 1971. Initially, the regime treated contacts with the Holy See as a chance to weaken the position of the Polish bishops at home. After the first round of talks, however, it became clear that such a goal was unrealistic. As one party expert put it, "We are under no illusion that the Vatican will do anything to complicate the position of the Church in Poland."[36] On June 28, 1972, the Holy See fully and permanently acknowledged Polish ecclesiastical jurisdiction over the western territories, a move facilitated by the ratification of the Polish-German border treaty by the Bundestag in May of that year. By July 1974, the Polish government and the Vatican had signed a protocol establishing "permanent working contacts" and the institution of special delegates for these contacts.[37]

Despite Piasecki's involvement in Polish-Vatican negotiations in the past, Gierek did not recruit him for talks with the Holy See. Piasecki's 1973 memorandum to Gierek on church-state relations in Poland and contacts with the Vatican contained some valuable points. For instance, Piasecki warned Gierek against ignoring the current religious revival, particularly among the workers. He observed that belief in the secularizing power of industrialization and urbanization was a harmful myth: the popular and traditional character of Polish Catholicism might be intellectually deficient, but it had a huge mobilizing impact on the masses.[38] Piasecki's suggestions had little effect, though, on Gierek. The fate of this memorandum followed that of other documents: it landed in the crammed and bottomless drawers of the Central Committee.

Instead of rebuking the leader of PAX, as Gomułka had done in the past, Gierek chose to mislead Piasecki. Piasecki grew excited each time he addressed or met with the first secretary. His associates consumed their energies by interpreting Gierek's gestures with the zeal and proficiency of ancient seers seeking a good augury.[39]

If Gierek's regime had no use for Piasecki, why did it continue to employ him? A decade earlier, Antoni Alster had made a vulgar but candid comment about Piasecki's usefulness: "We wanted him to be an abscess on Wyszyński's ass, but in the meantime we got it on our ass. However, nobody dares to cut it off. Some comrades still hope that he can be useful in the future."[40] Certainly, by 1972–73, Alster's opinion had lost its validity. Piasecki could no longer be used as a whip against the Church, and his nationalist credentials, useful on the front lines of 1968, were no longer needed.

Unlike Gomułka, Gierek was a pragmatic social engineer, given more to manipulation than to outright coercion and political crusades. His use of the nationalist card was calculated to produce general consensus rather than polarization: Gierek's order to rebuild the royal castle in Warsaw (destroyed during World War II) was a good indicator of this strategy. In comparison to Gomułka's era, references to nationalism and history in official discourse dramatically decreased under Gierek. Patriotism, the leader argued, was essentially the "patriotism of labor," consisting of support for state interests and daily fulfillment of civic duties.[41] War veterans no longer embodied supreme virtues or symbolized the system; now, the hero of the hour was a competent technocrat, as exemplified in one of the most hailed TV serials of the period, *Dyrektorzy* (The Managers). Gierek brushed aside war movies, ideological offensives, and austerity; instead, he brought jeans, Coca-Cola, modern popular entertainment, cars, and vacations on the Black Sea.

The most obvious reason why Piasecki remained on the political scene is that he did not pose any threat to the party. But there may be another explanation. Even as their ideological zeal decreased, the communists still engaged in socialist customs and rituals. In fact, under Gierek, mass rallies and ceremonies continued on a gigantic scale, reflecting the regime's claims of success in building a modern "Second Poland." Although the party did not have any illusions about the enthusiasm of its rank-and-file members, it continued to stage economically irrelevant "voluntary" labor services. Armed with shovels, Gierek's potbellied apparatchiks dripped with sweat on so-called social action days (*czyny społeczne*). For all the absurdity of the claim, the communists still presented themselves as the party of the working class. Apart from cultivating empty public gestures, they also showed a remarkable dependency on political arrangements and systematic solutions introduced during the pioneering years of communist rule. Hence, the communists never abandoned the fiction of a ruling coalition with the Peasant Party and the Democratic Party. Piasecki and his "progressive" Catholics were part of this formula; therefore, as powerless as it was, PAX was there to stay. In the end, the inertia of Piasecki's patrons enabled him to hang on as a fossil in a system that was itself becoming ossified.

Piasecki often criticized the government's policy of consumerism, its negligence of ideology, and its distortion of reality.[42] Chastising the regime for its self-described "propaganda of success" (*propaganda sukcesu*), which painted the picture of a prosperous and modern country about to make a great leap forward, he predicted that the policy of misinformation would have grave consequences for the communists.[43] Subsequent years would sub-stantiate this view. While Piasecki still believed in the power of an ideology-based mandate, Gierek chose pragmatism and, above all, manipulation when the Polish economy began running out of steam in the mid-1970s.[44]

When Piasecki urged the national leadership to inform the populace about the actual condition of the economy in order to prevent social unrest, he was quickly punished.[45] As Tejchma noted in his diary in July 1975, "[The government] ordered Piasecki to democratize the leadership [of PAX] in order to avoid a division between 'the leader' and 'the crowd.'"[46] In losing the title of chairman of PAX and becoming merely chairman of the High Council, Piasecki theoretically ceased to be the sole leader of his movement. He no longer had the right to convene the congress of PAX on his own, and he had to accept the government's interference in the elections to the supreme board.[47] "PAX has lost sovereignty to conduct its own affairs," observed a disgusted Hagmajer.[48]

It was not the end of Piasecki's misfortunes. On February 10, 1976, par-liament passed several amendments to the Polish constitution, declaring the communist party the ruling force, confirming the bogus system of a tripartite coalition government, and emphasizing the alliance with the Soviet Union. The amendments were passed with only one vote of abstention, from

Stanisław Stomma.[49] For Piasecki, the party's leading role and the alliance with the Soviet Union were a matter of record. The principle of a tripartite ruling coalition, by contrast, dashed his last hopes of ever becoming a coalition partner. Informed by Rakowski about Piasecki's frustration, Politburo member Edward Babiuch did not show any surprise: "Of course he must be depressed. After all, we deprived him of all hope that PAX would become the fourth political party in Poland."[50]

The Autumn of the Patriarch, 1976–79

The last years of Piasecki's political career overlapped with a new political context, that of the birth of the democratic opposition. By the summer of 1976, the Polish leaders no longer could bury their heads in the sand and ignore the failure of their ambitious economic policy. Economic growth rates began to drop. Misguided investment in obsolete heavy industries rivaled the incompetent management of the *nomenklatura*. Imported technology failed to produce the exportable products that were necessary to pay back the debts incurred. A trade deficit ensued as the government kept increasing real wages without adjusting prices.[51] In the end, Gierek resorted to the same solution that Gomułka had tried six years earlier: on June 24, 1976, the government announced a general increase of 30 to 100 percent in the prices of foodstuffs as of June 26.[52]

Strikes and demonstrations erupted in several cities. In Radom, southeast of the capital, demonstrators burned the local party headquarters. The police put down the protests with the utmost brutality, using among other methods the so-called paths of health (*ścieżki zdrowia*), in which detainees were forced to run between two lines of club-wielding police officers. Hundreds of people were tried and sentenced to prison terms or exorbitant fines, while others were fired and blacklisted. Ultimately, however, the government rescinded the price increases.

A group of Warsaw intellectuals formed the Committee for the Defense of Workers (Komitet Obrony Robotników, KOR), an organization to defend the arrested strikers and support their families. The group included former revisionists, leading personalities of the 1968 student movement, veterans of the noncommunist resistance movement, writers, and artists. Its major leaders included Jacek Kuroń, Antoni Macierewicz, Adam Michnik, and

Jan Józef Lipski.[53] KOR presented itself not as a political organization, but as a social movement paving the way for the establishment of an independent public sphere.[54] As David Ost has observed, however, KOR's struggle to rebuild civil society was indeed political, because it relied on the rights of free association and freedom of speech, both of which had been eliminated by communist authoritarianism.[55] Soon, KOR broadened its mandate to encompass other activities: the promotion of human rights, underground publishing, independent scientific courses, and the establishment of free trade unions. Setting aside fear of reprisals, members of KOR publicly revealed their names, addresses, and telephone numbers.[56] This formula of openness had a highly moral significance: its emphasis on legality demonstrated that people could pursue the goal of self-determination on their own.

Had the government responded with brutal repression, none of this could have happened. Members of KOR were subjected to detentions, occasional beatings, and police surveillance, but in comparison to the governments of other communist countries, the regime was quite tolerant in its policy toward the organization. As Gierek struggled to secure loans, he did not want to antagonize Western leaders by brutalizing dissidents. It also seems that he did not consider KOR a threat, but rather a safety valve, relieving intellectuals' criticism without attaining more than marginal importance. Commenting on the 1977 amnesty that freed arrested members of KOR, Gierek remarked, "In doing so, somehow we admitted that the communist government could live with KOR as with a small rash or other little ailment."[57]

The philosophy of KOR could hardly have appealed to Piasecki. The concepts of a civil society and an autonomous public sphere were completely incompatible with his authoritarian mindset and his cherished concept of a dualistic communist-nationalist state. Piasecki greeted the formation of KOR with outright hostility. Using rhetoric reminiscent of March 1968, Piasecki described the members of KOR as "people who consistently took positions in opposition to our national and political reasons for existence" and who served "the world coalition of imperialist forces, Zionists, and anti-Soviet hawks." Piasecki also rebuked one of the leaders of the committee, Michnik, for claiming that the joint efforts of the Church, the intelligentsia, and the working class would eventually force the government to make concessions: "In Poland, the Catholics contribute to moral-political unity on the basis of socialist ideology, which combines two major worldviews, one Christian, the other Marxist."[58]

This was, in fact, no longer the case. After the war, Piasecki had based his political program and practice on the belief that the Church would never fully ally itself with the Left. This premise might have held true in the case of the communists and the Church. Until the early 1970s, as well, Piasecki's opinion had proved valid with respect to the left-wing intelligentsia—the driving force behind the revisionist opposition and the March rebellion of 1968. Thereafter, however, the Church began to turn its attention to human and civil rights. In September 1976, Wyszyński even declared that it was "the clergy's duty to defend the workers against hasty and ill-considered government measures."[59]

To be sure, the majority of bishops and priests distrusted KOR, whose members included former communists and leftists. Rev. Jan Zieja and the archbishop of Kraków, Cardinal Karol Wojtyła, held meetings with the group's leader, Jacek Kuroń, and positively evaluated the writings of the opposition's philosophical father, Leszek Kołakowski. Their views, however, were in the minority.[60] In 1977, Wyszyński applauded the amnesty for detained workers and KOR members and praised Gierek's goodwill and realism. He told Kazimierz Kąkol, head of the Office for Religious Affairs, "One thing is sure: regardless of the development of the [political] situation, we will not pose problems [for the government]. The Church will not take any action which would undermine the system, question the needs of the state, and inflame [existing] conditions."[61]

At the same time, dissidents recognized the Church as the strongest autonomous institution in Poland capable of defending society against totalitarianism. This was the underlying message of Michnik's book *The Church and the Left* (Kościół, lewica, dialog), published in 1977.[62] There were a few villains in Michnik's book, and one of them was Piasecki. Michnik belittled Piasecki as a Soviet agent and attacked PAX as the fascist Right in Catholic disguise, espousing a totalitarian creed and readily accepting the communist system.[63]

These were undoubtedly unpleasant blows for Piasecki, but KOR was still a marginal group—or so it seemed. Far more significant was the flagging leadership of Gierek, who grew less and less capable of controlling the situation in Poland. "If Gierek does not understand the social and political roots of the current crisis, the masses will 'restore' order without him," Piasecki complained to Rakowski.[64] He conveyed the same message to the first secretary: if the government did not launch necessary economic reforms, catastrophic consequences would follow—whether implemented by the "street" or through Soviet intervention.[65]

Indeed, Gierek did not know how to improve the stagnating economy or to enhance the prestige of the party. He tried to cut investments and imports, but to no avail. As foreign debt ran into billions of dollars, the prospect of an economic catastrophe loomed. In a desperate attempt to improve his political standing, Gierek turned to the Church. He offered more building permits for churches and signaled the possibility of inviting the pope to visit Poland. Wyszyński was no longer an enemy, but a charismatic statesman and social arbiter.[66] In December 1977, Gierek traveled to Rome, where he met the pope. These gestures were welcomed by the Church and by Wyszyński, but they could not prevent the impending crisis of government.

Piasecki was in no position to intervene in the political and economic stalemate. Moreover, he had to devote more attention to the situation within PAX. Although he still commanded unwavering respect and support among the old guard, Piasecki's popularity among younger members had significantly waned. The young malcontents began criticizing the PAX leadership for its unfriendly policies toward the Church and other Catholic organizations, its sycophantic support of the party, and its ostensibly pro-Soviet propaganda.[67] The rise of the opposition only intensified these internal disputes. In Gdańsk, the local office of the association planned to hold a debate on "rethinking patriotic categories." Among the panelists invited was Bogdan Borusewicz, a KOR activist and organizer of free trade unions. Only the last-minute intervention of the local authorities prevented the debate from taking place.[68] The Movement in Defense of Human and Civil Rights (Ruch Obrony Praw Człowieka i Obywatela), another dissident organization, also attracted some PAX youth.[69] Established in March 1977, the group adopted the KOR's tenet of open struggle for human rights but took more nationalist and Catholic positions.[70]

Piasecki was unable to take swift action against those in his own organization who sympathized with the political opposition. He was no longer the powerful and resolute man he once had been. His health deteriorated rapidly, as years of stress, hard work, and chain-smoking took their toll. In the early 1970s, Piasecki had developed lung and heart problems. When climbing the stairs to his office on the second floor of PAX headquarters, he had to pause to catch his breath.[71] By 1978, he could barely walk at all. Piasecki had always ruled PAX singlehandedly, and his bad health seriously weakened the association, causing organizational chaos.[72] During Piasecki's prolonged absences, PAX was run by Przetakiewicz and Reiff. Because of their mutual animosity, this was not a happy arrangement. Civil and courteous, Reiff understood the grievances of the PAX youth, even if he did not share them. Przetakiewicz, by contrast, lived up to his reputation as Piasecki's ruthless watchdog. Highly unpopular among the younger activists and the more refined members of the establishment, he still had some support in the organization's middle-rank apparatus and among anti-Semitic small fry.[73]

As long as Piasecki was alive, he could prevent open conflict between his two most trusted lieutenants. He succeeded in bringing them together when he finally decided to expel the opposition sympathizers from PAX.[74] On October 6, 1978, Piasecki dragged himself to attend the presidium of PAX in what would prove to be his last public appearance. Addressing his followers, he announced the expulsion of ten high-ranking local activists.[75] He then proceeded to give his final public speech.

"We must remember that we are going through a difficult period in the life of our country," he said. "Perhaps, this situation will soon put our responsibility for the nation to the test. . . . We have nothing in common with the [people] who want to transform this crisis into a catastrophe, nor do we share the attitude of those who stand idly by while such a threat is looming." Poland needed PAX, he concluded, as a genuine political alternative from within the socialist system.[76] If Piasecki regarded this address as a farewell speech, he could not have been more consistent, nor could he have been more stubborn.

Ten days later, a more significant event detained him. On the evening of October 16, a crowd of lay Catholics and clergy gathered at the Saint Peter's Square in Rome to hear the verdict of the cardinals' conclave on the election of the new pope following the death of John Paul I. At last, there came the much-awaited puff of white smoke and the ritual phrase *"Habemus papam!"* (We have a pope), followed by the announcement of the new pontiff's name: Cardinal Wojtyła. Wojtyła's election was unexpected, at least for those who lacked knowledge of the Vatican's internal politics. Not only was he the first non-Italian Pope in five centuries, but he was also the first Slavic pontiff in history. Equally important was the fact that Wojtyła came from a communist country.[77]

Wojtyła's election caused widespread euphoria and boosted national pride in his native country. While the people celebrated, the regime was swept with a sense of humiliation, embarrassment, and panic. Eventually, it chose to reflect the general mood, greeting "the elevation of a son of the Polish nation."[78] But behind closed doors, party leaders unanimously agreed that the election of the Polish pope was a terrible blow.[79]

Piasecki's reaction to the election of the new pope combined both attitudes. On the one hand, as a Pole he clearly rejoiced at the news from Rome; on the other, he had his doubts about Wojtyła's suitability for the post. Piasecki was no friend of the new pope. Although Wojtyła had never shown a strong aversion to PAX in public, his warm ties with *Tygodnik powszechny* as well as his contacts with opposition intellectuals showed that he and Piasecki stood in two different political camps. Like the party bosses from the Central Committee, Piasecki viewed Wojtyła as an anticommunist.[80]

Whatever his private thoughts, Piasecki had no choice but to put a brave face on Wojtyła's election. "We are filled with joy, as a son of Polish soil and the shepherd of the historical Kraków archdiocese has been elected to head of the entire Catholic community," read his cable to the pontiff. "For us, this significant day in the history of the Church, and our nation, confirms the contribution of thousand-year-old Polish Catholicism to the mission of salvation embodied by the Universal Church."[81]

The naming of Wojtyła as Pope John Paul II also marked the end of the Marxist-Catholic philosophical and ideological dialogue in Poland. Neither the maximalist concept of Christianizing or enriching Marxism by Catholicism, as advocated by *Więź* and Piasecki's PAX, nor Stomma's and Znak's neopositivism, which recognized both Poland's dependence on the Soviet Union and communist party rule without endorsing its ideological system, mattered much in the late 1970s. The first approach had lost its relevance in the ideological demobilization of communism after 1968; the second strategy became obsolete after the birth of the democratic opposition in the 1970s. The election of Wojtyła in 1978 and his triumphant pilgrimage to Poland a year later left Polish Catholicism little incentive to conduct a dialogue with Marxism.

On October 28, Piasecki was taken to the intensive care unit of the hospital in Warsaw. He would not name his successor. Asked by Rev. Wacław Radosz if he had anybody in mind, Piasecki answered: "Nobody. They will plunder [and waste] everything."[82]

The end of the year brought a harsh winter. Heavy snowfalls and biting frost paralyzed the entire country. Thousands of people spent New Year's Eve stranded in snowbound cars and trains. Those who stayed at home were freezing in unheated rooms. Amid this natural cataclysm, in a quiet hospital room, the leader of PAX was on his deathbed. Surrounded by relatives and friends, Piasecki faced his death with calm. On December 31, he received the last rites. At about 2:00 a.m. on January 1, 1979, Piasecki died.[83]

Piasecki's funeral was scheduled for January 4. As a member of the Council of State, he was buried with all honors. His body was taken first to the Primate's Palace in Warsaw's Old Town district. The simple wooden coffin draped with the Polish flag was placed on a catafalque in the middle of the hall, before the neoclassical columns and below a plaque depicting the Polish white eagle. Soldiers from the Polish army's honor guard stood at attention. Members of the government, the Council of State, leaders of political and social associations, and representatives of PAX formed alternating guards of honor. Among the numerous veterans of Polish political life who came to pay tribute to Piasecki were Cyrankiewicz and Kliszko.[84]

At 11:00 a.m., accompanied by a drum roll, the coffin was carried out. It was snowing. The funeral procession moved slowly to Piasecki's parish church, Saint Michael's, in the Mokotów district. The mass was concelebrated by the parish priest and vicar-general of the Warsaw archdiocese, Rev. Stefan Piotrowski; the former chaplain of the Confederation of the Nation, Reverend Mieczysław Suwała; and Piasecki's confessor, Rev. Jan Twardowski. In his sermon, Piotrowski recalled Piasecki's services to the country: "A soldier, politician, social activist, he always served to the benefit of the fatherland." He also praised Piasecki for helping numerous people in the difficult postwar period and acknowledged his achievements in the field of Catholic culture. Piotrowski's benevolence toward the deceased reached its zenith when he told the mourners of a significant gesture by Wyszyński: on the day after Piasecki's death, the cardinal had said a mass for the deceased. But the sermon also included less-flattering undertones. Piotrowski stated, for example, that in his work for church-state dialogue, the leader of PAX had not escaped mistakes and errors. Perhaps the most telling of all were Piotrowski's opening words, reflecting the ambiguity of their subject: "Whoever decides to write the history of this life will face a difficult task."[85]

After the mass, the funeral procession began moving to Powązki Cemetery through the snowbound streets of Warsaw. At last, they reached the family grave, where Piasecki's wife and son were buried. There, shaking from the cold and his emotions, Jerzy Hagmajer delivered a final eulogy. He noted that throughout his life, Piasecki had always struggled to find the best way to serve his fatherland, sometimes in spite of the opinions of his contemporaries. "One thing is sure," he observed. "[Bolesław] always followed the difficult path."[86]

Conclusion

THE ABILITY OF THE COMMUNISTS to attract nationalists and to nationalize their societies without conceding their monopoly on power is one of the most interesting aspects of Eastern Europe in the postwar period. As the Italian socialist Ignazio Silone remarked on one occasion, "The first thing that the communists nationalize is socialism."[1] This was a dangerous game, since the communist government of each satellite state had to find a middle course between adherence to the Soviet Union and obligations to nationalism at home.[2] Only two Eastern European communist leaders, Tito and Enver Hoxha, managed to bypass this dilemma. In the Soviet bloc, the Romanian leader Nicolae Ceaușescu came closest to the implementation of national communism or, as Vladimir Tismăneanu suggests, to a "national Stalinism" independent of Moscow.[3] In Poland, all of the communists' attempts to win popular support through nationalism led to severe political and ideological crises: the growth of revisionism after 1956, the loss of ideological legitimacy following 1968, and lastly, the birth of Solidarity.

Piasecki's postwar career reflects the continuity of prewar political traditions. The trail of the East European Right is a peculiar one, and Piasecki's story is one of the most interesting examples of the persistence of the Right and of the pluralistic rather than totalitarian nature of East European communism. In his study of the Sovietization of East German, Czech, and Polish academia, John Connelly argues that there were many ways to work within communist structures to rebuild East European societies after World War II.[4] Indeed, Eastern Europe had access to a number of different political traditions, different social structures, and different cultural predispositions with which to work. The nationalist Piasecki, the Catholic Church, and the Znak

Catholics in Poland; the Zveno leader Kimon Georgiev in communist Bulgaria; the populist writers in Kadar's Hungary; the East German Protestant Church; various proregime associations and parties: all these noncommunist groups and individuals managed to maintain a modicum of independence under communism.

Piasecki played an important part in the nationalization of socialism in Poland. His formula for a nationalist-communist alliance preceded the official endorsement of nationalism and anti-Semitism by the communist leadership and paved the way for the recognition of a nationalist-communist kinship, which manifested itself in 1968 and came to full fruition under Wojciech Jaruzelski after 1981. Martial law proved that the party-state in Poland still possessed strong means of repression, suitable for defeating the opposition. The regime also faced the biggest crisis of legitimacy in its history, however. Solidarity successfully deployed national and noncommunist symbols against the symbols of the regime, offering an alternative vision of the fatherland. Its enormous popularity and the concurrent exodus of members from the party attested to the delegitimization of the party-state. Having lost their ideological superiority, the communists based their mandate on the concepts of the Polish raison d'état and "a lesser evil." In short, the Jaruzelski regime relied extensively on the rhetoric of nationalism, including old Piłsudskiite and Endek slogans, while also endorsing statism and further diminishing Marxist ideological discourse.

In his speech announcing martial law on December 13, 1981, Jaruzelski did not use the word "communism." Instead, he addressed the nation as a "soldier and the head of the Polish government."[5] It was the military and the government, the two pillars of Polish statehood, that were preventing Solidarity from leading the country toward a "national catastrophe." Jaruzelski claimed to be guided by "an instinct for the self-preservation of the nation."[6] In a veiled reference to the threat of Soviet intervention, he emphasized that Poland had to overcome the current crisis on its own. Jaruzelski expected his compatriots to accept the lesser evil of suspended liberties and hardships in the name of responsibility for the fate of the nation.[7]

Jaruzelski's message resembled the rhetoric of Sanacja: patriotic, authoritarian-militarist, all-embracing, but also extremely vague. It stood even closer to Piasecki's programmatic statements, especially his memorable "State Instinct" article of 1956. With his emphasis on national interest, patriotic responsibility, and the need for a strong government that sometimes had to act against popular sentiment, Jaruzelski walked in Piasecki's footsteps. In the end, socialist ideology did not matter. It was the Polish state that constituted the highest value. Those who did not share this notion of raison d'état, among them Solidarity leaders, were unpatriotic and anti-Polish.[8]

In 1982, the Jaruzelski regime established the Patriotic Movement for National Rebirth (Patriotyczny Ruch Odrodzenia Narodowego) to "unite the patriotic forces of the nation" and reflect a "pluralism of views and the differentiation of interests."[9] Both phrases clearly echoed Piasecki's old concept of the pluralism of worldviews, and the chairmanship of the new movement was given to one of Piasecki's old comrades, the Catholic writer Jan Dobraczyński.

The Patriotic Movement for National Rebirth hardly constituted an outlet for genuine independent groups. Instead, it soon became the laughingstock of public opinion, partly because of the advanced age of its leadership —men and women in their seventies—and partly because of its political irrelevance. But the movement also reflected the regime's ideological demobilization and its quest for alternative sources of legitimacy. In December 1981, both before and after the declaration of martial law, some of Jaruzelski's collaborators urged the general to dissolve the Polish United Workers' Party and create a new communist party.[10] The government soon embraced and exercised a "permissible pluralism," by which it sought to attract nonparty public figures—sometimes those with opposition credentials —to weaken the appeal of Solidarity and to demonstrate good relations with the episcopate.

The problem was that both the opposition and the Church also continued their efforts to monopolize national identity, sometimes separately and sometimes jointly. Solidarity's appropriation of numerous Catholic symbols and rituals helped legitimize the union in the eyes of a predominantly Catholic society, but it also confirmed the Church's position as the repository of national identity and moral truth, reinforcing the powerful appeal of ethnoconfessional identity. After the victory of the opposition in 1989, this emblematic dependence on Roman Catholicism posed serious challenges for both the new democratic elite and the clergy. But in the 1980s, it successfully challenged Jaruzelski's attempts to claim legitimacy through nationalism. The later endorsement of Mikhail Gorbachev's perestroika and subsequent dialogue with the opposition offered the communists an exit from this competition.

Since 1989, no significant political party in Poland has ever openly claimed Piasecki as its ideological patron. Perceived as a Soviet collaborator and communist stooge, Piasecki did not fit in.[11] His ethnoconfessional vision of national identity continued to hold a powerful appeal, however, due mostly to the dominant narrative of the postcommunist era, which portrayed Polish Catholicism, anticommunist opposition, and the struggle for sovereignty as synonymous.

Solidarity and the Church cooperated in the 1989 elections, but cracks began to show in this façade of harmonious alliance when several Solidarity candidates competed against Catholic independents supported by local bishops and parishes. During Lech Wałęsa's war at the top and the subsequent breakup of Solidarity into a number of political parties, the episcopate sided with those centrist and right-wing groups that promoted a confessional state and the *polak-katolik* ethnoreligious vision. Although some of these parties, particularly the short-lived Christian-National Union, adhered to Dmowski's legacy, they did not constitute a resurgence of Endecja. This was part of a general trend in post-1989 democratic Poland: despite some attempts at resurrection, the prewar political parties did not resurface. The new democratic nation-state had been shaped by the dynamics of the communist period. The powerful position of the Church, the display of religious symbols in public life, the clergy's participation in state ceremonies, and the unanimous adulation of Pope John Paul II all served to boost Catholic nationalism. The final version of the preamble to the 1997 constitution replaced the words "We Polish citizens" with "We the Polish nation" and included an *invocatio Dei*. In December 2009, the Polish parliament even passed a law protecting the display of the cross in the public sphere.[12]

Influencing voters, however, proved problematic. In 1991, Bishop Józef Michalik declared that a Catholic nation should not be ruled by "a non-Christian parliament" and that "a Catholic had the duty to vote for a Catholic, a Moslem for a Moslem, a Jew for a Jew, a Mason for a Mason."[13] Michalik's statement equated religious denomination with ethnic identity and political persuasion, hinting at anti-Semitic and xenophobic convictions and, more important, at least questioning if not outright denying the possibility of democratic consensus between citizens of different faiths. The majority of voters shunned such constructs. In the general and presidential elections of 1993, 1995, 2001, and most recently in 2010, candidates and parties endorsed by the episcopate or some of its members suffered defeat. Ethnoconfessional striving proved inferior to socioeconomic concerns. In the 2011 general elections, Janusz Palikot's anticlerical movement won 10 percent of the vote and became the third-largest force in parliament.

In her critically acclaimed study, *The Crosses of Auschwitz*, Genevieve Zubrzycki proposes that the erosion of ethnoreligious discourse in postcommunist Poland was inevitable. The collapse of communism and the construction of a legitimate national and pluralist state weakened the bond between religion and nation, as national identity found civic means of expression and Poles began redefining their vision of nationhood.[14] The evolving nature of church-state relations in recent years has gone beyond the duel between civic nationalism and an ethnoreligious concept of Poland. Enter the Law and Justice Party (Prawo i Sprawiedliwość, PiS), which moved from its original program of "civic nationalism" to that of Rev. Tadeusz Rydzyk, whose ethnoconfessional vision corresponds to Piasecki's creed.

In 1991, Rydzyk established a local religious radio station in Toruń, Radio Maryja. Three years later, the station expanded into a nationwide social movement of fundamentalist and ultranationalist Catholics, the Family of Radio Maryja. In 1998, Rydzyk's media company launched a Catholic daily, *Nasz dziennik*, with a circulation of two hundred thousand, and five years later it established the TV station Trwam (I Persist). The political credo of Rydzyk's media can be described as fundamentalist Catholic and nationalist extremist: anti-EU, anti-Western, and anti-Semitic. Foreigners, intellectuals, and members of liberal elites are the favored targets of broadcasters' and listeners' diatribes. In 2001, the radio station played midwife to the League of Polish Families, an ultranationalist party opposed to Poland's accession to the European Union. Cherished by the poor, uneducated, and unemployed, Rydzyk's station soon became the voice of those who had failed to advance and prosper in an environment dominated by the global market economy.[15]

The phenomenon of Radio Maryja is important for at least two reasons. First, the station remains independent of the Church. Numerous but rather feeble attempts by the Polish episcopate and the Vatican to discipline Rydzyk and dissuade him from broadcasting political propaganda have been largely unsuccessful. Second, Rydzyk has become a serious political player who oversees a highly disciplined and vocal electorate. His position is so strong that he was courted, successfully, by the Law and Justice Party of brothers Jarosław and Lech Kaczyński.

In its infancy, PiS preached anticorruption and decommunization while staying away from religious matters. Rydzyk's switch of allegiance from the League of Polish Families to the Kaczyńskis gained the brothers a victory in the 2005 parliamentary and presidential elections, but it also radicalized the rhetoric of their movement, which had hijacked the nationalist extremist and traditionalist Catholic electorate.

The 2005 elections took place just a few months after the death of John Paul II. His departure led to a power vacuum: the Polish church, hardly a monolith, lacked a leader who could step into the shoes of the late pontiff. It also silenced a voice that had influenced political and social debates in Poland. During his pontificate, and particularly after 1989, any attempt to confront the pope's opinions, views, and actions was considered taboo.[16]

The Kaczyńskis' alliance with Rydzyk suffered a serious setback in 2006 and 2007, in the wake of the attempted lustration of the Church. The PiS was seeking to delegitimize the entire post-1989 political system and to construct a Fourth Republic. The underpinning of this revolution was the lustration of the elites who, in the Kaczyńskis' view, had compromised with the communist establishment in 1989 and contributed to the overall climate of moral decay.[17]

As members of a private institution, the clergy did not have to undergo lustration. Its trial came in December 2006, with the scandal surrounding the nomination of Bishop Stanisław Wielgus to the post of archbishop of Warsaw, supported by Rydzyk's movement. The revelation of Wielgus's cooperation with the communist security services led to his resignation. Rydzyk defended the bishop. He even accused the PiS government of falling under the influence of the Jewish lobby.[18]

Rydzyk's vehement criticism of the government in the wake of the Wielgus affair slowed the impetus of decommunization and weakened the PiS, which lost early elections in 2007 to the centrist Civic Platform. But two subsequent events transformed the PiS into the guardians and advocates of the ethnoconfessional nationalism promoted by Rydzyk: the catastrophe involving the Polish presidential plane in April 2010 and the subsequent "Cross affair" in Warsaw. On April 10, 2010, the Polish equivalent of Air Force One crashed near Smolensk, Russia. There were no survivors. Among the ninety-six people on board was the president, Lech Kaczyński.

Kaczyński was up for reelection in the fall of 2010, and few expected him to retain his office.[19] But the Smolensk crash boosted the popularity of the surviving twin, Jarosław, who soon decided to run for president in his late brother's stead. The tragedy evoked feelings of grief, shock, and sorrow, generating spontaneous mass gestures of sympathy for the victims. Five days after the catastrophe, members of the Polish scouting organization planted a wooden cross in front of the Presidential Palace in Warsaw. Partly an appeal for a monument to Smolensk victims and partly a religious symbol of comfort, the cross gradually evolved into a meeting point for a small group of Catholic fundamentalists. It was a spontaneous, grassroots initiative, not the action of the Church, whose representatives never blessed the cross.

In the presidential election of July 2010, Bronisław Komorowski of the Civic Platform narrowly defeated Jarosław Kaczyński. In one of the first press interviews given after his victory, the president-elect, a practicing Catholic and moderate conservative, was asked how he felt about the cross in front of his future office. "The Presidential Palace is a sanctuary of state," he said. "The cross is a religious symbol, and as such it should be taken to a more appropriate place after consultations with the Church."[20] This remark emphasizing the separation of church and state would be no shocker in the Western world, particularly in the European Union. But in Poland, where segments of the clergy and the political elite preached the unity of national identity and Catholicism, it was a significant statement, and Komorowski's defeated opponent took notice.

"If President Komorowski removes the cross," Kaczyński announced, "then it will be clear who he is and whose side he is on regarding debates about Polish history."[21] After an unsuccessful attempt to move the cross to a Warsaw church in August 2010, he declared that Komorowski had implemented *Zapateryzm* (meaning "atheism"; Kaczyński coined this term from the name of Spain's socialist prime minister José Zapatero) in Poland.[22] What Kaczyński implied was that the president belonged to the unpatriotic and anti-Catholic minority. Gone was Kaczyński's emphasis on anticommunism. Moderate Catholics, centrists, atheists, and those members of the pre-1989 opposition who contested the PiS and its vision of Poland's history became the main enemy.

Rydzyk's ethnoconfessional nationalism, anti-Semitism, Germanophobia, rejection of a secular nation state, and anti-intellectual bias make him a fitting heir to Piasecki. But his extremism also contains astonishing hostility toward those who opposed communism from liberal Catholic, left-wing, and centrist positions. Essentially, Rydzyk is carrying forward the worldview of

Piasecki and, incidentally, of those elements within the Polish communist party that orchestrated the anti-Semitic campaign of the 1960s. By adopting this approach, he and Jarosław Kaczyński, former dissident and self-described champion of the anticommunist crusade, may find themselves on a political journey back to Piasecki, Moczar, and Dmowski, those who fathered and carried out the most aggressive manifestation of Polish nationalism.

Notes

Abbreviations

AAN	New Documents Archive (Archiwum Akt Nowych)
AKS CC	Archive of the Catholic Association Civitas Christiana (Archiwum Katolickiego Stowarzyszenia Civitas Christiana)
AUW	Archive of the University of Warsaw (Archiwum Uniwersytetu Warszawskiego)
HIA	Hoover Institution Archives
IPN	Institute for National Remembrance (Instytut Pamięci Narodowej)

Preface

1. Wojciech Wasiutyński, *Prawą stroną labiryntu* (Gdańsk: Exter, 1996); Wojciech Wasiutyński, *Czwarte pokolenie* (London: Odnowa, 1982); Zygmunt Przetakiewicz, *Od ONR-u do PAX-u* (Warsaw: Wydawnictwo Książka Polska, 1994); Włodzimierz Sznarbachowski, *300 lat wspomnień* (London: Aneks, 1995); Jan Dobraczyński, *Tylko w jednym życiu* (Warsaw: PAX, 1970); Andrzej Micewski, *Katolicy w potrzasku* (Warsaw: BGW, 1993); Ryszard Reiff, *Gra o życie* (Warsaw: Unicorn, 1993).

Introduction

1. "Endeks" were followers of Roman Dmowski's National Democratic Party (Narodowa Demokracja), commonly known as "Endecja" from the organization's initials in Polish, ND.
2. There are at least two outstanding books examining the entanglement of nationalism and communism in Romania: see Katherine Verdery, *National Ideology under Socialism: Identity and Cultural Politics in Ceauşescu's Romania* (Berkeley: University of California Press, 1991), and Vladimir Tismăneanu, *Stalinism for All*

Seasons: A Political History of Romanian Communism (Berkeley: University of California Press, 2003). Studies by Rogers Brubaker and Timothy Snyder provide excellent sociological analyses of Polish and other regional nationalisms. Rogers Brubaker, *Nationalism Reframed: Nationalism and the National Question in the New Europe* (New York: Cambridge University Press, 1996); Timothy Snyder, *The Reconstruction of Nations: Poland, Ukraine, Lithuania, Belarus, 1569–1999* (New Haven, Conn.: Yale University Press, 2004). Marcin Zaremba devoted his work to the incorporation of nationalism into the communists' ideological and cultural discourse, whereas John Connelly has explored the much overlooked phenomenon of pluralism within communism and the persistence of different political and cultural traditions that East European communists had to deal and work with. John Connelly, *Captive University* (Chapel Hill: University of North Carolina Press, 2000); Marcin Zaremba, *Komunizm, legitymizacja, nacjonalizm: Nacjonalistyczna legitymizacja władzy komunistycznej w Polsce* (Warsaw: Trio, 2001). Books by Walter Kemp and Amir Weiner discuss the Soviet experience and how the Stalinist regimes experimented with their own brand of nationalism, using its appeal to legitimize their rule and create new nationalist canons. Walter A. Kemp, *Nationalism and Communism in Eastern Europe and the Soviet Union* (New York: St. Martin's, 1999); Amir Weiner, *Making Sense of War: The Second World War and the Fate of the Bolshevik Revolution* (Princeton, N.J.: Princeton University Press, 2001). Fewer scholars have produced studies on modern nationalism and religion in East Central Europe. While Brian Porter's and Paul Hanebrink's groundbreaking works on Polish and Hungarian nationalism remain primarily focused on the late nineteenth and early twentieth century, Genevieve Zubrzycki is attentive to postcommunist Poland. Brian Porter, *When Nationalism Began to Hate* (New York: Oxford University Press, 2000); Paul Hanebrink, *In Defense of Christian Hungary: Religion, Nationalism, and Antisemitism, 1890–1944* (Ithaca, N.Y.: Cornell University Press, 2006); Genevieve Zubrzycki, *The Crosses of Auschwitz: Nationalism and Religion in Post-Communist Poland* (Chicago: University of Chicago Press, 2006).

3. Bolesław Piasecki, *Duch czasów nowych a Ruch Młodych* (Warsaw: n.p., 1935), 36.

4. Instytut Pamięci Narodowej (IPN), Teczka osobowa Bolesława Piaseckiego, IPN 0259/6, Osobiste oświadczenie Bolesława Piaseckiego, May 22, 1945; Archiwum Katolickiego Stowarzyszenia Civitas Christiana (AKS CC), I/91, Piasecki to Władysław Gomułka, August 18, 1946.

5. Bolesław Piasecki, introduction to *Zagadnienia istotne* (Warsaw: PAX, 1954).

6. Western scholarship on Piasecki is thin and poorly researched. The significant exception is Norbert A. Żmijewski's work on Catholic-Marxist dialogue in postwar Poland. Although Żmijewski's work contains valuable insights, it does not provide a thorough examination of Piasecki's politics. See Norbert A. Żmijewski, *The Catholic-*

Marxist Ideological Dialogue in Poland, 1945–1980 (Brookfield, Vt.: Dartmouth, 1991). The British journalist and former Bundist Lucjan Blit offers a popular biography of Piasecki. Blit acknowledges Piasecki as a leading personage on the political map of the Soviet bloc. Based on scattered secondhand sources and anonymous interviews, however, the book is more anecdotal than informative and full of errors. See Lucjan Blit, *The Eastern Pretender* (London: Hutchinson, 1965). Polish scholarship on Piasecki reveals problems of a different nature. It often demonstrates a deficient methodological approach based on old-fashioned historicism and a lack of emotional distance from the subject. Prominent among Polish studies is Antoni Dudek and Grzegorz Pytel's biography of Piasecki, a rigorously chronological account that is nonetheless riddled with conflicting and often unverified information and lacks a basic thesis. See Antoni Dudek and Grzegorz Pytel, *Bolesław Piasecki: Próba biografii politycznej* (London: Aneks, 1990).

7. Having researched Piasecki's activism on the Catholic front, I disagree with those who represent him as a communist stooge, a Trojan horse working for the destruction of the Church from the inside. Compare the opinion of the Polish primate, Cardinal Stefan Wyszyński, who described Piasecki as a "thief secretly opening the doors of the Church to the Communists." Hoover Institution Archives (HIA), Peter Raina Collection, box 3, folder 1, Notatka, November 3, 1966.

8. Hermann Broch, *The Spell* (San Francisco: North Point, 1989), 188.

Chapter 1: The Early Years, 1915–35

1. Other military conflicts that took place after November 1918 included the Polish-Ukrainian war in the former Austrian province of Galicia, an anti-German revolt in the area of Prussian Poland in 1919, and border skirmishes with Czechoslovakia and Lithuania.

2. Elected by the national assembly thanks to votes of the Left, the centrist PSL, and national minorities, Narutowicz was vilified by the nationalist Right and assassinated by a follower of Dmowski after only five days in office. Piłsudski blamed Endecja for Narutowicz's death. He retired in protest against the formation of Witos's government, which included Dmowski's party.

3. Henryk Dembiński, "Defilada umarłych bogów," *Żagary*, September (1931).

4. Michael Mann, *Fascists* (Cambridge: Cambridge University Press, 2004), 39–40.

5. Antony Polonsky, *Politics in Independent Poland, 1921–1939: The Crisis of Constitutional Government* (Oxford: Clarendon, 1972), vii.

6. Joseph Rothschild, *Pilsudski's Coup d'État* (New York: Columbia University Press, 1966), 353–54.

7. Eva Plach, *The Clash of Moral Nations: Cultural Politics in Piłsudski's Poland, 1926–1935* (Athens: Ohio University Press, 2006), 6–7, 15–16.

8. Joseph Rothschild, *East Central Europe between the Two World Wars* (Seattle: University of Washington Press, 1974), 60.

9. Roman Wapiński, *Narodowa Demokracja, 1893–1939* (Wrocław: Ossolineum, 1980), 236–37.

10. Roman Dmowski, *Pisma*, vol. 10, *Od Obozu Wielkiej Polski do Stronnictwa Narodowego* (Częstochowa: Antoni Gmachowski, 1939), 34.

11. Jerzy Borejsza, *Mussolini był pierwszy* (Warsaw: Czytelnik, 1979), 177.

12. Wapiński, *Narodowa Demokracja,* 264–66.

13. Szymon Rudnicki, *Obóz Narodowo-Radykalny: Geneza i działalność* (Warsaw: Czytelnik, 1985), 22–23.

14. Plach, *Clash of Moral Nations,* 34.

15. Brian Porter, *When Nationalism Began to Hate* (New York: Oxford University Press, 2000), 143–55, 182–223.

16. Ibid., 136, 151.

17. Wojciech Wasiutyński, *Prawą stroną labiryntu* (Gdańsk: Exter, 1996), 96.

18. Wapiński, *Narodowa Demokracja,* 269.

19. Ibid., 276.

20. Andrzej Pilch, *Rzeczpospolita akademicka* (Kraków: Księgarnia Akademicka, 1997), 93.

21. *Akademik polski,* February 10, 1927.

22. Porter, *When Nationalism Began to Hate,* 230–31.

23. Irina Livezeanu, *Cultural Politics in Greater Romania: Regionalism, Nation Building, and Ethnic Struggle, 1918–1930* (Ithaca, N.Y.: Cornell University Press, 1995), 267.

24. Polonsky, *Politics in Independent Poland,* 247, 250.

25. Roman Dmowski, *Wybór pism Romana Dmowskiego* (New York: Instytut Romana Dmowskiego, 1988), 4:90.

26. Tom Buchanan and Martin Conway, eds., *Political Catholicism in Europe, 1918–1965* (Oxford: Clarendon, 1996), 15, 22.

27. Paul A. Hanebrink, *In Defense of Christian Hungary: Religion, Nationalism, and Anti-Semitism, 1890–1944* (Ithaca, N.Y.: Cornell University Press, 2006), 2–4, 92.

28. R. J. B. Bosworth, *Mussolini* (London: Hodder Education, 2002), 238, 258.

29. Porter, *When Nationalism Began to Hate,* 153–56.

30. Krzysztof Kawalec, *Narodowa Demokracja wobec faszyzmu* (Warsaw: PIW, 1989), 106–7.

31. Jarosław Piasecki to the author, February 4, 2002.

32. Ibid. Among Zamoyski's graduates was the rising star of Endecja, Jan Mosdorf. At the time of Piasecki's enrollment, the institution was run by Henryk

Lipski, a National Democratic member of parliament. Count Maurycy Zamoyski was Endecja's presidential candidate in 1922. On the Zamoyski school, see Stanisław Konarski, "Warszawskie średnie szkolnictwo ogólnokształcące w latach 1918–1939," in *Warszawa II Rzeczypospolitej, 1918–1939*, ed. Marian M. Drozdowski, vol. 5 (Warsaw: PWN, 1973), 179–97.

33. Antoni Dudek and Grzegorz Pytel, *Bolesław Piasecki: Próba biografii politycznej* (London: Aneks, 1990), 12.

34. Jarosław Piasecki to the author, February 4, 2002.

35. Archiwum Akt Nowych (AAN), Komisariat Rządu miasta stołecznego Warszawy, Wydział Bezpieczeństwa Komisariatu Rządu, 297-I-2, Sprawozdanie z wyborów do Sejmu i Senatu z 1930 r. na terenie m.st. Warszawy.

36. Andrzej Garlicki, *Dzieje Uniwersytetu Warszawskiego* (Warsaw: PWN, 1982), 127.

37. Wasiutyński, *Prawą stroną labiryntu*, 77–80.

38. Archiwum Uniwersytetu Warszawskiego (AUW), Bolesław Piasecki, WP 37500.

39. Marian M. Drozdowski, "Skład i struktura społeczna ludności Warszawy przedwojennej," in Drozdowski, *Warszawa II Rzeczypospolitej*, 1:31.

40. Mikołaj Bierdiajev, *Nowe Średniowiecze*, trans. Marian Reutt (Warsaw: Rój, 1936); Mikołaj Bierdiajev, *Problem komunizmu*,trans. Marian Reutt (Warsaw: Rój, 1937); Jacques Maritain, *Nauka i mądrość*, trans. Marian Reutt (Warsaw: Rój, n.d.).

41. Wasiutyński, *Prawą stroną labiryntu*, 103.

42. Marian Reutt, preface to Bierdiajev, *Problem komunizmu*, 5–14.

43. Marian Reutt, preface to Bierdiajev, *Nowe Średniowiecze*, 5–9.

44. Wasiutyński, *Prawą stroną labiryntu*, 156–57.

45. Ibid., 88.

46. Oddział Akademicki O.W.P., *Wytyczne w sprawach: Żydowskiej, mniejszości słowiańskich, niemieckiej, zasad polityki gospodarczej* (Warsaw, 1932), 3–6.

47. Ibid., 6–8.

48. Ibid., 8–10.

49. Ibid., 10–12.

50. Mann, *Fascists*, 7.

51. Rudnicki, *Obóz Narodowo-Radykalny*, 127, 148–49.

52. *Kurier poranny*, November 30, 1932.

53. *Kurier poranny*, November 11, 1932.

54. *W sprawie nowej ustawy o szkołach akademickich* (Lwów, 1933).

55. In the town of Radziłów in Białystok province, the rioters attacked a local police precinct. Police reinforcements used firearms, killing two people. *Kurier poranny*, March 24, 1933. In 1941, Radziłów and the neighboring town of Jedwabne saw the massacre of the Jews by their Polish neighbors. See Jan T. Gross, *Neighbors:*

The Destruction of the Jewish Community in Jedwabne, Poland (Princeton, N.J.: Princeton University Press, 2001).

56. *Akademik polski,* January 23, 1933.

57. Mann, *Fascists,* 27.

58. *Akademik polski,* February 14, 1933.

59. *Akademik polski,* March 15, 1933.

60. *Akademik polski,* June 17, 1933.

61. *Akademik polski,* October 10, 1933.

62. Mann, *Fascists,* 13–16.

63. Rudnicki, *Obóz Narodowo-Radykalny,* 174.

64. Wasiutyński, *Prawą stroną labiryntu,* 98–99, emphasis added.

65. Jacek Majchrowski, *Geneza politycznych ugrupowań katolickich: Stronnictwo Pracy, grupa "Dzis i Jutro"* (Paris: Libella, 1986), 85.

66. Tadeusz Bielecki, *W szkole Dmowskiego* (Gdańsk: Exter, 2000), 169–70.

67. Wasiutyński, *Prawą stroną labiryntu,* 96.

68. Dudek and Pytel, *Bolesław Piasecki,* 38.

69. Jan Grabowski, "Wynik pięcioletniej pracy," *Ruch młodych* 2 (February 1937): 33.

70. *Sztafeta,* April 15, 1934.

71. Majchrowski, *Geneza politycznych ugrupowań katolickich,* 90.

72. *Kurier warszawski,* April 15, 1934; *Myśl narodowa,* April 22, 1934.

73. *Robotnik,* April 15, 17, 1934.

74. *Kurier poranny,* April 18, 1934.

75. AAN, Bezpartyjny Blok Współpracy z Rządem, 62-II-25, Aleksander Kawałkowski, Zagadnienia młodzieży w Polsce.

76. Majchrowski, *Geneza politycznych ugrupowań katolickich,* 93.

77. Włodzimierz Sznarbachowski, *300 lat wspomnień* (London: Aneks, 1997), 82; Dudek and Pytel, *Bolesław Piasecki,* 40.

78. Rudnicki, *Obóz Nardowo-Radykalny,* 237.

79. Their most notorious assault was the beating of Professor Marceli Handelsman (1882–1945), a renowned historian of Jewish origin and propagator of the Annales School in Poland. *Sztafeta,* April 15, 1934. Handelsman participated in the resistance movement and in this capacity served in the Home Army Office of Information and Propaganda (Biuro Informacji i Propagandy Armii Krajowej). In 1944, he was denounced to the Gestapo by members of the National Armed Forces (Narodowe Siły Zbrojne), a far-right group. Handelsman died in a concentration camp in 1945.

80. *Sztafeta,* May 13, 1934.

81. Rudnicki, *Obóz Narodowo-Radykalny,* 250–51.

82. *Sztafeta,* May 30, 1934.

83. *Sztafeta,* June 10, 1934.

84. Ibid.

85. The nationalist youth had by the late 1920s adopted as its symbol the sword of Polish king Bolesław Chrobry, the Szczerbiec. The ONR inherited the sword from the OWP.

86. Zygmunt Przetakiewicz, *Od ONR-u do PAX-u* (Warsaw: Wydawnictwo Książka Polska, 1994), 12.

87. Dudek and Pytel, *Bolesław Piasecki,* 43.

88. Sznarbachowski, *300 lat wspomnień,* 84.

89. Following the collapse of the ONR, Mosdorf returned to journalism. After the defeat of Poland in September 1939, he rejoined the National Party and participated in the anti-Nazi resistance. Arrested in 1940, Mosdorf was sent to Auschwitz. The accounts left by fellow inmates testify to Mosdorf's exemplary conduct in the camp. Approached by the Germans with an offer of release in exchange for collaboration, Mosdorf refused. He was executed in October 1943. Witold Nieciuński, interview by author, tape recording, Warsaw, September 14, 1999.

90. Majchrowski, *Geneza politycznych ugrupowań katolickich,* 93–94.

91. Sznarbachowski, *300 lat wspomnień,* 94; *ABC,* July 8, 1934.

92. Stanisław Mackiewicz, *Historia Polski od 11 listopada 1918 r. do 17 wrzesnia 1939 r.* (Warsaw: Głos, 1989), 245.

Chapter 2: The National Radical Movement, 1934–39

1. Włodzimierz Sznarbachowski, *300 lat wspomnień* (London: Aneks, 1997), 94–96.

2. On Bereza, see Wojciech Śleszyński, "Utworzenie i funkcjonowanie obozu odosobnienia w Berezie Kartuskiej," *Dzieje najnowsze* 2 (June 2003): 35–53.

3. Sznarbachowski, *300 lat wspomnień,* 118–24. Wasiutyński suggested that Piasecki elaborated his plan only in 1935. Wojciech Wasiutyński, *Prawą stroną labiryntu* (Gdańsk: Exter, 1996), 93.

4. Bogumił Grott, *Nacjonalizm chrześcijański* (Kraków: Ostoja, 1996), 235–46. Rossman's ONR ABC also rejected the principle of a one-party state. Though viciously anti-Semitic, Rossman elevated national identity over ethnocentrism, a logical choice for a party whose leaders had German-sounding names. Following Rossman's death in 1937, the ONR ABC zigzagged between monarchism and corporatism.

5. For this explanation, see Stanley Payne, *A History of Fascism, 1914–1945* (Madison: University of Wisconsin Press, 1995), 321. *Falanga* was launched before the outbreak of the Spanish Civil War, before the Polish nationalists turned their attention to the Iberian state. It was Zygmunt Dziarmaga, the first publisher of

Falanga, who came up with the title, which resembled his own three-syllable surname ending with an "a" (Wasiutyński, *Prawą stroną labiryntu,* 164). Before the emergence of Piasecki's movement, the word did not necessarily carry fascist connotations in prewar Poland. For instance, Falanga was also the name of a Polish film company.

6. Zygmunt Przetakiewicz, *Od ONR-u do PAX-u* (Warsaw: Wydawnictwo Książka Polska, 1994), 13–14.

7. Bolesław Piasecki, *Duch czasów nowych a Ruch Młodych* (Warsaw, 1935), 6–11.

8. Ibid., 15–18.

9. Ibid., 19–24.

10. Ibid., 26–30.

11. Ibid., 30–31.

12. Ibid., 32–36.

13. Ibid., 40–45.

14. Ibid., 55–63.

15. Brian Porter, *When Nationalism Began to Hate* (New York: Oxford University Press, 2000), 223.

16. Payne, *History of Fascism,* 272.

17. Paul A. Hanebrink, *In Defense of Christian Hungary: Religion, Nationalism, and Antisemitism, 1890–1944* (Ithaca, N.Y.: Cornell University Press, 2006), 141–43.

18. Constantin Iordachi, "God's Chosen Warriors: Romania," in *Comparative Fascist Studies: New Perspectives,* ed. Constantin Iordachi (London: Routledge, 2010), 339–52.

19. On Léon Degrelle, see Martin Conway, *Collaboration in Belgium: Léon Degrelle and the Rexist Movement, 1940–1944* (New Haven, Conn.: Yale University Press, 1993).

20. On Mounier's flirtation with fascism, see Zeev Sternhell, *Neither Right nor Left: Fascist Ideology in France* (Berkeley: University of California Press, 1986), 215–19, 276–91.

21. *Sztafeta,* May 13, 1935.

22. *Falanga* reprinted Piasecki's article in June 1939, shortly before the outbreak of World War II. See Antoni Dudek and Grzegorz Pytel, *Bolesław Piasecki: Próba biografii politycznej* (London: Aneks, 1990), 62.

23. According to Sznarbachowski, who served in the army at the same time, such sentiments were particularly evident among junior officers. See Sznarbachowski, *300 lat wspomnień,* 130.

24. This temporary collective included Cimoszyński, Dziarmaga, Kwasieborski, Reutt, Staniszkis (designated by Piasecki as his deputy), Szpakowski, and Wasiutyński. Szymon Rudnicki, *Obóz Narodowo-Radykalny: Geneza i działalność* (Warsaw: Czytelnik, 1985), 281; Dudek and Pytel, *Bolesław Piasecki,* 57.

25. Quoted in Dudek and Pytel, *Bolesław Piasecki*, 57.

26. Jacek Majchrowski, *Geneza politycznych ugrupowań katolickich: Stronnictwo Pracy, grupa "Dziś i Jutro"* (Paris: Libella, 1986), 115; Andrzej Micewski, *Współrządzić czy nie kłamać? Pax i Znak w Polsce, 1945–1976* (Paris: Libella, 1978), 14.

27. AAN, KRZ, 297-VII-8, February 1938; AAN, KRZ, 297-VII-9, September 1938.

28. Sznarbachowski, *300 lat wspomnień*, 152.

29. AAN, KRZ, 297-VII-8, Miesięczne sprawozdania sytuacyjne, April 1938; Rudnicki, *Obóz Narodowo-Radykalny*, 282.

30. Jerzy Borejsza, *Mussolini był pierwszy* (Warsaw: Czytelnik, 1979), 232.

31. In his letter to the Italian Ministry of Culture, Arone praised Piasecki's press for "the utmost comprehension and enthusiasm for fascism." Ibid., 235–38.

32. *Ruch młodych* 1 (October 1935).

33. *Falanga*, July 12, 1936.

34. Led by young National Democrat Adam Doboszyński, the anti-Semitic "march on Myślenice" constituted a small nationalist insurrection. The rioters, mostly local peasants, armed themselves and took control of the town. Police restored order only after a gun battle with Doboszyński's men.

35. Szymon Rudnicki, "Anti-Jewish Legislation in Interwar Poland," in *Antisemitism and Its Opponents in Modern Poland*, ed. Robert Blobaum (Ithaca, N.Y.: Cornell University Press, 2005), 148–70.

36. AAN, Komisariat Rządu Miasta Stołecznego Warszawy, 297-VII-14, Sprawozdania kwartalne z życia polskich legalnych stowarzyszeń i związków, April 1936.

37. Przetakiewicz, *Od ONR-u do PAX-u*, 20.

38. Onufry Kopczyński, "Narodowa rewolucja kulturalna," *Ruch młodych* 11 (November 1936): 2.

39. The episode of the Committee of the Young Press constitutes one of the least-known chapters in the biography of Jerzy Giedroyc, founder of a literary institute in Paris and the review *Kultura*, the most prestigious Polish émigré periodical after World War II. On Giedroyc, see Timothy Snyder, *The Reconstruction of Nations: Poland, Ukraine, Lithuania, Belarus, 1569–1999* (New Haven, Conn.: Yale University Press, 2003), 217–31.

40. *Falanga*, November 15, 1936.

41. *Falanga*, November 25, 1936.

42. Przetakiewicz, *Od ONR-u do PAX-u*, 22–23.

43. Rudnicki, "Anti-Jewish Legislation," 165–66.

44. Piasecki's call for the creation of Polish colonies echoed Sanacja's feeble and often grotesque attempts to gain overseas possessions in places like Brazil, Liberia, and the former German empire.

45. Bolesław Piasecki, *Wytyczne Narodowo-Radykalnej myśli gospodarczej* (Warsaw, 1937), 4–8.

46. *Zasady programu Narodowo-Radykalnego* (Warsaw, 1937), 2–8.

47. Ibid., 8–9.

48. Ibid., 15–16.

49. Quoted in *Ruch młodych* 5 (May 1937): 10–12.

50. Ibid., 11.

51. Wojciech Kwasieborski, "Problem polityki katolikiej," *Ruch młodych* 1 (January 1937): 22–26.

52. Kondrad Sadkowski, "Clerical Nationalism and Antisemitism: Catholic Priests, Jews, and Orthodox Christians in the Lublin Region, 1918–1939," in Blobaum, *Antisemitism and Its Opponents in Modern Poland*, 172.

53. Michael Mann, *Fascists* (Cambridge: Cambridge University Press, 2004), 45.

54. Edward D. Wynot, Jr., *Polish Politics in Transition: The Camp of National Unity and the Struggle for Power, 1935–1939* (Athens: University of Georgia Press, 1974), 50–51.

55. Jacek Majchrowski, *Silni-zwarci-gotowi: Myśl polityczna Obozu Zjednoczenia Narodowego* (Warsaw: PWN, 1985), 35–36.

56. Edward Rydz-Śmigły, *Byście o sile nie zapomnieli: Rozkazy, artykuły, mowy, 1904–1936* (Warsaw: Książnica Atlas, 1936), 257–61.

57. Wynot, *Polish Politics in Transition*, 61.

58. Antony Polonsky, *Politics in Independent Poland, 1921–1939: The Crisis of Constitutional Government* (Oxford: Clarendon, 1972), 423–24.

59. Majchrowski, *Silni-zwarci-gotowi*, 49.

60. On the "nationalizing state," see Rogers Brubaker, *Nationalism Reframed: Nationalism and the National Question in the New Europe* (Cambridge: Cambridge University Press, 1996), 84–103.

61. AAN, Instytucje Wojskowe 1918–1939. Ministerstwo Spraw Wojskowych. Gabinet Ministra—Komunikaty Informacyjne Wydziału Bezpieczeństwa, 296-III-37, Komunikat informacyjny nr. 28, March 2, 1937; *Ruch młodych* 2 (February 1937): 2.

62. Majchrowski, *Geneza politycznych ugrupowań katolickich*, 115.

63. Przetakiewicz, *Od ONR-u do PAX-u*, 24; Wasiutyński, *Prawą stroną labiryntu*, 163; Sznarbachowski, *300 lat wspomnień*, 130.

64. Open Society Archives (HU OSA), Records of the Polish Unit. Polish Bio Files, Bolesław Piasecki, item no. 7819–55—Bolesław Piasecki's collaboration with Rydz-Śmigły regime, September 16, 1955.

65. Wojciech Wasiutyński, *Czwarte pokolenie* (London: Odnowa, 1982), 74.

66. *Falanga*, May 9, 1937; Przetakiewicz, *Od ONR-u do PAX-u*, 24.

67. *Warszawski dziennik narodowy*, May 2, 1937.

68. Bolesław Piasecki, *Przełom narodowy* (Warsaw, 1937), 3–5.

69. In the city of Radom, RNR activists broke into the Adventist church and "lectured" them about the harmfulness of their religious beliefs. *Falanga*, September 14, 1937.

70. Quoted in Majchrowski, *Silni-zwarci-gotowi*, 168.

71. *Ruch młodych* 7–8 (July–August 1937): 5–6.

72. Bogusław Miedziński, "Sprostowanie spoza grobu," *Zeszyty historyczne* 22 (1972): 144; HU OSA, Records of the Polish Unit, Polish Bio Files, Bolesław Piasecki, item no. 7819/55, Bolesław Piasecki's collaboration with Rydz-Śmigły regime.

73. Wynot, *Polish Politics in Transition*, 147.

74. Majchrowski, *Silni-zwarci-gotowi*, 166.

75. Sznarbachowski, *300 lat wspomnień*, 148–49.

76. Majchrowski, *Geneza politycznych ugrupowań katolickich*, 116.

77. Tadeusz Jędruszczak and Artur Leiwand, eds., *Archiwum polityczne Ignacego Paderewskiego* (Wrocław: Ossolineum, 1974), 4:149–50.

78. Ibid., 149.

79. Majchrowski, *Geneza politycznych ugrupowań katolickich*, 118.

80. During World War II, Modelski remained Sikorski's trusted aide, and in 1940 he drafted a report about the causes of Polish defeat in 1939, in which he blamed Sanacja and proposed courts-martial and detention camps for the regime's survivors and sympathizers.

81. Andrzej Ajnenkiel, *Polska po przewrocie majowym* (Warsaw: PWN, 1980), 571.

82. *Falanga*, November 9, 23, 1937.

83. Sznarbachowski, *300 lat wspomnień*, 134.

84. Dudek and Pytel, *Bolesław Piasecki*, 88.

85. Stanisław Cat-Mackiewicz, "Bolesław Piasecki—znak zapytania w życiu naszem," *Słowo*, November 2, 1937.

86. *Falanga*, December 7, 1937; Dudek and Pytel, *Bolesław Piasecki*, 89.

87. Bolesław Piasecki, "Trzy czynniki siły Ruchu Narodowo-Radykalnego," *Ruch młodych* 1 (January 1938): 1–3.

88. Miedziński, "Sprostowanie spoza grobu," 144.

89. Wynot, *Polish Politics in Transition*, 183.

90. Mann, *Fascists*, 45.

91. Rudnicki, "Anti-Jewish Legislation," 160–61, 164, 168.

92. Wasiutyński, *Prawą stroną labiryntu*, 94, 103; Dudek and Pytel, *Bolesław Piasecki*, 93.

93. *Falanga*, May 15, 1938.

94. AAN, KRZ, 297-VII-9, Miesięczne sprawozdania sytuacyjne, December 1938.

95. AAN, KRZ, 297-VII-9, Miesięczne sprawozdania sytuacyjne, June 1938.

96. *Falanga*, June 28, 1938.

97. Ibid.

98. *Falanga,* May 15, 1938.

99. *Falanga,* May 10, 1938.

100. *Falanga,* May 24, 1938.

101. *Falanga,* October 2, 1938; AAN, KRZ, 297-VII-9, Miesięczne sprawozdania sytuacyjne, September 1938.

102. Polonsky, *Politics in Independent Poland,* 442.

103. AAN, KRZ, 297-VII-9, Miesięczne sprawozdania sytuacyjne, December 1938.

104. AAN, KRZ, 297-VII-13, Wydział Bezpieczeństwa Publicznego, Sprawozdania miesięczne, January and February 1939.

105. Sznarbachowski, *300 lat wspomnień,* 138–42.

106. Ibid., 176.

107. Stanisław Brochwicz, *Bohaterowie czy zdrajcy? Wspomnienia więźnia politycznego* (Warsaw: Wydawnictwo Nowoczesne, 1940), 53, 57.

108. Sznarbachowski, *300 lat wspomnień,* 165–69.

109. Brochwicz, *Bohaterowie czy zdrajcy,* 64.

110. Przetakiewicz, *Od ONR-u do PAX-u,* 31–32.

111. Wasiutyński, *Prawą stroną labiryntu,* 114.

112. AAN, Halina Krahelska—spuścizna, 383-II-3, dzienniki, March 3, 1940.

113. Polonsky, *Politics in Independent Poland,* 508.

114. William W. Hagen, "Before the 'Final Solution': Toward a Comparative Analysis of Political Anti-Semitism in Interwar Germany and Poland," *Journal of Modern History* 68 (June 1996): 352.

115. *Falanga,* April 11–18, 1937.

116. Alfred Łaszowski, "Papierowa rewolucja," *Ruch młodych* 11 (November–December 1937): 30.

117. *Falanga,* June 7, 1938.

118. *Ruch młodych* 3 (March 1936): 5.

119. *Falanga,* August 14–21, 1938.

120. *Falanga,* May 16, 1937.

121. Jan Józef Lipski, *Katolickie państwo narodu polskiego* (London: Aneks, 1994), 152.

Chapter 3: The War Years, 1939–44

1. Tadeusz Kutrzeba, *Bitwa nad Bzurą* (Warsaw: MON, 1957), 481.

2. Tadeusz Jurga, *Obrona Polski, 1939* (Warsaw: PAX, 1990), 744–46.

3. Rajmund Szubiński, *Polska broń pancerna, 1939* (Warsaw: MON, 1982), 256–61.

4. HU OSA, Records of the Polish Unit, Bio Files: Bolesław Piasecki, item no. 15559/56—Bolesław Piasecki "Progressive Catholic" Leader, February 13, 1956.

5. Jurga, *Obrona Polski*, 686.

6. Antoni Dudek and Grzegorz Pytel, *Bolesław Piasecki: Próba biografii politycznej* (London: Aneks, 1990), 107.

7. After the collapse of France in 1940, the phrase referring to the General Gouvernement as "the Polish occupied territories" was deleted.

8. AAN, Delegatura Rządu na Kraj, 202-II-22, Uwagi do raportu t. Próby utworzenia polskiego ruchu narodowo-socjalistycznego w 1939–1940.

9. For more on Studnicki, see Mikołaj Kunicki, "Unwanted Collaborators: Leon Kozłowski, Władysław Studnicki, and the Problem of Collaboration among Polish Conservative Politicians in World War II," *European Review of History* 8, no. 2 (2001): 203–20.

10. Tomasz Szarota, *U progu zagłady: Zajścia antyżydowskie i pogromy w okupowanej Europie* (Warsaw: Wydawnictwo Sic!, 2000), 50–64.

11. Fred Taylor, ed., *The Goebbels Diaries, 1939–1941* (New York: Penguin, 1982), 25.

12. On the ideological background of the Nazi invasion, see Alexander B. Rossino, *Hitler Strikes Poland: Blitzkrieg, Ideology, and Atrocity* (Lawrence: University Press of Kansas, 2003).

13. Mark Mazower, *Hitler's Empire: How the Nazis Ruled Europe* (New York: Penguin, 2008), 73.

14. Włodzimierz Sznarbachowski, *300 lat wspomnień* (London: Aneks, 1997), 190–94.

15. Zygmunt Przetakiewicz, *Od ONR-u do PAX-u* (Warsaw: Wydawnictwo Książka Polska, 1994), 53.

16. Dudek and Pytel, *Bolesław Piasecki*, 110.

17. Kunicki, "Unwanted Collaborators," 206.

18. *Dziś i jutro*, October 31, 1948.

19. In her wartime diaries, left-wing social activist Halina Krahelska reported that Piasecki led the organization from the underground, while Świetlicki acted as a titular leader. AAN, Halina Krahelska—spuścizna, 383-II-3, 158.

20. AAN, Delegatura Rządu na Kraj, 202-II-22, Uwagi do raportu t. Próby utworzenia polskiego ruchu narodowo-socjalistycznego w 1939–1940.

21. On Brochwicz's arrest, see chapter 2.

22. Luciana Frassati, *Il Destino passa per Varsavia* (Milan: Bompiani, 1985), 90.

23. Ibid.

24. Luciana Frassati-Gawrońska (1902–2007) received numerous Polish decorations for her services. In 1993, President Lech Wałęsa awarded her the Polish Republic's Medal of Merit with Star, one of the highest Polish honors.

25. Frassati, *Il Destino*, 91.

26. Ibid., 93.

27. Ibid., 94–96.

28. Sznarbachowski, *300 lat wspomnień*, 196.

29. R. J. B. Bosworth, *Mussolini* (London: Hodder Education, 2002), 363.

30. Cimoszyński died in combat in 1939. Szpakowski was killed at Katyń. Marian Reutt, who joined the Home Army, died in Gross-Rosen in January 1945. Przetakiewicz served in the Polish armed forces in the West.

31. Stefan Korboński, *The Polish Underground State* (New York: Hippocrene, 1981), 15–33.

32. The Central Committee of Organizations for Independence was the creation of Ryszard Świętochowski, a confidant of General Sikorski. The tactic of tolerating two rival organizations, each claiming a mandate from the government in exile, was abandoned in the spring of 1940 when Sikorski authorized the ZWZ to unify the clandestine forces. Ibid., 41.

33. On the National Armed Forces, see Zbigniew S. Siemaszko, *Narodowe Siły Zbrojne* (London: Odnowa, 1982).

34. HIA, Tadeusz Komorowski Collection, box 4, file Zestawienie ugrupowań politycznych i odpowiednich im organizacji wojskowych, January 1942, 5.

35. Kazimierz Krajewski, *Uderzeniowe Bataliony Kadrowe, 1942–1944* (Warsaw: PAX, 1993), 36–37.

36. Leon Całka [Bolesław Piasecki], *Wielka ideologia narodu polskiego* (Warsaw, 1940), 2.

37. Ibid., 7–9, 13.

38. Ibid., 11.

39. Ibid., 15.

40. Ibid., 18–19.

41. Ibid., 19–20.

42. Istvan Deak, "Hungary," in *The European Right: A Historical Profile*, ed. Hans Rogger and Eugen Weber (Berkeley: University of California Press, 1965), 393.

43. Michael Mann, *Fascists* (Cambridge: Cambridge University Press, 2004), 246.

44. Całka, *Wielka ideologia*, 17.

45. Krajewski, *Uderzeniowe Bataliony Kadrowe*, 37.

46. HIA, Tadeusz Komorowski Collection, box 4, file Zestawienie ugrupowań politycznych i odpowiednich im organizacji wojskowych, October 1, 1941, 5–6; HIA, Tadeusz Komorowski Collection, box 5, Zestawienie ugrupowań politcznych. Załącznik II. Ugrupowania narodowo-centrowe, July 1942, 4–5.

47. AAN, Opracowania, 76-III-56, 1; AAN, Konfederacja Narodu, 336-II, Raporty sprawozdawcze, September 22, 1942.

48. HIA, Tadeusz Komorowski Collection, box 5, file Zestawienie ugrupowań politycznych. Załącznik II. Ugrupowania Narodowo-Centrowe, July 1942; *Fakty na tle idei*, November 15, 1941; *Do broni*, June 29, 1942.

49. *Nowa Polska,* May 31, 1941.

50. Andrzej Paczkowski, *Pół wieku dziejów Polski, 1939–1989* (Warsaw: PWN, 1998), 66–67.

51. *Fakty na tle idei,* September 15, 1941.

52. *Nowa Polska,* August 19, 1941.

53. *Nowa Polska,* January 20, 1942.

54. In the summer of 1942, *Nowa Polska* did not hesitate to declare Sikorski's political entourage an enemy to be fought for the good of Poland. *Nowa Polska,* June 3, 1942.

55. HIA, Tadeusz Komorowski Collection, box 5, file Sytuacja wewnętrzno-polityczna nr. 3/41, December 10, 1941, 4; AAN, 76-III-56, 4.

56. AAN, 336-II, 60–62.

57. AAN, Konfederacja Narodu, 336-II, Dowództwo Dzielnicy Polski Centralnej i Północnej, Raport lustracyjny,"February 4, 1942.

58. AAN, 336-II, 63; AAN, 336-I, 60–62.

59. AAN, 336-II, Wytyczne do programu kursu dla młodych dowódców, 1942.

60. AAN, 336-II, Nowe ogólne wytyczne szkoleniowe "Pionu Uderzeniowego," February 25, 1942.

61. Zofia Kobylańska, *Konfederacja Narodu w Warszawie* (Warsaw: PAX, 1999), 176.

62. Ibid., 123–24.

63. HIA, Jan Karski Collection, box 2, folder 4, Prasa tajna, 4.

64. None of them survived the war. Wacław Bojarski died in a German prison in June 1943. Andrzej Trzebiński was killed in mass execution in November 1943. Tadeusz Gajcy was killed in action during the Warsaw Uprising in August 1944.

65. Jan Kott, "Zły wygląd," *Gazeta wyborcza,* March 24–25, 2001.

66. Maciej z Gdańska, "Czarna sprawa," *Nowa Polska,* October 15, 1941.

67. AAN, Konfederacja Narodu, 336-I, Życie i Śmierć dla Polski, 1942.

68. "Inny świat," *Do broni,* August 11, 1942.

69. "Likwidacja żydostwa," *Nowa Polska,* August 12, 1942.

70. "Trzeci front w Warszawie," *Nowa Polska,* May 5, 1943.

71. AAN, Konfederacja Narodu, 336-I, Życie i Śmierć dla Polski, 1942.

72. AAN, Konfederacja Narodu, 336-II, Rozkaz nr. 3 dla Komendy Pionu Uderzeniowego, n.p., n.d.

73. AAN, Konfederacja Narodu, 336-II, Welanowski, Analiza do rozkazu uderzenia, Warsaw, February 5, 1942.

74. Wojciech z Królewca, "Wojna w Polsce czy wojna dla Polski," *Nowa Polska,* December 23, 1942.

75. Norman Naimark, *Fires of Hatred* (Cambridge, Mass.: Harvard University Press, 2001), 123–24.

76. Dudek and Pytel, *Bolesław Piasecki,* 127.

77. Wojciech z Królewca, "Po przezwyciężeniu samych siebie—zwycięstwo," *Nowa Polska*, November 15, 1941; Wojciech z Królewca, "Bolszewicy w granicach Polski—to walka," *Nowa Polska*, January 20, 1942.

78. AAN, Konfederacja Narodu, 336-II, Rozkaz nr. 5/42, Warsaw, March 14, 1942.

79. Krajewski, *Uderzeniowe Bataliony Kadrowe*, 53.

80. AAN, Konfederacja Narodu, 336-I, Wołkowyski, Raport z podróży organizacyjnej odbytej dnia 10–13.02.42, February 15, 1942.

81. AAN, Konfederacja Narodu, 336-I, Komendant Roch, Raport nr. 1, Biała Podlaska, March 5, 1942.

82. AAN, Armia Krajowa. Komenda Główna—Oddział II, 203-III-128, Report on the KN, February 15, 1943.

83. HIA, Jan Karski Collection, box 2, folder 4, Karski's report on the KN action, n.p., n.d.

84. Krajewski, *Uderzeniowe Bataliony Kadrowe*, 77; AAN, Konfederacja Narodu, 336-II, Report on the expedition to the Sterdyńskie woods, 1942.

85. Wojciech z Królewca, "Oczekiwanie i czyn," *Nowa Polska*, November 11, 1942.

86. AAN, Konfederacja Narodu, 336-II, Report on the expedition to the Sterdyńskie woods, 1942.

87. AAN, Konfederacja Narodu, 336-II, Report on the expedition to the Sterdyńskie woods, 1942; Krajewski, *Uderzeniowe Bataliony Kadrowe*, 86.

88. According to one version, German patrols found the partisans while combing the area for Jews in hiding (Krajewski, *Uderzeniowe Bataliony Kadrowe*, 89). By another account, the Poles were betrayed by Nazi informers (AAN, Konfederacja Narodu, 336-II, Report on the expedition to the Sterdyńskie woods, 1942).

89. AAN, Konfederacja Narodu, 336-II, Report on the expedition to the Sterdyńskie woods, 1942; Krajewski, *Uderzeniowe Bataliony Kadrowe*, 94.

90. AAN, Konfederacja Narodu, 336-II, Report on the expedition to the Sterdyńskie woods, 1942.

91. Rowecki to Sikorski, Meldunek organizacyjny nr. 190 za czas od 1.IX.42 do 1.III.43, March 1, 1943, published in *Armia Krajowa w dokumentach, 1939–1945* (Wrocław: Ossolineum, 1990), 2:452.

92. *Nowa Polska*, May 5, 1943.

93. In one encounter, Piasecki's forces wiped out a People's Guard detachment, killing nineteen communist partisans. AWIH, Armia Krajowa, Obszar Białystok, III/32/12, Partyzantka polska, 1943; Krajewski, *Uderzeniowe Bataliony Kadrowe*, 176.

94. Władysław Pobóg-Malinowski, *Najnowsza historia polityczna Polski*, vol. 2, *Okres 1939–1945* (Gdansk: Oficyna Wydawnicza "Graf," 1989), 309–403.

95. Rowecki to Sikorski, January 12, 1943, in *Armia Krajowa w dokumentach,* 2:401–4.

96. Sikorski to Rowecki, February 6, 1943, in ibid., 2:412–14.

97. Rowecki to Sikorski, June 19, 1944, in ibid., 3:28–32.

98. Pobóg-Malinowski, *Najnowsza historia Polski,* 1:405–6; Paczkowski, *Pół wieku dziejów Polski,* 110.

99. AWIH, Armia Krajowa, Komenda Główna Oddział I, Materiały dotyczące struktury organizacyjnej oddziałów i wcielenia do AK Konferederacji Narodu, III/21/4, Komendant Sił Zbrojnych w Kraju, L.DZ.109/I, August 17, 1943.

100. AWIH, Armia Krajowa, Obszar Białystok, III/32/15, Bekas, July 30, 1943; AWIH, Armia Krajowa, Obszar Białystok, III/32/12, Raport sabotażowo-dywersyjny za miesiąc listopad 43 r, Pełnia, December 5, 1943.

101. AAN, Opracowania, 76/II-56, 6; Krajewski, *Uderzeniowe Bataliony Kadrowe,* 290.

102. Dudek and Pytel, *Bolesław Piasecki,* 139; Krajewski, *Uderzeniowe Bataliony Kadrowe,* 332–60.

103. Wincenty Borodziewicz, "Rozmowy polsko-litewskie w Wilnie, 1942–1944," *Przegląd historyczny* 1 (1989): 328–29.

104. AAN, Delegatura Rządu na Kraj, Departament Spraw Wewnętrznych, Biuro Wschodnie, 202/II-49, quoted in ibid., 329.

105. Krajewski, *Uderzeniowe Bataliony Kadrowe,* 376–80.

106. Jan Erdman, *Droga do Ostrej Bramy* (London: Odnowa, 1984), 242.

107. Ibid., 276–77.

108. Komorowski to Sosnkowski, Meldunek organizacyjny nr. 240 za okres od 1.IX.43 do 29.II.44," March 1, 1944, in *Armia Krajowa w dokumentach,* 3:343.

109. Wojciech z Królewca, "Decyzja Polska," *Do broni,* January 25, 1944.

110. Komorowski to Sosnkowski, Depesza—szyfr. Rozkaz do Akcji Burza, November 26, 1943, in *Armia Krajowa w dokumentach,* 3:209–13; Korboński, *Polish Underground State,* 153–54.

111. "Tezy programowe Nowej Polski," *Nowa Polska,* May 15, 1944.

112. Włodzimierz z Halicza, "Polityka w prasie," *Nowa Polska,* May 5, 1943.

113. Erdman, *Droga do Ostrej Bramy,* 259–60.

114. Ibid., 246–55.

115. Józef Świda, "Wyjaśnienia dotyczące okresu, 1943–1944," *Zeszyty historyczne* 73 (1983): 74–80.

116. Such was the case of Adolf Pilch. Like Świda, Pilch concluded a non-aggression pact with the Germans, who in December 1943 supplied him with two heavy machine guns, four mortars, and ammunition. Erdman, *Droga do Ostrej Bramy,* 252.

117. Borodziewicz, "Rozmowy polsko-litewskie w Wilnie," 317–37.

118. Romuald J. Misiunas and Rein Taagepera, *The Baltic States: Years of Dependence, 1940–1990* (Berkeley: University of California Press, 1993), 59; Borodziewicz, "Rozmowy polsko-litewskie w Wilnie," 334–35.

119. Erdman, *Droga do Ostrej Bramy,* 315, 324.

120. AAN, Opracowania, 76/III-56, 9.

121. Dudek and Pytel, *Bolesław Piasecki,* 138.

122. Erdman, *Droga do Ostrej Bramy,* 278–79.

123. Ibid., 331.

124. Ibid., 319–21.

125. Ibid., 332.

126. Krajewski, *Uderzeniowe Bataliony Kadrowe,* 486–87.

127. Krzyżanowski to Komorowski, July 10, 1944, in *Armia Krajowa w dokumentach,* 3:512.

128. Krzyżanowski to Komorowski, July 15, 1944, ibid., 3:560.

129. Colonel Ignacy Blumski to the AK High Command, July 17, 1944, ibid., 3:561.

130. Erdman, *Droga do Ostrej Bramy,* 413–16.

131. Krajewski, *Uderzeniowe Bataliony Kadrowe,* 491.

132. Ryszard Reiff, *Gra o życie* (Warsaw: Unicorn, 1993), 16; Wojciech Kętrzyński's testimony, in Erdman, *Droga do Ostrej Bramy,* 369.

133. Instytut Pamięci Narodowej (IPN), Teczka osobowa Bolesława Piaseckiego, IPN 0259/6, Protokół dochodzenia, November 14, 1944; Reiff, *Gra o życie,* 19.

134. IPN, Teczka osobowa Bolesława Piaseckiego, IPN 0259/6, Protokół dochodzenia, November 14, 1944.

135. Jarosław Piasecki, interview by author, Warsaw, September 24, 2002.

136. IPN, Teczka osobowa Bolesława Piaseckiego, IPN 0259/6, Protokół oględzin dowodów rzeczowych, May 19, 1945.

137. IPN, Teczka osobowa Bolesława Piaseckiego, IPN 0259/6, Protokół dochodzenia, November 15, 1944; Reiff, *Gra o życie,* 60.

138. IPN, Teczka osobowa Bolesława Piaseckiego, IPN 0259/6, Protokół dochodzenia, November 16, 1944.

139. IPN, Teczka osobowa Bolesława Piaseckiego, IPN 0259/6, Protokół dochodzenia, Ryszard Romanowski's confession, November 17, 1944.

140. IPN, Teczka osobowa Bolesława Piaseckiego, IPN 0259/6, k.1.

Chapter 4: Under the Cross and the Red Flag, 1945–56

1. Tony Judt, *Postwar: A History of Europe since 1945* (New York: Penguin, 2005), 48.

2. Ryszard Reiff, *Gra o życie* (Warsaw: Unicorn, 1993), 215–16.

3. Brian Porter, *When Nationalism Began to Hate* (New York: Oxford University Press, 2000), 220–21.

4. A. F. Noskova, ed., *Iz Varshavy: Moskva, tovarishchu Beriia; Dokumenty NKVD SSSR o pol'skom podpol'ye, 1944–1945 gg.* (Moscow: Sibirskii Khronograf, 2001), 96–97.

5. Investigators from the Institute for National Remembrance who searched the former NKVD villa in Włochy found numerous inscriptions on the building's walls, one of which read: "I was locked up here—Bolesław Piasecki." See Michał Maciej Piotrowski, "Pamiątki po generale Sierowie," *Rzeczpospolita*, October 2, 2001.

6. IPN, Teczka osobowa Bolesława Piaseckiego, IPN 0259/6, Protokół dochodzenia, November 15, 1944, k.39–44.

7. Serov stayed in Lublin from August 1944 to February 1945. See Nikita Petrov, *Ivan Serov: Pervyi predsedatel' KGB* (Moscow: Materik, 2005), 35–39.

8.Jarosław Piasecki, interview by author, August 23, 2004.

9. HU OSA, Records of the Polish Unit, Bio Files: Józef Światło, transcript of "Inside Story of Bezpieka and the Party," September 1, 1955.

10. Teresa Torańska, *Oni* (London: Aneks, 1985), 285.

11. Władysław Gomułka, *Pamiętniki*, ed. Andrzej Werblan (Warsaw: BGW, 1995), 2:517.

12. Archiwum Dokumentacji Historycznej PRL, Jan Ptasiński's unpublished manuscript, 189.

13. IPN, Teczka osobowa Bolesława Piaseckiego, IPN 0259/6, Osobiste oświadczenia Bolesława Piaseckiego, May 22, 1945, k.100.

14. IPN BU MBP 283, quoted in Romuald Niedzielko and Bartłomiej Noszczak, "Bolesława Piaseckiego przepustka do wolności," *Przegląd powszechny* 5 (May 2006): 98–107.

15. Ibid., 107–10.

16. IPN 0259/6, "Postanowienie o przekazaniu materiałów śledczych," April 10, 1945.

17. IPN 0259/6, Piasecki's statement, May 22, 1945.

18. IPN 0259/6, Osobiste oświadczenie Bolesława Piaseckiego, May 22, 1945.

19. Krystyna Kersten, *The Establishment of Communist Rule in Poland, 1943–1948* (Berkeley: University of California Press, 1991), 130.

20. The sixteen arrested included General Okulicki; the government delegate Jan Jankowski; members of the Home Council of Ministers Adam Bień, Antoni Pajdak, and Stanisław Jasiukowicz; and leaders of the Democratic, National, Peasant, and Socialist parties. Okulicki, Jankowski, and Jasiukowicz died in Soviet prison.

21. Antoni Dudek, *Państwo i Kościół w Polsce, 1945–1970* (Kraków: Wydawnictwo PiT, 1995), 7.

22. Kersten, *Establishment of Communist Rule*, 212.

23. See, e.g., AAN, Sekretariat KC PPR, 295/VII-43, List pasterski biskupa katowickiego księdza doktora Stanisława Adamskiego, February 18, 1945.

24. Michał Jagiełło, *Próba rozmowy: Szkice o katolicyzmie odrodzeniowym i "Tygodniku Powszechnym," 1945–1953* (Warsaw: Biblioteka Narodowa, 2001), 2:7.

25. Jerzy Giedroyc, *Autobiografia na cztery ręce* (Warsaw: Czytelnik, 1994), 49.

26. HIA, Tadeusz Komorowski Collection, box 5, folder Załącznik X. Charakterystyka ogólna położenia politycznego w kraju za okres do września 1941 r., July 1942.

27. Stefan Kisielewski, *Abecadło Kisiela* (Warsaw: Oficyna Wydawnicza INTERIM, 1990), 11.

28. Jerzy Borejsza's report is in Andrzej Micewski, *Katolicy w potrzasku* (Warsaw: BGW, 1993), 22–29.

29. Wojciech Kętrzyński, "Na przełomie 1944–1945," *Więź* 11 (November–December 1967): 164–70.

30. Archiwum Katolickiego Stowarzyszenia Civitas Christiana (AKS CC), I/90, Memoriał przedstawiony Tow. Gomułce w lipcu 1945.

31. Inessa Iazhborovskaia, "The Gomułka Alternative: The Untravelled Road," in *The Establishment of Communist Regimes in Eastern Europe, 1944–1949*, ed. Norman Naimark and Leonid Gibianskii (Boulder: Westview, 1997), 126–35.

32. Gomułka, *Pamiętniki*, 2:516–17.

33. Jacek Majchrowski, *Geneza politycznych ugrupowań katolickich: Stronni-ctwo Pracy, grupa "Dziś i Jutro"* (Paris: Libella, 1984), 156.

34. Antoni Dudek and Grzegorz Pytel, *Bolesław Piasecki: Próba biografii politycznej* (London: Aneks, 1990), 161.

35. Kersten, *Establishment of Communist Rule*, 212.

36. Ibid., 205–6.

37. See appropriate sections in the firsthand accounts and memoirs of PSL, SP, and PPS leaders: Stefan Korboński, *Warsaw in Chains* (London: Allen and Unwin, 1959); Karol Popiel, *Od Brześcia do Polonii* (London: Odnowa, 1967); Zygmunt Żuławski, *Wspomnienia* (Warsaw: Nowa, 1980).

38. IPN, IPN 0648/49 t.1, Informacja dot. Stowarzyszenia PAX ze szczególnym uwzględnieniem okresu 1956–1960, Warsaw, December 12, 1961.

39. Mikołaj Rostworowski, *Słowo o PAX-ie* (Warsaw: PAX, 1968), 24–25. Jerzy Pietrzak raises doubts about Hlond's donation in "Prymas Polski kardynał August Hlond a grupa katolików 'Dziś i Jutro,'" in *Komu służył PAX*, ed. Sabina Bober (Warsaw: PAX, 2008), 96.

40. When Piasecki sent his associates to meet Hlond in Poznań in October 1945, he chose Bieńkowski and Dobraczyński, whom the primate had known since the 1930s. Jan Dobraczyński, *Tylko w jednym życiu* (Warsaw: PAX, 1970), 363.

41. Pietrzak, "Prymas Polski kardynał August Hlond a grupa katolików 'Dziś i Jutro,'" 95.

42. Ibid., 98.

43. IPN 0648/46, t.1, security police report on *Dziś i jutro* and *Tygodnik Powszechny*, n.d., k.184.

44. Jagiełło, *Próba rozmowy*, 2:25.

45. Ibid., 2:52.

46. Bolesław Piasecki, "Po prostu," *Dziś i jutro*, November 25, 1945.

47. Bolesław Piasecki, "Zagadnienia istotne," *Dziś i jutro*, November 25, 1945.

48. Bolesław Piasecki, "Kierunki," *Dziś i jutro*, January 20, 1946.

49. Bolesław Piasecki, "Kierunki," *Dziś i jutro*, February 3, 1946.

50. Bolesław Piasecki, "Kierunki," *Dziś i jutro*, March 17, 1946.

51. On the phenomenon of Western European Left Catholicism, see Gerd-Rainer Horn and Emmanuel Gerard, eds., *Left Catholicism: Catholics and Society in Western Europe at the Point of Liberation, 1943–1955* (Leuven: Leuven University Press, 2001).

52. On Mounier, see John Hellman, *Emmanuel Mounier and the New Catholic Left, 1930–1950* (Toronto: University of Toronto Press, 1981).

53. Horn and Gerard, *Left Catholicism*, 30, 61.

54. Emmanuel Mounier, *Be Not Afraid: A Denunciation of Despair*, trans. Cynthia Rowland (New York: Sheed and Ward, 1951), 172–73.

55. Piotr Kosicki, "Promieniowanie Personalizmu: Mounier, 'Esprit,' i początki 'Więzi,'" *Więź* 2–3 (February–March 2008): 113–14.

56. Ibid., 114.

57. Kersten, *Establishment of Communist Rule*, 281–82.

58. AKS CC, I/91, Do Obywatela Wiesława Gomułki Vice-premiera Rządu, Warsaw, August 18, 1946.

59. AKS CC, I/91, Do Jego Eminencji Prymasa Polski Księdza Kardynała Augusta Hlonda, Warsaw, August 9, 1946.

60. Dobraczyński, *Tylko w jednym życiu*, 370.

61. *Rzeczpospolita*, November 20, 1946.

62. In September 1946, the bishops urged lay Catholics to vote only for candidates whose programs did not contest Catholic teachings. They also criticized "modern, allegedly democratic regimes that in their pursuit of absolute power ignored the opinion of their societies." AAN, KC PPR, 295/VII-43, Orędzie Episkopatu Polski w sprawie wyborów do Sejmu, September 10, 1946.

63. Wacław Bitner, the leader of a splinter faction that had provoked the breakup of the Labor Party, unsuccessfully tried to win the communists' support for his Catholic Social Movement. AAN, KC PPR, 295/VII-43, Katolicki Ruch Społeczny, December 8, 1946.

64. Dobraczyński, *Tylko w jednym życiu*, 372.

65. Ibid., 339.

66. Bolesław Piasecki, "Ruch nie nazwany," *Dziś i jutro*, April 6–13, 1947.

67. AKS CC, V-128, Bishop Stefan Wyszyński to the editors of *Dziś i jutro,* Lublin, January 30, 1947.

68. IPN, IPN 0648/155, Hlond to Bieńkowski, March 12, 1947.

69. Jagiełło, *Próba rozmowy,* 96.

70. Stanisław Stomma, "O pozornym maksymaliznie i urojonym defetyźmie," *Tygodnik powszechny,* April 20, 1947.

71. Stanisław Stomma and Jerzy Turowicz, "Katolicy w Polsce Ludowej," *Tygodnik powszechny,* December 10, 1947.

72. AKS CC, Sprawozdanie z działalności grupy 'Dziś i Jutro,' March 1948.

73. Kersten, *Establishment of Communist Rule,* 407.

74. Tomasz Łabuszewski and Kazimierz Krajewski, eds., *Od "Łupaszki" do "Młota," 1944–1949: Materiały źródłowe do dziejów V i VI Brygady Wileńskiej AK* (Warsaw: Oficyna Wydawnicza Volumen, 1994), 270–72, 285–305.

75. IPN, IPN 0648/46 t.3, Doniesienie agenturalne, May 20, 1948.

76. AKS CC, I/1, Bolesław Piasecki's Correspondence 1947–59, Jerzy Śmiechowski's letter, July 14, 1954. According to Piasecki's own estimates, some four hundred to five hundred Home Army men and women benefited from his interventions. AKS CC, Piasecki's speech of February 17, 1963.

77. In a conversation with the author, Andrzej Micewski dismissed these rumors as groundless. Andrzej Micewski, interview by author, tape recording, Warsaw, September 16, 2001.

78. Reiff, *Gra o życie,* 224–25.

79. Piasecki set a good example by marrying Barbara Kolendo, a sister of his close associate Janina Kolendo. They would have five children: Halina (1949–), Bożena (1951–), Marzenna (1952–), Zdzisław (1959–), and Ładysław (1961–). Jarosław Piasecki to the author, May 28, 2003.

80. IPN 0648/155, Request to the Ministry of Education, July 31, 1951; AKS CC, I/1, Bolesław Piasecki's correspondence 1947–1959, Bolesław Piasecki to Mieczysław Suwała, December 9, 1950. Education was another field in which Piasecki invested a great deal. In 1949, *Dziś i jutro* opened Saint Augustine High School, a quasi-private institution with a Catholic profile—a rare phenomenon in Stalinist Poland.

81. Micewski interview, September 16, 2001.

82. IPN, IPN 0648/155, Relacja agenta, December 11, 1949; Linia taktyczna Dziś i Jutro, December 6, 1949.

83. Jonathan Luxmore and Jolanta Babiuch, *The Vatican and the Red Flag* (London: Chapman, 1999), 41–43.

84. Stefan Wyszyński, *A Freedom from Within* (San Diego, Calif.: Harcourt Brace Jovanovich, 1983), 17–18, 40–46.

85. AKS CC, Bolesław Piasecki to Primate Wyszyński, January 22, 1949.

86. AKS CC, Bolesław Piasecki, Ocena możliwości rozmów z Watykanem, August 23, 1949.

87. Antoni Dudek and Ryszard Gryz, *Komuniści i Kościół w Polsce, 1945–1989* (Kraków: Znak, 2003), 33–34.

88. AKS CC, V-129, Appeal to the Pope, June 7, 1948.

89. AKS CC, transcript of Vatican Radio broadcast, July 14, 1949.

90. Jarosław Piasecki, interview by author, August 23, 2004.

91. Micewski interview by author, September 16, 2001; Ryszard Reiff, phone interview by author, June 16, 2001.

92. HU OSA, Records of the Polish Unit, Subject Files, 845.01, Wykaz księży współpracujących z reżimem komunistycznym; Antoni Dudek, "Sutanny w służbie Peerelu," *Karta* 25, no. 8 (1998): 110–14.

93. Andrzej Micewski, *Współrządzić czy nie kłamać? Pax i Znak w Polsce, 1945–1976* (Paris: Libella, 1978), 41–44.

94. Micewski interview, September 16, 2001.

95. Stefan Wyszyński, *Dzieła zebrane* (Warsaw: Soli Deo, 1991), 1:80.

96. AKS CC, Piasecki to Wyszyński, January 13, 1950; AKS CC, Wyszyński to Piasecki, January 21, 1950.

97. The Polish accord served as a model for a church-state agreement in communist Hungary signed in August 1950. See Luxmore and Babiuch, *Vatican and the Red Flag,* 75–76.

98. "Porozumienie zawarte między przedstawicielami Rządu R. i Episkopatu Polskiego," in Wyszyński, *Dzieła zebrane,* 1:243–44.

99. Wyszyński, *Freedom from Within,* 20.

100. Bolesław Piasecki, "Skala wydarzenia," *Dziś i jutro,* April 30, 1950.

101. AKS CC, Wytyczne ideowo-polityczne, 1950.

102. IPN 0648/155, security police report on a conference of Catholic activists, n.d., k.340.

103. Micewski, *Współrządzić czy nie kłamać,* 48–49.

104. Luxmore and Babiuch, *Vatican and the Red Flag,* 102.

105. Piasecki sided with the government in the conflict over the western dioceses. Micewski, *Współrządzić czy nie kłamać,* 49.

106. AKS CC, Statut Stowarzyszenia PAX, May 7, 1952.

107. IPN 0648/155, Report on Dziś i Jutro, August 8, 1952.

108. IPN 0648/155, Sekretariat Episkopatu Polski do Stowarzyszenia PAX, June 20, 1952.

109. Wytyczne ideowo-polityczne, December 6, 1952, quoted in Dudek and Pytel, *Bolesław Piasecki,* 199–200.

110. Peter Raina, *Kościół w PRL: Kościół katolicki a państwo w świetle dokumentów, 1945–1989* (Poznań: W Drodze, 1994), 1:392.

111. Andrzej Micewski, *Cardinal Wyszyński* (San Diego, Calif.: Harcourt Brace Jovanovich, 1984), 108, 110–11.

112. AKS CC, II.4/1953, Bolesław Piasecki, Trudności w przestawianiu się Kościoła, 8.

113. *Słowo powszechne*, March 2, 1953; Micewski, *Cardinal Wyszyński*, 111–12.

114. Jacek Żakowski, *Pół wieku pod włos czyli życie codzienne "Tygodnika Powszechnego" w czasach heroicznych* (Kraków: Znak, 1995), 19–21, 57.

115. In Raina, *Kościół w PRL*, 1:427.

116. Andrzej Paczkowski, *Pół wieku dziejów Polski, 1939–1989* (Warsaw: PWN, 1995), 279.

117. AKS CC, II.4/1953, Bolesław Piasecki, Trudności w przestawianiu się Kościoła, 2–3.

118. Ibid., 6.

119. Ibid., 12.

120. Wyszyński, *Freedom from Within*, 285.

121. Micewski, *Współrządzić czy nie kłamać*, 59.

122. "Uchwała Prezydium Rządu Polskiej Rzeczypospolitej Ludowej z dnia 24 września 1953 roku—nr. 700/53," in Wyszyński, *Dziela zebrane*, 2:233.

123. Sprawozdanie K. Łubieńskiego z rozmów z E. Ochabem o aresztowaniu Prymasa Polski, Warsaw, September 28, 1953, in Raina, *Kościół w PRL*, 1:444.

124. Micewski, *Współrządzić czy nie kłamać*, 59–60; Dudek and Pytel, *Bolesław Piasecki*, 208.

125. "Deklaracja Episkopatu Polski o stworzeniu warunków dla normalizacji stosunków między Państwem a Kościołem," September 28, 1953, in Raina, *Kościół w PRL*, 1:446.

126. AKS CC, II 2/1953, Bolesław Piasecki, Zagadnienia programowe dla wydziału ideologicznego, October 19, 1953.

127. Ibid.

128. AKS CC, Piasecki to Bierut, Warsaw, June 20, 1955.

129. Micewski, *Współrządzić czy nie kłamać*, 66.

130. Bolesław Piasecki, "Przedmowa do książki 'Zagadnienia istotne,'" in *Kierunki, 1945–1960* (Warsaw: PAX, 1960), 182–84.

131. Ibid., 185–86.

132. Ibid., 189–90.

133. Ibid., 193.

134. Ibid., 194, 197.

135. Philippe Burrin, "Political Religion: The Relevance of a Concept," *History and Memory* 9, no. 1–2 (1997): 326.

136. J. L. Talmon, *Political Messianism: The Romantic Phase* (New York: Praeger, 1960), 30.

137. Porter, *When Nationalism Began to Hate*, 104–34.

138. Leo XIII, *Rerum novarum*, in Paul E. Sigmund, *St. Thomas Aquinas on Politics and Ethics* (New York: W. W. Norton, 1987), 155–60.

139. Norbert A. Żmijewski, *The Catholic-Marxist Ideological Dialogue in Poland, 1945–1980* (Brookfield, Vt.: Dartmouth, 1991), 62.

140. Kisielewski, *Abecadło Kisiela*, 88.

141. Dudek and Pytel, *Bolesław Piasecki*, 216.

142. Józef Bocheński, *Wspomnienia* (Kraków: Philed, 1993), 218.

143. Peter Raina, *Piasecki na indeksie watykańskim* (Warsaw: Wydawnictwo von Borowiecky, 2002), 23–40.

144. IPN, IPN 0648/53, t.2, Doniesienie agenturalne, October 19, 1955.

145. Paczkowski, *Pół wieku dziejów Polski*, 293–95.

146. IPN, IPN 0648/49, t.1, Informacja dotycząca Stowarzyszenia PAX ze szczególnym uwzględnieniem okresu 1956–1960, Warsaw, December 10, 1961.

147. ASK CC, Notatka w sprawie założenia Komitetu Polonia, May 27, 1955.

148. IPN, IPN 0648/49 t.1, Informacja, December 10, 1961.

149. Raina, *Piasecki na indeksie watykańskim*, 41.

150. Ibid., 43–50.

151. Suprema Sacra Congregation Sancti Officii, "Decretum," *L'Osservatore romano*, June 29, 1955.

152. AKS CC, Ustawienie zagadnienia umieszczenia na indeksie 'Zagadnień istotnych' i Dziś i Jutro.

153. Jerzy Zawieyski, *Kartki z dziennika, 1955–1969* (Warsaw: PAX, 1983), 47.

154. Micewski, *Współrządzić czy nie kłamać*, 70.

155. IPN, IPN 0648/46, t.1, Piasecki to Bishop Wacław Majewski, Warsaw, July 1955.

156. Bishop Klepacz to Cardinal Pizzardo, Warsaw, August 11, 1955, in Raina, *Piasecki na indeksie watykańskim*, 60–61.

157. AKS CC, Piasecki's note concerning the meeting with Mazur, July 28, 1955.

158. "Wielkie sprzeniewierzenie," *Po prostu*, November 11, 1956; AKS CC, "Fronda," letter to Piasecki, May 17, 1955.

159. Micewski, *Współrządzić czy nie kłamać*, 76.

160. AKS CC, Fronda, Zarządzenie nr. 4/55, September 9, 1955. Within a year, members of Fronda had allied themselves with the Catholic group Znak. In 1958, they launched a monthly, *Więź* (The Link). In the course of the 1970s and 1980s, Tadeusz Mazowiecki, the former leader of Fronda, became one of the leading figures in the democratic opposition. On August 24, 1989, he was sworn in as the first non-communist prime minister in Central Europe in forty years.

161. Jan Nowak [Zdzisław Jeziorański], *Wojna w eterze: Wspomnienia* (London: Odnowa, 1985), 201–4.

162. HU OSA, Records of the Polish Unit, Polish Bio Files: Bolesław Piasecki, RFE, "Poznajmy się bliżej," August 14, 1955.

163. HU OSA, Records of the Polish Unit, Polish Bio Files: Józef Światło, RFE, "Za kulisami bezpieki i partii," date September 1, 1955.

164. IPN, IPN 0648/57, Zjazd organizowany przez PAX z okazji uroczystości 10-lecia Ruchu Postępowego Katolików Polskich, October 30–November 2, 1955.

165. IPN, IPN 0648/57, Notatka informacyjna, November 15, 1955.

166. Warszawski to Piasecki, Rome, January 7, 1956, in Raina, *Piasecki na indeksie watykańskim*, 80–81.

167. It is important to mention that both factions included former Stalinists. Another noteworthy observation applies to the Natolin: the conservatives were the first to call for Gomułka's return to the politburo. See Torańska, *Oni*, 177.

168. Micewski, *Współrządzić czy nie kłamać*, 71.

169. AKS CC, Mikołaj Rostworowski, Spostrzeżenia z podróży do Rzymu 27 IV-25 V 56.

170. IPN, IPN 0648/53 t.2, "Doniesienie agenturalne," April 27, 1956.

171. *Times* (London), May 10, 1956.

Chapter 5: Years of Hope and Disapointment, 1956–67

1. Jerzy Giedroyc, interview, Polish TV, Channel 2, broadcast date June 28, 1996.

2. Bolesław Piasecki, "Konsekwencje," *Kierunki*, May 20, 1956.

3. IPN, IPN 0648/53, t.2, Doniesienie agenturalne, Warsaw, May 3, 1956.

4. Andrzej Paczkowski, *Pół wieku dziejów Polski, 1939–1989* (Warsaw: PWN, 1995), 300.

5. Andrzej Friszke, *Opozycja polityczna w PRL, 1945–1980* (London: Aneks, 1994), 71.

6. Aleksander Ziemkowski, "Ofiary i straty ludzkie," in *Poznański czerwiec 1956*, ed. Jarosław Maciejewski and Zofia Trojanowiczowa (Poznań: Wydawnictwo Poznańskie, 1990), 112–20.

7. IPN 0648/53, t.2, Doniesienie agenturalne, August 23, 1956.

8. Antoni Dudek and Grzegorz Pytel, *Bolesław Piasecki: Próba biografii politycznej* (London: Aneks, 1990), 231–32.

9. IPN 0648/53, t.2, Doniesienie agenturalne, October 17, 1956.

10. Andrzej Micewski, *Współrządzić czy nie kłamać? PAX i Znak w Polsce, 1945–1976* (Paris: Libella, 1978), 83–84.

11. IPN 0648/53, t.2, Doniesienie agenturalne, October 23, 1956.

12. Ibid., October 5, 1956.

13. *Słowo powszechne,* October 16, 1956.

14. *Słowo powszechne,* October 19, 1956.

15. *Express wieczorny,* October 17, 1956.

16. Witold Jedlicki, *Klub Krzywego Koła* (Paris: Instytut Literacki, 1963), 78.

17. Micewski, *Współrządzić czy nie kłamać,* 86; *Życie Warszawy,* October 23, 1956.

18. William Taubman, *Khrushchev: The Man and His Era* (New York: Norton, 2003), 293; HIA, ANEKS Collection, box 7, Władysław Gomułka's notes from the meeting with Khrushchev, October 19, 1956.

19. Taubman, *Khrushchev,* 293–94; Nikita Sergeevich Khrushchev, *Khrushchev Remembers: The Glasnost Tapes,* trans. and ed. Jerrold L. Schecter with Vyacheslav V. Luchkov (Boston: Little, Brown, 1990), 115–16.

20. Paczkowski, *Pół wieku dziejów Polski,* 304.

21. IPN 0648/53, t.2, Doniesienie agenturalne, October 24, 1956; Micewski, *Współrządzić czy nie kłamać,* 86.

22. Micewski, *Współrządzić czy nie kłamać,* 87.

23. Visited by Gomułka's emissaries, Zenon Kliszko and Władysław Bieńkowski, the primate agreed to leave his internment, subject to several conditions. He required the new government to nullify the 1953 decree on ecclesiastical appointments and to reinstate the arrested and ousted bishops. Wyszyński traveled to Warsaw only after he had won Gomułka's consent. See Stefan Wyszyński, *A Freedom from Within* (San Diego, Calif.: Harcourt Brace Jovanovich, 1983), 349–54.

24. AKS CC, R-II-14/1956, List Bolesława Piaseckiego do Zespołu Stowarzyszenia PAX, October 28, 1956.

25. AKS CC, R-II-14/1956, results of a vote of confidence in Piasecki's leadership.

26. Micewski, *Współrządzić czy nie kłamać,* 89.

27. Dudek and Pytel, *Bolesław Piasecki,* 246.

28. Leopold Tyrmand, "Sprawa Piaseckiego," *Świat,* November 18, 1956.

29. Peter Raina, *Kościół w PRL: Kościół katolicki a państwo w świetle dokumentów, 1945–1989* (Poznań: W Drodze, 1994–95), 1:575–76, 583.

30. Andrzej Friszke, *Koło posłów "Znak" w Sejmie PRL, 1957–1976* (Warsaw: Wydawnictwo Sejmowe, 2002), 11–12.

31. Ibid., 13.

32. Ibid., 159.

33. Teresa Torańska, *Oni* (London: Aneks, 1985), 152.

34. AKS CC, Piasecki to Gomułka, December 17, 1956.

35. Dudek and Pytel, *Bolesław Piasecki,* 250.

36. AAN, Prokuratura Generalna PRL, 16/493, Prosecutor Jerzy Smoleński, Analiza śledztwa w sprawie uprowadzenia i zabójstwa Bohdana Piaseckiego, December 16, 1961.

37. AAN, Prokuratura Generalna PRL, 17/184, t.7, Protokół sądowo-lekarski oględzin zwłok, December 9, 1958.

38. AAN, Prokuratura Generalna PRL, 16/516, Projekt opinii sądowo-lekarskiej w sprawie zabójstwa Bohdana Piaseckiego, October 6, 1972.

39. AAN, Prokuratura Generalna PRL, 16/493, Smoleński, Analiza śledztwa.

40. AAN, Prokuratura Generalna PRL, 17/187, Prosecutor Tadeusz Olekiewicz's note, August 26, 1959; Protokół przesłuchania świadka Adama Góreckiego, October 25, 1962, in Peter Raina, *Mordercy uchodzą bezkarnie: Sprawa Bohdana P.* (Warsaw: Wydawnictwo von Borowiecky, 2000), 26.

41. AAN, Prokuratura Generalna PRL, 17186, Prosecutor Olekiewicz's note, June 25, 1959.

42. AAN, Prokuratura Generalna PRL, 17/212, Captain Stanisław Włodarski and Prosecutor Józef Gurgul, Notatka dotycząca sprawy zabójstwa Bohdana Piaseckiego, December 15, 1975. According to Jarosław Piasecki, Zenon Kliszko told him that the decision to drop the charges against Ekerling had been approved by Gomułka. Jarosław Piasecki, interview by author, Warsaw, June 28, 2001.

43. The investigators estimated that by March 1959, PAX had submitted 175 documents related to the case. AAN, 17/181, Wyciąg z ewidencji MSW materiałów dostarczonych przez PAX, March 1959.

44. AAN, 17/180, Wnioski Bolesława Piaseckiego przedstawione władzom MSW i Prokuratury, September 12, 1958.

45. IPN 0648/55, t.1, Notatka służbowa, January 31, 1959.

46. Tadeusz Różewicz, "Świadkowie albo nasza mała stabilizacja," *Dialog,* no. 5 (1962): 5–26.

47. Jan B. de Weydenthal, *The Communists of Poland: An Historical Outline* (Stanford, Calif.: Hoover Institution Press, 1978), 100.

48. Marcin Zaremba, *Komunizm, legitymizacja, nacjonalizm: Nacjonalistyczna legitymizacja władzy komunistycznej w Polsce* (Warsaw: Trio, 2001), 255–56.

49. Ibid., 264.

50. AKS CC, Piasecki to Gomułka, memo, September 30, 1957.

51. Ibid.

52. IPN, IPN 0648/49, t.2, Notatka służbowa dotycząca Stowarzyszenia PAX, September 15, 1958.

53. Asked by high Vatican officials in 1957 to elaborate on the differences between PAX and Znak, Wyszyński gave the following answer: "PAX is involved in ideological cooperation with the communists whereas Znak aims at cooperation on the institutional level but views the ideological differences [between the Catholics

and the Marxists] as irreproachable." HIA, Peter Raina Collection, box 3, folder Wyszyński, Informacja dotycząca pobytu delegacji Episkopatu w Rzymie, August 13, 1957. Piasecki and Wyszyński met several times after 1956. On these occasions, Wyszyński refused to be drawn into political discussions. IPN, IPN 0296/156, t.8, Informacje o PAX-ie odczytane przez księdza W, n.d., n.p.

54. Friszke, *Koło posłów "Znak" w sejmie PRL,* 27.

55. On the link between the Endek and communist treatment of the Piast and commonwealth periods and role of nationalist historians in the postwar historiographical discourse, see Maciej Górny, *Przede wszystkim ma być naród: Marksistowskie historiografie w Europie Środkowo-Wschodniej* (Warsaw: Trio, 2007), 57, 188–89.

56. On the Novena, see Jan Kubik, *The Power of Symbols against the Symbols of Power: The Rise of Solidarity and the Fall of State Socialism in Poland* (University Park: Pennsylvania State University Press, 1994), 110–17, 127–28.

57. Friszke, *Koło posłów "Znak" w sejmie PRL,* 52, 56.

58. IPN, Materiały do Koła Poselskiego *"ZNAK,"* IPN 0648/51, Informacja służbowa, August 8, 1958.

59. Friszke, *Koło posłów "Znak" w sejmie PRL,* 65, 70.

60. Ibid., 30.

61. Friszke, *Opozycja polityczna w PRL,* 198.

62. IPN 0648/51, *ZNAK* to the government, memo, March 7, 1958.

63. IPN 0648/51, Doniesienie informacyjne, May 19, 1959.

64. AKS CC, R-II, 17/1959, Piasecki's speech delivered at the PAX information meeting, May 19, 1959.

65. IPN 0648/49, t.2, Informacja dot. Stowarzyszenia PAX, April 14, 1958.

66. Bolesław Piasecki, "O socjalistycznym zaangażowaniu narodu," *Słowo powszechne,* May 10, 1957.

67. IPN 0201/260, t.1, Analiza składu oddziałów Stowarzyszenia PAX w województwie warszawskim, January 14, 1966.

68. AAN, Urząd do spraw Wyznań, 129/11, Posłowie ze Stowarzyszenia PAX. Kwestionariusze osobowe, dane biograficzne, życiorysy, 1969.

69. Micewski, *Współrządzić czy nie kłamać,* 114–15.

70. Congratulating Piasecki on the occasion of the fifteenth anniversary of *Dziś i jutro,* Mackiewicz wrote: "I remember that many years ago, when you were still a young politician, I told you: 'Stake everything on your abilities.' Today, I see you as the only great Polish politician." AKS CC, I/3, Mackiewicz to Piasecki, Warsaw, November 22, 1960.

71. Of the three writers, only Kossak-Szczucka remained loyal to Piasecki until her death in 1968. Wańkowicz provoked Piasecki's animosity when he began criticizing Gomułka's crackdown on freedom of speech. In 1964, he signed the "Letter

of 34" sent to the government by a group of public intellectuals as a protest against censorship. In the fall of the same year, he was put on trial. Sentenced to two years in prison, Wańkowicz owed his immediate release to advanced age and the public outcry that forced Gomułka to pardon the writer. Mackiewicz cooperated with the PAX press until 1965, when he was prosecuted for contributing to the émigré journal *Kultura.*

72. IPN 0299/156, t.8, Informacje o PAX-ie odczytane przez księdza W, n.p., n.d; IPN 0648/49, t.2, Informacja dotycząca przeprowadzonej rozmowy przez Zofię Kossak-Szczucką, Jana Dobraczyńskiego i Władysława Grabskiego z kardynałem Wyszyńskim w dniu 15 stycznia 1959, January 22, 1958. In private, Wyszyński characterized Piasecki's moral crusade as a farce: "The front for moral renewal is led by the alcoholic Przetakiewicz, whereas the people attending PAX's rallies are on [Piasecki's] payroll." IPN 0296, 165, t.2, Informacje o PAX-ie.

73. Micewski, *Współrządzić czy nie kłamać,* 100.

74. IPN 0648/49, t.2, Informacja dotycząca rozmowy, January 22, 1959.

75. Zygmunt Przetakiewicz, "Przeciwko indyferentyzmowi," *Kierunki,* March 23, 1958.

76. IPN 0648/49, t.1, Informacja dotycząca Stowarzyszenia PAX ze szczególnym uwzględnieniem okresu 1956–1960, December 10, 1961.

77. Bolesław Piasecki, "Patriotyzm polski," in Piasecki, *Kierunki, 1945–1960* (Warsaw: PAX, 1960), 298.

78. AKS CC, R-II, 16/1959, Piasecki's speech at PAX meeting, March 23, 1959.

79. AAN, 237/XIX-171, fragments of Piasecki's speeches at PAX, November 1959 and February 27, 1960.

80. AAN, 237/XIX-171, Bolesław Piasecki, Wyjątki z materiałów pomocniczych na zebrania PAX w marcu 1960, March 1960.

81. Ibid.

82. AAN, 237/XIX-171, Piasecki's speech at PAX meeting, February 27, 1960.

83. IPN 0648/63, t.3, Notatka służbowa, November 11, 1961.

84. IPN 0648/62, t.1, Streszczenie rozmowy Mazowieckiego i Micewskiego, December 16, 1960.

85. IPN 0648/62, t.2, Notatka służbowa, January 26, 1961.

86. IPN 0648/65, t.2, transcript of Radio Free Europe broadcast, September 28, 1960.

87. Dudek and Pytel, *Bolesław Piasecki,* 273.

88. *Słowo powszechne,* December 17–18, 1960.

89. IPN 0648/49, t.1, Informacja dotycząca działalności Stowarzyszenia PAX w okresie ostatnich dwóch miesięcy, January 25, 1961.

90. *Słowo powszechne,* December 17–18, 1960.

91. AAN, Urząd do spraw Wyznań, 129/11, Rozmowa Towarzysza Władysława Gomułki z przedstawicielami PAX-u, January 25, 1961.

92. Ibid.

93. Ibid.

94. IPN 0648/49, t.1, Informacja dotycząca posiedzenia Zarządu Głównego PAX, February 10, 1961.

95. IPN 0648/55, t.1, Notatka służbowa, March 15, 1961.

96. The prerogatives adopted by the party shortly after the meeting with Piasecki were aimed at preventing the economic expansion of PAX. IPN 0648/49, t.1, Wyciąg z posiedzenia na którym omówiono realizację postanowień Kierownictwa Partii w odniesieniu do stowarzyszenia PAX, January 28, 1961; IPN 0648/49, t.1, Wydział Administracyjny KC PZPR, Wnioski, March 20, 1961.

97. IPN 0648/55, t.2, Notatka służbowa, April 8, 1961.

98. IPN 0648/56, t.1, Notatka służbowa, December 23, 1961. Shortly after his discovery, Piasecki installed a costly soundproofing system.

99. IPN 0648/56, t.1, "Notatka służbowa," November 3, 1961.

100. Instytut Studiów Politycznych Polskiej Akademii Nauk (ISP PAN), documents from Tsentr Khraneniia Sovremennykh Dokumentov (TsKhSD, currently Rossiiskii Gosudarstvennyi Arkhiv Noveishei Istorii), Dokumental'nye Materialy TsK KPSS, transcript of V. A. Karpov's conversation with Piasecki, April 27, 1957.

101. IPN 0648/49, t.2, Informacja dotycząca kontaktów kierownictwa PAX z przedstawicielami krajów socjalistycznych, November 1958.

102. Ibid.

103. IPN 0648/49, t.2, Informacja dotycząca działalności Stowarzyszenia PAX, November 25, 1958.

104. Ibid.

105. IPN 0648/52, Ulysses report, November 4, 1965.

106. IPN 0648/54, t.3, Notatka ze spotkania z t.w. "Konrad," September 11, 1964.

107. Martin Rissmann, *Kaderschulung in der Ost-CDU, 1949–1971* (Düsseldorf: Droste, 1995), 37.

108. Michael Richter, *Die Ost-CDU, 1948–1952* (Düsseldorf: Droste, 1990), 19.

109. Gerald Götting, *Christliche Mitverantwortung im Sozialismus* (Berlin: Union Verlag, 1965); Götting, *Erkenntnishilfe und Wegweisung: Lenins Werk und wir Christen heute* (Berlin: Union Verlag, 1970).

110. Gerald Götting, "Nierozerwalna przyjaźń," speech given at the twentieth annivarsary of PAX, in *Słowo powszechne*, November 27–28, 1965.

111. IPN 0648/49, t.1, Informacja dotycząca działalności Stowarzyszenia PAX w okresie ostatnich dwóch miesięcy, January 25, 1961.

112. In 1945 the Soviets relegalized four political parties in their zone: the Communists, the Social Democrats, the Christian Democrats, and the Liberals.

113. Béla Kézai, "Katoliccy pionierzy pokoju i postępu nad Wisłą i Dunajem," *Słowo powszechne*, November 27–28, 1965.

114. In March 1961, the episcopate forbade the clergy from engaging in any contact with the Caritas priests. See Antoni Dudek and Ryszard Gryz, *Komuniści i Kościół w Polsce (1945–1989)* (Kraków: Znak, 2003), 192.

115. IPN 0648/55, t.2, Notatka służbowa, April 10, 1961. "The plan of organizing the clergy around Caritas," Piasecki observed in April 1960, "will not work because it relies on administrative measures, not on priests' convictions." IPN 0648/49, t.1, Informacja dotycząca obrad Zarządu Głównego PAX w dniach od 23 do 26.V.1961, June 3, 1961.

116. When Stomma, who opposed the bill, approached Hagmajer, head of the PAX caucus, to see if Znak and PAX could agree on the vote, Piasecki advised his deputy: "Go and talk to him, but do not make any decisions." IPN 0648/56, t.1, Notatka służbowa, July 8, 1961.

117. Bogdan Szajkowski, *Next to God . . . Poland: Politics and Religion in Contemporary Poland* (London: Pinter, 1983), 26.

118. IPN 0648/56, t.1, Notatka służbowa, October 11, 1961.

119. Szajkowski, *Next to God*, 27.

120. IPN 0648/55, t.1, Notatka służbowa, February 11, 1961.

121. "W oczekiwaniu soboru," *Słowo powszechne*, October 29, 1962.

122. Jan Dobraczyński, "O otwartej postawie," *Słowo powszechne*, April 25, 1963.

123. Witold Jankowski, "Lewica katolicka w Polsce wobec stosunków kościelno-państowych," *Słowo powszechne*, April 25, 1963.

124. Dudek and Gryz, *Komuniści i Kościół w Polsce*, 207.

125. Jonathan Luxmore and Jolanta Babiuch, *The Vatican and the Red Flag* (London: Chapman, 1999), 125.

126. Ibid., 110, 112–13.

127. "Z dyskusji o encyklice 'Pacem in Terris' w klubie im. Włodzimierza Pietrzaka," *Słowo powszechne*, June 15–16, 1963.

128. Luciana Frassati, *Il Destino passa per Varsavia* (Milan: Bompiani, 1985), 97; IPN 0648/65, t.1, Podsłuch rozmów telefonicznych polskich dziennikarzy i działaczy katolickich przebywających na soborze, December 4, 1962.

129. Tom Buchanan and Martin Conway, eds. *Political Catholicism in Europe, 1918–1965* (Oxford: Clarendon, 1996), 18, 32–33.

130. Ibid., 32.

131. On new perspectives on Wyszyński's Nowenna campaign, see James Bjork, "Bulwark or Patchwork?" in *Christianity and Modernity in Eastern Eu-*

rope, ed. Bruce R. Berglund and Brian Porter-Szücs (Budapest: CEU Press, 2010), 129–58.

132. IPN 0648.54, t.3, Ocena kampanii propagandowej i incydentów wywołanych we Francji przez notę kardynała Wyszyńskiego, July 27, 1964.

133. IPN 0648/54, t.3, Wyszyński's note quoted by *La France catholique,* June 5, 1964.

134. IPN 0648.54, t.3, Ocena kampanii propagandowej i incydentów wywołanych we Francji przez notę kardynała Wyszyńskiego, July 27, 1964.

135. In Paris, Aleksander Bocheński contacted *Le Monde* and categorically refuted all the charges that had been brought against Piasecki and his organization. IPN 0648/54, t.3, Aleksander Bocheński to Hubert Beure-Méry, July 13, 1964.

136. IPN 0201/260, t.1, Departament IV MSW, Informacja nr. 43/II/64 dotyczy: listu otwartego PAX i związanej z tym sytuacji na odcinku katolickim, October 13, 1964.

137. IPN 0648/54, t.3, Doniesienie, September 9, 1964.

138. IPN 0201/260, t.1, Informacja nr. 43/II/64. During the affair, Znak refrained from issuing public statements because of its own conflict with Wyszyński. In October 1963, Stomma sent to the Papal State Secretariat a memorandum calling for the establishment of diplomatic relations between Poland and the Vatican. Wyszyński viewed this initiative as an attempt to negotiate with the Vatican behind his back. As a result, the first few months of 1964 saw the deterioration in relations between the primate and Znak.

139. IPN 0648/52, Wyciąg z notatki służbowej, November 23, 1965.

140. AKS CC, I-112, Piasecki to Kliszko, August 3, 1966.

141. Letter of the Polish Bishops to the German Bishops, November 18, 1965, in Raina, *Kościół w PRL,* 2:362.

142. Zaremba, *Komunizm, legitymizacja, nacjonalizm,* 304.

143. Dudek and Gryz, *Komuniści i Kościół w Polsce,* 230.

144. Aleksandra Klich, "Kardynał Bolesław Kominek," *Gazeta wyborcza,* March 12, 2004; Luxmore and Babiuch, *Vatican and the Red Flag,* 139.

145. Luxmore and Babiuch, *Vatican and the Red Flag,* 139.

146. Antoni Dudek, *Państwo i Kościół w Polsce, 1945–1970* (Kraków: Wydawnictwo PiT, 1995), 190.

147. "Wbrew własnym słowom," *Słowo powszechne,* December 10, 1965; "Oświadczenie," *Słowo powszechne,* December 28, 1965.

148. AKS CC, I-112, Piasecki to Kliszko, July 25, 1966.

149. The rivalry between the Church and the government held some grotesque undertones. In Gniezno, the mass celebrated by Bishop Karol Wojtyła was interrupted by a deafening salvo of guns announcing the arrival of Spychalski at a state-organized rally. "Protokół z posiedzenia Prezydium Komisji Partyjno-Rządowej

d/s Uroczystości Tysiąclecia," April 8, 1966, in *Tajne dokumenty: Państwo-kościół, 1960–1980* (London: Aneks, 1996), 235–36.

150. Antoni Dudek and Tomasz Marszałkowski, *Walki uliczne w PRL, 1956–1989* (Kraków: Wydawnictwo Geo, 1999), 133–35.

151. Bolesław Piasecki, *Siły rozwoju* (Warsaw: PAX, 1971), 227–28.

152. Dudek, *Państwo i Kościół w Polsce,* 194.

153. Luxmore and Babiuch, *Vatican and the Red Flag,* 156–57.

154. AKS CC, I/111, Piasecki to Kliszko, March 24, 1966.

155. AKS CC, I/111, Piasecki to Kliszko, June 20, 1966; July 9, 1966.

156. AKS CC, I/111, Piasecki's notes, August 4, 22, 1966.

157. AKS CC, I/111, Piasecki to Kliszko, November 21, 1966.

158. Report of the Polish Ministry of Internal Affairs on Casaroli's stay in Poland, May 1967, in *Tajne dokumenty,* 275–85.

159. AKS CC, I/112, Piasecki to Kliszko, March 6, 1967.

160. Andrzej Werblan's note on the conversation with Casaroli, April 6, 1967, *Tajne dokumenty,* 272.

Chapter 6: The Last Crusade

1. Leszek Kołakowski, *Main Currents of Marxism.* Vol. 3. *The Breakdown* (Oxford: Oxford University Press, 1981), 466.

2. Antoni Dudek and Grzegorz Pytel, *Bolesław Piasecki: Próba biografii politycznej* (London: Aneks, 1990), 285.

3. Shortly before his downfall in 1948, Gomułka complained to Stalin about the large presence of Jews in the party and their outright hostility toward him. Anastas Mikoyan reminded Gomułka of the episode in October 1956. HIA, ANEKS Collection, box 7, Władysław Gomułka's notes from the meeting with Khrushchev, October 19, 1956.

4. Mieczysław Franciszek Rakowski, *Dzienniki polityczne, 1963–1966* (Warsaw: Iskry, 1999), 55, 73.

5. The name of the group—"the Partisans"—was coined by Ernest Halperin, a correspondent for *Neue Zürcher Zeitung,* and popularized by Arthur Olsen of the *New York Times.* Halperin and Olsen used it as a reference to the protagonists of a book published in 1961 containing interviews with twelve People's Army partisan commanders. Marcin Zaremba, *Komunizm, legitymizacja, nacjonalizm: Nacjonalistyczna legitymizacja władzy komunistycznej w Polsce* (Warsaw: Trio, 2001), 289.

6. Ibid.

7. Joanna Wawrzyniak, *ZBOWiD i pamięć drugiej wojny światowej, 1949–1969* (Warsaw: Trio, 2009), 275–76.

8. In a 1964 address delivered at the commemoration of the 1944 Warsaw Uprising, Zenon Kliszko went so far as to deny that there were any divisions among former resistance fighters. Quoted in Wawrzyniak, *ZBOWiD i pamięć drugiej*, 269–70.

9. Mieczysław Moczar, *Barwy walki* (Warsaw: Wydawnictwo MON, 1961).

10. Paweł Wieczorkiewicz, "Walka o władzę w kierownictwie PZPR w marcu 68," in *Marzec 1968: Trzydzieści lat później*, ed. Marcin Kula, Piotr Osęka, and Marcin Zaremba (Warsaw: PWN, 1998), 1:43.

11. In an article published in *Trybuna ludu* in April 1968, Moczar lamented the postwar "arrival in our country . . . of certain politicians dressed in officers' uniforms, who later were of the opinion that it was only they—the Zambrowskis, the Radkiewiczes, and the Bermans—who had a monopoly on deciding what was right for the Polish nation." Quoted in Jan B. de Weydenthal, *The Communists of Poland: An Historical Outline* (Stanford, Calif.: Hoover Institution Press, 1978), 131.

12. Krzysztof Lesiakowski, *Mieczysław Moczar "Mietek": Biografia polityczna* (Warsaw: Rytm, 1998), 222–23; Zaremba, *Komunizm, legitymizacja, nacjonalizm*, 287–91. Among the leading voices of the Partisans was Colonel Zbigniew Załuski, who glorified nineteenth-century insurrections and emphasized the link between the Polish communists and the independence movement. See Zbigniew Załuski, *Siedem polskich grzechów głównych* (Warsaw: MON, 1962).

13. Quoted in Zaremba, *Komunizm, legitymizacja, nacjonalizm*, 289.

14. Jerzy Eisler, *Polski rok 1968* (Warsaw: IPN, 2006), 516; Zaremba, *Komunizm, legitymizacja, nacjonalizm*, 290.

15. On the rivalry between Moczar and Alster, see Franciszek Szlachcic, "Wspomnienia z okresu pracy w organach bezpieczeństwa i Ministerstwa Spraw Wewnętrznych: Napisane dla wewnętrznego użytku MSW," mimeograph, Ministry of Internal Affairs, Warsaw, 1988, 129.

16. IPN 0648/55, t.1, Notatka służbowa, January 31, 1959.

17. IPN 0648/46, t.3, Doniesienie, September 12, 1962.

18. IPN 0648/56, t.2, Notatka służbowa, January 22, 1962.

19. Ibid.

20. IPN, MSW II 31145, Bolesław Piasecki, O twórczą kontynuację historii Polski Ludowej, 9–10.

21. Bolesław Piasecki, "Bieżące i perspektywiczne problemy dyskusji," speech delivered on March 9, 1963, in Piasecki, *Siły rozwoju* (Warsaw: PAX, 1971), 159–61.

22. Józef Wójcik, "Barwy walki," *Kierunki* 14 (1962): 8.

23. Lesiakowski, *Mieczysław Moczar*, 318.

24. IPN 0648/56, t.1, Stenogram z posiedzenia sekretariatu PAX odbytego w dniu 26.IX. 1961, September 28, 1961.

25. IPN 0648/48, t.1, Doniesienie, June 29, 1962.

26. Mieczysław Franciszek Rakowski, *Dzienniki polityczne, 1967–1968* (Warsaw: Iskry, 1999), 112.

27. Adam Schaff, *Marksizm i jednostka ludzka* (Warsaw: PWN, 1965).

28. Quoted in Zaremba, *Komunizm, legitymizacja, nacjonalizm*, 299.

29. Zaremba, *Komunizm, legitymizacja, nacjonalizm*, 300.

30. AAN, Biuro Prasy KC PZPR, 237/XIX-353, Bolesław Piasecki, Niektóre zagadnienia socjalistyczno-patriotycznego ruchu umysłowego w Polsce, transcript of a speech given on October 28, 1966.

31. Ibid.

32. Bolesław Piasecki, "O rozwojową ciągłość historii Polski Ludowej," speech delivered at PAX training center in December 1966, in Piasecki, *Siły rozwoju*, 267.

33. IPN, MSW II 31145, Bolesław Piasecki, O twórczą kontynuację historii Polski Ludowej, February 1967, 5–6.

34. Ibid., 20–21.

35. IPN, MSW II 31145, Bolesław Piasecki, O twórczą kontynuację historii Polski Ludowej, February 1967, 38–40.

36. Bolesław Piasecki, "Przewidywania i dążenia," speech given on May 21, 1967, in Piasecki, *Siły rozwoju*, 296–300.

37. M. K. Dziewanowski, *The Communist Party of Poland* (Cambridge, Mass.: Harvard University Press, 1976), 299.

38. Rakowski, *Dzienniki polityczne, 1967–1968*, 63.

39. Ibid., 61.

40. Zaremba, *Komunizm, legitymizacja, nacjonalizm*, 334.

41. Gomułka did not consult Politburo members regarding the speech. After he delivered the address, Ochab and Minister of Foreign Affairs Adam Rapacki strongly objected to the reference to a fifth column, which was dropped from the published version of the speech. Teresa Torańska, *Oni* (London: Aneks, 1985), 47.

42. Stola, *Kampania antysyjonistyczna w Polsce*, 274.

43. For Rakowski, the meaning of Gomułka's remarks was obvious: "In short, he asked them [the Jews] to leave the country." Rakowski, *Dzienniki polityczne, 1967–1968*, 65.

44. Zaremba, *Komunizm, legitymizacja, nacjonalizm*, 336–38.

45. For this view, see Dziewanowski, *Communist Party of Poland*, 299–300.

46. Zaremba, *Komunizm, legitymizacja, nacjonalizm*, 337.

47. AAN, Kolekcja Mieczysława Moczara, Andrzej Werblan, Szkic tez dla odpowiedzi na pytania dotyczące rzekomego antysemityzmu w Polsce Ludowej, November 1970.

48. The purge led to the dismissal of fourteen generals and two hundred colonels. Andrew Michta, *Red Eagle: The Army in Polish Politics, 1944–1988* (Stanford, Calif.: Hoover Institution Press, 1990), 55.

49. Zaremba, *Komunizm, legitymizacja, nacjonalizm,* 339–40.

50. Andrzej Friszke, *Opozycja polityczna w PRL, 1945–1980* (London: Aneks, 1994), 240–42.

51. The term was coined by communist propagandists in order to demonstrate that the student rebels had been in the vanguard of Zionist action against Poland.

52. Because of their diversity, it is almost impossible to provide a coherent portrayal of the 1968 student militants. Generalizations may lead to the elevation of some individuals at the cost of neglecting others. For the most unbiased survey of the commandos, see Friszke, *Opozycja polityczna w PRL,* 227–39.

53. Ibid., 241–42.

54. On the scale of the March protests and police repression, consult Jerzy Eisler, *Marzec 1968* (Warsaw: PWN, 1991); Friszke, *Opozycja polityczna w PRL;* and Antoni Dudek and Tomasz Marszałkowski, *Walki uliczne w PRL, 1956–1989* (Kraków: Wydawnictwo Geo, 1999).

55. Eisler, *Polski rok 1968,* 684. As a veteran of the AK and anticommunist underground, Zabłocki respected Moczar's efforts to bring former Home Army soldiers into the Veterans' Union and promote reconciliation between members of rival resistance groups. He even conferred with Moczar on several occasions. See Janusz Zabłocki, *Dzienniki, 1956–1966* (Warsaw: IPN, 2008), 375, 472–74, 614–15.

56. Friszke, *Opozycja polityczna w PRL,* 217–19.

57. Eisler, *Polski rok 1968,* 703.

58. He told his collaborators in November 1967, "In Poland we are witnessing a change of cadres: the socialist-patriotic forces are [gradually] replacing the socialist-cosmopolitan elements and the Zionist circles." AKS CC, Piasecki's speech at the meeting of the PAX supreme board, November 27, 1967.

59. Jan Engeldard to the author, December 14, 2003.

60. *Słowo powszechne,* March 11, 1968.

61. Ibid.

62. Stola, *Kampania antysyjonistyczna w Polsce,* 99.

63. Ibid., 100–102.

64. Consider Klaudiusz Hrabyk, a former activist of the Camp of Great Poland and the National Radical Camp, whose contributions to the anti-Semitic campaign earned him the prize of the Ministry of Foreign Affairs. Rakowski, *Dzienniki polityczne, 1967–1968,* 321.

65. On March 8, Gomułka, Kliszko, and Spychalski were not in Poland; they were attending a meeting of communist leaders in Sofia. Thus, the first measures against students were carried out by Moczar.

66. Dariusz Stola, "Rok 1968," in *Centrum władzy w Polsce, 1948–1970,* ed. Andrzej Paczkowski (Warsaw: ISP PAN, 2003), 215.

67. Zaremba, *Komunizm, legitymizacja, nacjonalizm,* 342–45.

68. On April 8, 1968, speaking to Politburo members, Gomułka recommended the moderation of anti-Jewish propaganda. Stola, "Rok 1968," 241–42.

69. Torańska, *Oni,* 68.

70. AAN, Biuro Prasy KC PZPR, 237-XIX-353, Zygmunt Przetakiewicz, "Charakterystyka obozu przewrotu w Polsce," a speech given in Bydgoszcz on April 6, 1968.

71. Ibid. Przetakiewicz was referring to Gierek's speech in Katowice on March 14. The party boss of Silesia promised to "break the bones of all remnants of the old regime, revisionists, Zionists, and imperialist lackeys" if these groups dared to stir unrest in his province. See Weydenthal, *Communists of Poland,* 127.

72. Rakowski, *Dzienniki polityczne, 1967–1968,* 252–53. Gomułka received the full text of Przetakiewicz's speech in late April 1968. See AAN, Biuro Prasy KC PZPR, 237-XIX-353, Olszowski to Gomułka and Kliszko, April 23, 1968.

73. Piasecki, "O twórczą kontynuację ustroju i władzy," in Piasecki, *Siły rozwoju,* 352–53.

74. Ibid., 346–52.

75. Ibid., 348.

76. *Słowo powszechne,* April 30, 1968; *Kierunki,* April 28, 1968.

77. AAN, Urząd d/s Wyznań, 129/10, Piasecki's speech at the meeting of PAX board, May 3, 1968, 2.

78. Ibid., 3–4, emphasis added.

79. Ibid., 5–6.

80. Ibid., 12, 24.

81. Dudek and Pytel, *Bolesław Piasecki,* 299.

82. Paczkowski, *Pół wieku dziejów Polski,* 372.

83. Eisler, *Polski rok 1968,* 623.

84. Gomułka criticized the "overflow of publications on Zionism" and recommended that censors limit such publications. He also ordered publications not to mention the Jewish origin of "the instigators of March events" and victims of purges, and he urged the elimination of materials that glorified the nationalist right. AAN, KC PZPR, Biuro Listów, Wydarzenia marcowe w Polsce, 237/XIX-347, instructions for censors, June 1968.

85. Maciej Górny, "Wydarzenia marcowe w opinii czechosłowackiej," in *Marzec 1968: Trzydzieści lat później,* ed. Marcin Kula, Piotr Osęka, and Marcin Zaremba (Warsaw: Wydawnictwo Naukowe PWN, 1998), 1:208.

86. Ibid., 208–17.

87. Weydenthal, *Communists of Poland,* 141.

88. Stola, *Kampania antysyjonistyczna w Polsce,* 213.

89. Piasecki, *Siły rozwoju,* 425.

90. Zaremba, *Komunizm, legitymizacja, nacjonalizm,* 351.

91. Kołakowski, *Main Currents of Marxism,* 3:467.

92. David Ost, *Solidarity and the Politics of Anti-Politics: Opposition and Reform in Poland since 1968* (Philadelphia: Temple University Press, 1990), 49.

93. Andrzej Walicki, *Marxism and the Leap to the Kingdom of Freedom :The Rise and Fall of the Communist Utopia* (Stanford, Calif.: Stanford University Press, 1995), 520.

Chapter 7: The Exit of the Crusader, 1970–79

1. IPN 0201/260 t.7, Bolesław Piasecki, "Sytuacja ideowo-polityczna i zadania Stowarzyszenia PAX," transcript of a speech, January 26, 1972.

2. Józef Tejchma, *Kulisy dymisji: Z dzienników ministra kultury, 1974–1977* (Kraków: Oficyna Cracovia, 1991), 104.

3. Antoni Dudek and Grzegorz Pytel, *Bolesław Piasecki: Próba biografii politycznej* (London: Aneks, 1990), 299–300.

4. Piasecki, "Polska—NRF," speech, October 7, 1970, in Piasecki, *Siły rozwoju* (Warsaw: PAX, 1971), 486–93.

5. Roman Laba, *The Roots of Solidarity* (Princeton, N.J.: Princeton University Press, 1991), 19–20.

6. For detailed coverage of the December 1970 events, see ibid., 21–70.

7. *Trybuna ludu,* December 21, 1970.

8. Laba, *Roots of Solidarity,* 80–81.

9. IPN 0201/260, t.3, Pióro, Notatka informacyjna, January 25, 1971.

10. AKS CC, I/121, draft of Piasecki's memo to Gierek on the political advancement of PAX, December 26, 1970.

11. AKS CC, I/112, Piasecki to Gierek, December 31, 1970.

12. AKS CC, I/121, Bolesław Piasecki, Tezy, January 197.

13. Franciszek Szlachcic, *Gorzki smak władzy* (Warsaw: Fakt, 1990), 49.

14. Dudek and Pytel, *Bolesław Piasecki,* 304.

15. AKS CC, I/123, Piasecki to Gierek, January 24, 1971.

16. AAN, Ud/sW, 129/10, Piasecki's parliamentary speech, February 13, 1971.

17. Dudek and Pytel, *Bolesław Piasecki,* 304.

18. Mieczysław Franciszek Rakowski, *Dzienniki polityczne, 1969–1971* (Warsaw: Iskry, 2001), 389.

19. IPN, IPN 0201/260, t.3, Bishop Bronisław Dąbrowski to the board of PAX, July 8, 1971.

20. Stefan Kisielewski, *Dzienniki* (Warsaw: Iskry, 1996), 593.

21. IPN, IPN0201/260, t.4, Sprawozdanie z zebrania poszerzonego zarządu Oddziału Wojewódzkiego PAX w Warszawie, July 7, 1972.

22. Ibid.

23. Ryszard Skwarski, *Za zieloną kurtyną: PAX lat 1975–1982* (London: Polska Fundacja Kulturalna, 1990), 7.

24. Edward Gierek, *Smak życia: Pamiętniki* (Warsaw: BGW, 1993), 32.

25. Ibid., 15–16.

26. Ibid., 20, 31.

27. Ibid., 102.

28. Janusz Rolicki, *Edward Gierek: Przerwana dekada* (Warsaw: Wydawnictwo Fakt, 1990), 74.

29. Andrzej Friszke, *PRL wobec Kościoła: Akta Urzędu do Spraw Wyznań, 1970–1978* (Warsaw: Biblioteka Więzi, 2010), 26.

30. Gierek, *Smak życia*, 114.

31. Friszke, *PRL wobec Kościoła*, 27, 39.

32. Ibid., 28.

33. Ibid., 38.

34. Antoni Dudek and Ryszard Gryz, *Komuniści i Kościół w Polsce (1945–1989)* (Kraków: Znak, 2003), 277–78, 283.

35. Ibid., 287–89.

36. Ibid., 299.

37. Jonathan Luxmore and Jolanta Babiuch, *The Vatican and the Red Flag* (London: Chapman, 1999), 166.

38. AKS CC, I-9/374, Bolesław Piasecki, Problem Kościoła i Katolicyzmu w Polsce Ludowej, memo to Gierek, February 1973, 11–15, 45.

39. By contrast, Gierek never mentioned Piasecki in his autobiography.

40. Mieczysław Franciszek Rakowski, *Dzienniki polityczne, 1958–1962* (Warsaw: Iskry, 1998), 259.

41. Marcin Zaremba, *Komunizm, legitymizacja, nacjonalizm: Nacjonalistyczna legitymizacja władzy komunistycznej w Polsce* (Warsaw: Trio, 2001), 372.

42. IPN, IPN 0639/223, Informacja dotycząca posiedzenia zarządu Stowarzyszenia PAX w dniu 31.I.1974 r., February 1, 1974, 111.

43. IPN, IPN 0639/223, Informacja dotycząca posiedzenia zarządu Stowarzyszenia PAX w dniach 16–17.V.1974 r., May 20, 1974, 20.

44. Reminiscing on the social strategy of his regime, Gierek admitted: "At the turn of 1974 and 1975 we had the choice of telling society the whole truth about the new situation and the necessity of tightening our belts or adopting various preventive measures, known only to the leadership, without informing them about the state of affairs. Acting with my consent, we chose the second option." See Gierek, *Smak życia*, 104.

45. IPN, IPN 0639/223, Notatka dotycząca ocen kierownictwa Stowarzyszenia PAX na odcinku sytuacji rynkowej kraju, April 1975.

46. Tejchma, *Kulisy dymisji*, 104.

47. IPN, DSA 1672, Statut Stowarzyszenia PAX, January 25, 1976.

48. Skwarski, *Za zieloną kurtyną,* 43.

49. The vote on the constitution assured the disintegration of Znak, as well as Stomma's exit from official politics. He was not reelected to parliament in 1976. The leadership of Znak passed into the hands of a more accommodating Konstanty Łubieński.

50. Mieczysław Franciszek Rakowski, *Dzienniki polityczne, 1976–1978,* (Warsaw: Iskry, 2002), 37.

51. Ivan T. Berend, *Central and Eastern Europe, 1944–1993: Detour from the Periphery to the Periphery* (Cambridge: Cambridge University Press, 1996), 229.

52. Ibid., 255.

53. Jan Józef Lipski, *KOR: A History of the Workers' Defense Committee in Poland* (Berkeley: University of California Press, 1984), 52–58; Friszke, *Opozycja polityczna w PRL,* 347.

54. KOR based its philosophy on the political writings of the philosopher Leszek Kołakowski (namely, his 1971 essay "Theses on Hope and Hopelessness") and the work of two of its founding fathers, Kuroń (his 1974 article "Political Opposition in Poland" published in the Paris-based *Kultura* journal) and Michnik (*A New Evolutionism,* a book published in exile in 1976). See David Ost, *Solidarity and the Politics of Anti-Politics: Opposition and Reform in Poland since 1968* (Philadelphia: Temple University Press, 1990), 58–68.

55. Ost, *Solidarity,* 71.

56. Lipski, *KOR,* 44.

57. Rolicki, *Edward Gierek,* 141.

58. *Słowo powszechne,* January 29–30, 1977.

59. Timothy Garton Ash, *The Polish Revolution: Solidarity, 1980–1982* (London: Granta Books, 1983), 20.

60. Luxmore and Babiuch, *Vatican and the Red Flag,* 195–96.

61. Friszke, *PRL wobec Kościoła,* 61–64.

62. Adam Michnik, *The Church and the Left,* trans. David Ost (Chicago: University of Chicago Press, 1993).

63. Ibid., 40, 173–75, 189.

64. Rakowski, *Dzienniki polityczne, 1976–1978,* 168–69.

65. Ibid., 165.

66. Gierek, *Smak życia,* 118.

67. Skwarski, *Za zieloną kurtyną,* 142.

68. AAN, Urząd do Spraw Wyznań, 127/291, Urząd Wojewódzki w Gdańsku, Wydział d/s Wyznań to Urząd d/s Wyznań w Warszawie, Informacja na temat działalności Stowarzyszenia PAX na tutejszym terenie, January 16, 1978.

69. AAN, Urząd do Spraw Wyznań, 127/291, Informacja służbowa dot. działalności Stowarzyszenia PAX na terenie województwa legnickiego w okresie od czerwca 1975 r. do grudnia 1977 r., January 1978.

70. Friszke, *Opozycja polityczna w PRL,* 452–68.

71. Jan Engelgard to the author, December 14, 2003.

72. AAN, Urząd do spraw Wyznań, A.R., Notatka na temat działalności Stowarzyszenia PAX, 1978.

73. Skwarski, *Za zieloną kurtyną,* 61, 72–75.

74. AAN, Urząd do spraw Wyznań, 127/291, Śliwiński, Notatka z rozmowy ze Zbigniewem Lesiewskim, przewodniczącym Oddziału Stołecznego Stowarzyszenia PAX, April 12, 1978.

75. Skwarski, *Za zieloną kurtyną,* 61–62.

76. IPN, DSA 1673, Referat sprawozdawczy Komisji Rewizyjnej Stowarzyszenia PAX na walne zgromadzenie w dniu 8 czerwca 1980 r., June 1980.

77. Luxmore and Babiuch, *Vatican and the Red Flag,* 203.

78. Garton Ash, *Polish Revolution,* 28; Gierek, *Smak życia,* 125.

79. The following anecdote illustrates the sense of panic that swept the party at the news of Wojtyła's election. On October 16, a member of the Politburo, Kazimierz Barcikowski, went to Kraków to discuss with the local party committee "how to resist the antisocialist activism of Cardinal Wojtyła." During a break, a cleaning lady entered the room and announced Wojtyła's election. The flamboyant communist writer Władysław Machejek, who participated in the meeting, responded: "I am buying everyone a liter of vodka, because from today we will kiss the Catholics' asses." See Adam Michnik, Józef Tischner, and Jacek Żakowski, *Między panem a plebanem* (Kraków: Znak, 2001), 280.

80. Skwarski, *Za zieloną kurtyną,* 63–64.

81. IPN, DSA 1673, Piasecki to the pope, telegram, October 16, 1978.

82. Jan Engeldard to the author, December 14, 2003.

83. Dudek and Pytel, *Bolesław Piasecki,* 322; Skwarski, *Za zieloną kurtyną,* 65.

84. "Ostatnia droga śp. Bolesława Piaseckiego," *WTK,* January 14, 1979.

85. Rev. Stefan Piotrowski's sermon, *WTK,* January 14, 1979.

86. Jerzy Hagmajer's eulogy, *WTK,* January 14, 1979.

Conclusion

1. Quoted in Walter A. Kemp, *Nationalism and Communism in Eastern Europe and the Soviet Union* (New York: St. Martin's, 1999), xi.

2. Ibid., 123.

3. Vladimir Tismăneanu, *Stalinism for All Seasons: A Political History of Romanian Communism* (Berkeley: University of California Press, 2003), 32–35.

4. John Connelly, *Captive University* (Chapel Hill: University of North Carolina Press, 2000).

5. Wojciech Jaruzelski, *Przemówienia, 1981–1982* (Warsaw: KiW, 1983), 213.

6. Ibid., 215.

7. Ibid., 219–21.

8. Marcin Zaremba, *Komunizm, legitymizacja, nacjonalizm* (Warsaw: Trio, 2001), 385–89.

9. Gale Stokes, *The Walls Came Tumbling Down: The Collapse of Communism in Eastern Europe* (New York: Oxford University Press, 1993), 110.

10. Andrzej Paczkowski, *The Spring Will Be Ours: Poland and the Poles from Occupation to Freedom*, trans. Jane Cave (University Park: Pennsylvania State University Press, 2003), 466.

11. The tiny National Rebirth of Poland (Narodowe Odrodzenie Polski) is the only political group that openly claims to be the incarnation of the prewar National Radicals.

12. See "Uchwała Sejmu Rzeczypospolitej Polskiej z 3 grudnia 2009 w sprawie ochrony wolności wyznania i wartości będących wspólnym dziedzictwem narodów Europy," available at http://isasejm.gov.pl.

13. *Niedziela*, October 27, 1991.

14. Genevieve Zubrzycki, *The Crosses of Auschwitz: Nationalism and Religion in Post-Communist Poland* (Chicago: University of Chicago Press, 2006).

15. On Radio Maryja, see Stanisław Burdziej, "Voice of the Disinherited? Religious Media after the 2005 Presidential and Parliamentary Elections in Poland," *East European Quarterly* 42, no. 2 (2008): 207–21.

16. Joanna Kurczewska, *Patriotyzmy polskich polityków* (Warsaw: Wydawnictwo IFiS PAN, 2002), 75–77.

17. The 2006 lustration law stipulated that all nominees to public posts born before 1972 had to undergo a process of lustration verifying that they had not cooperated with communist security services in repressing the democratic opposition, violating human and civil rights, or advancing the goals of a totalitarian state. Members of the central and local governments, administration employees, academics, lawyers, journalists—all these professionals became responsible for procuring a document that confirmed their clean hands before 1989. Those found guilty of collaborating with communist security were to be banned from their posts and to have their names revealed to the public. Ustawa z dnia 18 października 2006 roku o ujawnianiu informacji o dokumentach organów bezpieczeństwa państwa z lat 1944–1990 oraz treści tych dokumentów.

18. *Wprost*, July 9, 2007.

19. Before the catastrophe, the president had suffered low approval rates. He was often viewed as incompetent, lacking international prestige, and completely dependent on his brother Jarosław (March 2010 opinion survey "Społeczny portret prezydenta Lecha Kaczyńskiego w roku wyborczym," available at http://www.cbos.pl).

Between 18 and 20 percent of respondents declared Lech Kaczyński as their candidate (March 2010 opinion survey "Wybory prezydenckie—preferencje Polaków przed prawyborami w PO," available at http://www.cbos.pl).

20. "Komorowski: Chodzi o to, żeby ludzi nie bolało," *Gazeta wyborcza*, July 9, 2010.

21. Polish Press Agency daily news, July 16, 2010, available at http://www.pap.pl.

22. Jarosław Kaczyński's response to the chief editor of *Rzeczpospolita*, Paweł Lisiecki, August 6, 2010, available at http://www.pis.org.pl.

Bibliography

Archives

Archiwum Akt Nowych, Warsaw
Archiwum Dokumentacji Historycznej PRL, Warsaw
Archiwum Katolickiego Stowarzyszenia Civitas Christiana, Warsaw
Archiwum Universytetu Warszawskiego, Warsaw
Archiwum Wojskowego Instytutu Historycznego, Warsaw
Centralne Archiwum Wojskowe, Warsaw
Hoover Institution Archives, Stanford
Instytut Pamięci Narodowej, Warsaw
Instytut Studiów Politycznych Polskiej Akademii Nauk, Warsaw
Open Society Archives, Budapest

Periodicals

Akademik polski
Czas
Daily Worker
Do broni
Dzień akademicki
Dziś i jutro
Express wieczorny
Fakty na tle idei
Falanga
Gazeta polska
Gazeta wyborcza
Ilustrowany kurier codzienny
Kierunki
Kultura-oświata-nauka
Kurier poranny
Kurier warszawski

L' Osservatore romano
Ład
Merkuryusz polski
Myśl narodowa
Niedziela
Nowa kultura
Nowa Polska
Nowa sztafeta
Polityka
Po prostu
Przełom
Robotnik
Ruch młodych
Rzeczpospolita
Słowo
Słowo powszechne
Sztafeta
Świat
Times (London)
Tygodnik powszechny
Warszawski dziennik narodowy
Wielka Polska
Wprost
WTK
Znak
Żagary
Życie Warszawy

Primary Sources

Armia Krajowa w dokumentach, 1939–1945. 6 vols. Wrocław: Ossolineum, 1990–92.
Bielecki, Tadeusz. W szkole Dmowskiego. Gdańsk: Exter, 2000.
Bocheński, Józef. Wspomnienia. Kraków: Philed, 1993.
Brochwicz, Stanisław. Bohaterowie czy zdrajcy? Wspomnienia więźnia politycznego. Warsaw: Wydawnictwo Nowoczesne, 1940.
Całka, Leon [Bolesław Piasecki]. Wielka ideologia narodu polskiego. Warsaw, 1940.
Dmowski, Roman. Pisma. 10 vols. Częstochowa: Antoni Gmachowski, 1938–39.
———. Wybór pism Romana Dmowskiego. 4 vols. New York: Instytut Romana Dmowskiego, 1988.
Dobraczyński, Jan. Tylko w jednym życiu. Warsaw: PAX, 1970.

Frassati, Luciana. *Il Destino passa per Varsavia*. Milan: Bompiani, 1985.

Giedroyc, Jerzy. *Autobiografia na cztery ręce*. Warsaw: Czytelnik, 1994.

Gierek, Edward. *Smak życia: Pamiętniki*. Warsaw: BGW, 1993.

Gomułka, Władysław. *Pamiętniki*. Edited by Andrzej Werblan. 2 vols. Warsaw: BGW, 1995.

Götting, Gerald. *Christliche Mitverantwortung im Sozialismus*. Berlin: Union Verlag, 1965.

————. *Erkenntnishilfe und Wegweisung: Lenins Werk und wir Christen heute*. Berlin: Union Verlag, 1970.

Jaruzelski, Wojciech. *Przemówienia, 1981–1982*. Warsaw: KiW, 1983.

Jędruszczak, Tadeusz, and Artur Leiwand, eds. *Archiwum polityczne Ignacego Paderewskiego*. 4 vols. Wrocław: Ossolineum, 1973–74.

Kętrzyński, Wojciech. "Na przełomie 1944–1945." *Więź* 11 (November–December 1967): 158–71.

Khrushchev, Nikita Sergeevich. *Khrushchev Remembers: The Glasnost Tapes*. Translated and edited by Jerrold L. Schecter with Vyacheslav V. Luchkov. Boston: Little, Brown, 1990.

Kisielewski, Stefan. *Abecadło Kisiela*. Warsaw: Oficyna Wydawnicza INTERIM, 1990.

————. *Dzienniki*. Warsaw: Iskry, 1996.

Korboński, Stefan. *Warsaw in Chains*. London: Allen and Unwin, 1959.

Miedziński, Bogusław. "Sprostowanie spoza grobu." *Zeszyty historyczne* 22 (1972): 140–54.

Mounier, Emmanuel. *Be Not Afraid: A Denunciation of Despair*. Translated by Cynthia Rowland. New York: Sheed and Ward, 1951.

Noskova, A. F., ed. *Iz Varshavy: Moskva, tovarishchu Beriia; Dokumenty NKVD SSSR o pol'skom podpol'ye, 1944–1945 gg*. Moscow: Sibirskii Khronograf, 2001.

Nowak, Jan [Zdzisław Jeziorański]. *Wojna w eterze: Wspomnienia*. 2 vols. London: Odnowa, 1985–88.

Oddział Akademicki O.W.P. *Wytyczne w sprawach: Żydowskiej, mniejszości słowiańskich, niemieckiej, zasad polityki gospodarczej*. Warsaw, 1932.

Piasecki, Bolesław. *Duch czasów nowych a Ruch Młodych*. Warsaw, 1935.

————. *Kierunki, 1945–1960*. Warsaw: PAX, 1960.

————. *Patriotyzm polski*. Warsaw: PAX, 1958.

————. *Przełom narodowy*. Warsaw, 1937.

————. *Siły rozwoju*. Warsaw: PAX, 1971.

————. *Wytyczne Narodowo-Radykalnej myśli gospodarczej*. Warsaw, 1937.

————. *Zagadnienia istotne*. Warsaw: PAX, 1954.

Popiel, Karol. *Od Brześcia do Polonii*. London: Odnowa, 1967.

Przetakiewicz, Zygmunt. *Od ONR-u do PAX-u*. Warsaw: Wydawnictwo Książka Polska, 1994.

Raina, Peter. *Kościół w PRL: Kościół katolicki a państwo w świetle dokumentów, 1945–1989.* 2 vols. Poznań: W Drodze, 1994–95.

———. *Piasecki na indeksie watykańskim.* Warsaw: Wydawnictwo von Borowiecky, 2002.

Rakowski, Mieczysław Franciszek. *Dzienniki polityczne, 1958–1962.* Warsaw: Iskry, 1998.

———. *Dzienniki polityczne, 1963–1966.* Warsaw: Iskry, 1999.

———. *Dzienniki polityczne, 1967–1968.* Warsaw: Iskry, 1999.

———. *Dzienniki polityczne, 1969–1971.* Warsaw: Iskry, 2001.

———. *Dzienniki polityczne, 1976–1978.* Warsaw: Iskry, 2002.

Reiff, Ryszard. *Gra o życie.* Warsaw: Unicorn, 1993.

Rolicki, Janusz. *Edward Gierek: Przerwana dekada.* Warsaw: Fakt, 1990.

Rydz-Śmigły, Edward. *Byście o sile nie zapomnieli: Rozkazy, artykuły, mowy, 1904–1936.* Warsaw: Książnica Atlas, 1936.

Szlachcic, Franciszek. *Gorzki smak władzy.* Warsaw: Fakt, 1990.

———. "Wspomnienia z okresu pracy w organach bezpieczeństwa i Ministerstwa Spraw Wewnętrznych: Napisane dla wewnętrznego użytku MSW." Warsaw: MSW, 1988.

Sznarbachowski, Włodzimierz. *300 lat wspomnień.* London: Aneks, 1997.

Świda, Józef. "Wyjaśnienia dotyczące okresu 1943–1944." *Zeszyty historyczne* 73 (1983): 74–80.

Tajne dokumenty: Państwo-kościół, 1960–1980. London: Aneks, 1996.

Tejchma, Józef. *Kulisy dymisji: Z dzienników ministra kultury, 1974–1977.* Kraków: Oficyna Cracovia, 1991.

Torańska, Teresa. *Oni.* London: Aneks, 1985.

Wałek-Czarnecki, Tadeusz. *Sprawa szkół akademickich.* Warsaw:, 1933.

Wasiutyński, Wojciech. *Czwarte pokolenie.* London: Odnowa, 1982.

———. *Prawą stroną labiryntu.* Gdańsk: Exter, 1996.

Wyszyński, Stefan. *Dzieła zebrane.* 2 vols. Warsaw: Soli Deo, 1991–93.

———. *A Freedom from Within.* San Diego, Calif.: Harcourt Brace Jovanovich, 1983.

Zabłocki, Janusz. *Dzienniki, 1956–1966.* Warsaw: IPN, 2008.

Zasady programu Narodowo-Radykalnego. Warsaw, 1937.

Zawieyski, Jerzy. *Kartki z dziennika, 1955–1969.* Warsaw: PAX, 1983

Żuławski, Zygmunt. *Wspomnienia.* Warsaw: Nowa, 1980.

Secondary Sources

Ajnenkiel, Andrzej. *Polska po przewrocie majowym.* Warsaw: PWN, 1980.

Ambroziewicz, Jerzy, Walery Namiotkiewicz, and Jan Olszewski. *Na spotkanie ludziom z AK.* Warsaw: Iskry, 1956.

Berend, Ivan T. *Central and Eastern Europe, 1944–1993: Detour from the Periphery to the Periphery.* Cambridge: Cambridge University Press, 1996.

Bierdiajev, Mikołaj. *Nowe Średniowiecze.* Translated by Marian Reutt. Warsaw: Rój, 1936.

———. *Problem komunizmu.* Translated by Marian Reutt. Warsaw: Rój, 1937.

Bjork, James. "Bulwark or Patchwork? Religious Exceptionalism and Regional Diversity in Postwar Poland." In *Christianity and Modernity in Eastern Europe,* edited by Bruce R. Berglund and Brian Porter-Szücs, 129–58. Budapest: CEU Press, 2010.

Blit, Lucjan. *The Eastern Pretender.* London: Hutchinson, 1965.

Blobaum, Robert, ed. *Antisemitism and Its Opponents in Modern Poland.* Ithaca, N.Y.: Cornell University Press, 2005.

Borejsza, Jerzy. *Mussolini był pierwszy.* Warsaw: Czytelnik, 1979.

Borodziewicz, Wincenty. "Rozmowy polsko-litewskie w Wilnie, 1942–1944." *Przegląd historyczny* 1 (1989): 317–37.

Bosworth, R. J. B. *Mussolini.* London: Hodder Education, 2002.

Broch, Hermann. *The Spell.* San Francisco: North Point, 1989.

Brubaker, Rogers. *Nationalism Reframed: Nationalism and the National Question in the New Europe.* New York: Cambridge University Press, 1996.

Buchanan, Tom, and Martin Conway, eds. *Political Catholicism in Europe, 1918–1965.* Oxford: Clarendon, 1996.

Burdziej, Stanisław. "Voice of the Disinherited? Religious Media after the 2005 Presidential and Parliamentary Elections in Poland." *East European Quarterly* 42, no. 2 (2008): 207–21.

Burrin, Philippe. "Political Religion: The Relevance of a Concept." *History and Memory* 9, no. 1–2 (1997): 320–40.

Connelly, John. *Captive University.* Chapel Hill: University of North Carolina Press, 2000.

Conway, Martin. *Collaboration in Belgium: Léon Degrelle and the Rexist Movement, 1940–1944.* New Haven, Conn.: Yale University Press, 1993.

De Felice, Renzo. *Fascism: An Informal Introduction to Its Theory and Practice.* New Brunswick, N.J.: Transaction Books, 1976.

———. *Interpretations of Fascism.* Cambridge, Mass.: Harvard University Press, 1977.

Drozdowski, Marian M., ed. *Warszawa II Rzeczypospolitej, 1918–1939.* 5 vols. Warsaw: PWN, 1968–73.

Dudek, Antoni. *Państwo i Kościół w Polsce, 1945–1970.* Kraków: Wydawnictwo PiT, 1995.

———. "Sutanny w służbie Peerelu." *Karta* 25, no. 8 (1998): 110–20.

Dudek, Antoni, and Ryszard Gryz. *Komuniści i Kościół w Polsce (1945–1989).* Kraków: Znak, 2003.

Dudek, Antoni, and Tomasz Marszałkowski. *Walki uliczne w PRL, 1956–1989.* Kraków: Wydawnictwo Geo, 1999.

Dudek, Antoni, and Grzegorz Pytel. *Bolesław Piasecki: Próba biografii politycznej.* London: Aneks, 1990.

Dziewanowski, M. K. *The Communist Party of Poland.* Cambridge, Mass.: Harvard University Press, 1976.

Eisler, Jerzy. *Marzec 1968* (Warsaw: PWN, 1991).

———. *Polski rok 1968.* Warsaw: IPN, 2006.

Erdman, Jan. *Droga do Ostrej Bramy.* London: Odnowa, 1984.

Friszke, Andrzej. *Koło posłów "Znak" w Sejmie PRL, 1957–1976.* Warsaw: Wydawnictwo Sejmowe, 2002.

———. *Opozycja polityczna w PRL, 1945–1980.* London: Aneks, 1994.

———. *PRL wobec Kościoła: Akta Urzędu do Spraw Wyznań, 1970–1978.* Warsaw: Biblioteka Więzi, 2010.

Garlicki, Andrzej. *Dzieje Uniwersytetu Warszawskiego.* Warsaw: PWN, 1982.

Garton Ash, Timothy. *The Polish Revolution: Solidarity, 1980–1982.* London: Granta Books, 1983.

Górny, Maciej. *Przede wszystkim ma być naród: Marksistowskie historiografie w Europie Środkowo-Wschodniej.* Warsaw: Trio, 2007.

———. "Wydarzenia marcowe w opinii czechosłowackiej." In *Marzec 1968: Trzydzieści lat później,* 2 vols., edited by Marcin Kula, Piotr Osęka, and Marcin Zaremba. 1:206–18. Warsaw: Wydawnictwo Naukowe PWN, 1998.

Gross, Jan T. *Neighbors: The Destruction of the Jewish Community in Jedwabne, Poland.* Princeton, N.J.: Princeton University Press, 2001.

Grott, Bogumił. *Nacjonalizm chrześcijański.* Kraków: Ostoja, 1996.

Hagen, William W. "Before the 'Final Solution': Toward a Comparative Analysis of Political Anti-Semitism in Interwar Germany and Poland." *Journal of Modern History* 68 (June 1996): 351–81.

Hanebrink, Paul A. *In Defense of Christian Hungary: Religion, Nationalism, and Anti-Semitism, 1890–1944.* Ithaca, N.Y.: Cornell University Press, 2006.

Hellman, John. *Emmanuel Mounier and the New Catholic Left, 1930–1950.* Toronto: University of Toronto Press, 1981.

Horn, Gerd-Rainer, and Emmanuel Gerard, eds. *Left Catholicism: Catholics and Society in Western Europe at the Point of Liberation, 1943–1955.* Leuven: Leuven University Press, 2001.

Iordachi, Constantin. "God's Chosen Warriors: Romania." In *Comparative Fascist Studies: New Perspectives,* edited by Constantin Iordachi, 339–52. London: Routledge, 2010.

Jagiełło, Michał. *Próba rozmowy: Szkice o katolicyzmie odrodzeniowym i "Tygodniku Powszechnym," 1945–1953.* 2 vols. Warsaw: Biblioteka Narodowa, 2001.

Jedlicki, Witold. *Klub Krzywego Koła.* Paris: Instytut Literacki, 1963.

Judt, Tony. *Postwar: A History of Europe since 1945.* New York: Penguin, 2005.

Jurga, Tadeusz. *Obrona Polski, 1939.* Warsaw: PAX, 1990.

Kawalec, Krzysztof. *Narodowa Demokracja wobec faszyzmu.* Warsaw: PIW, 1989.

Kemp, Walter A. *Nationalism and Communism in Eastern Europe and the Soviet Union.* New York: St. Martin's, 1999.

Kersten, Krystyna. *The Establishment of Communist Rule in Poland, 1943–1948.* Berkeley: University of California Press, 1991.

Kobylańska, Zofia. *Konfederacja Narodu w Warszawie.* Warsaw: PAX, 1999.

Kołakowski, Leszek. *Main Currents of Marxism.* Vol. 3. *The Breakdown.* Oxford: Oxford University Press, 1982.

Korboński, Stefan. *The Polish Underground State.* New York: Hippocrene, 1981.

Kosicki, Piotr. "Promieniowanie personalizmu: Mounier, 'Esprit,' i początki 'Więzi.'" *Więź* 2–3 (February–March 2008): 111–22.

Krajewski, Kazimierz. *Uderzeniowe Bataliony Kadrowe, 1942–1944.* Warsaw: PAX, 1993.

Kubik, Jan. *The Power of Symbols against the Symbols of Power.* University Park: Pennsylvania State University Press, 1994.

Kunicki, Mikołaj. "Between Accommodation, Resistance, and Dialogue: Church-State Relations in Communist Poland, 1945–1989." In *Peaceful Coexistence or Iron Curtain: Austria, Neutrality, and Eastern Europe in the Cold War and Détente, 1955–1989,* edited by Arnold Suppan and Wolfgang Mueller, 393–411. Vienna: LIT, 2009.

———. "The Red and the Brown: Bolesław Piasecki, the Polish Communists, and the Anti-Zionist Campaign in Poland, 1967–1968." *East European Politics and Societies* 19, no. 2 (2005): 185–225.

———. "Unwanted Collaborators: Leon Kozłowski, Władysław Studnicki, and the Problem of Collaboration among Polish Conservative Politicians in World War II." *European Review of History* 8, no. 2 (2001): 203–20.

Kurczewska, Joanna. *Patriotyzmy polskich polityków.* Warsaw: Wydawnictwo IFiS PAN, 2002.

Kutrzeba, Tadeusz. *Bitwa nad Bzurą.* Warsaw: MON, 1957.

Laba, Roman. *The Roots of Solidarity.* Princeton, N.J.: Princeton University Press, 1991.

Lesiakowski, Krzysztof. *Mieczysław Moczar "Mietek": Biografia polityczna.* Warsaw: Rytm, 1998.

Lipski, Jan Józef. *Katolickie państwo narodu polskiego.* London: Aneks, 1994.

———. *KOR: A History of the Workers' Defense Committee in Poland.* Berkeley: University of California Press, 1984.

Livezeanu, Irina. *Cultural Politics in Greater Romania: Regionalism, Nation Building, and Ethnic Struggle, 1918–1930.* Ithaca, N.Y.: Cornell University Press, 1995.

Luxmore, Jonathan, and Jolanta Babiuch. *The Vatican and the Red Flag.* London: Chapman, 1999.

Łabuszewski, Tomasz, and Kazimierz Krajewski, eds. *Od "Łupaszki" do "Młota," 1944–1949.* Warsaw: Oficyna Wydawnicza Volumen, 1994.

Machcewicz, Paweł. *Polski rok 1956.* Warsaw: Oficyna Wydawnicza Mówią Wieki, 1993.

Maciejewski, Jarosław, and Zofia Trojanowiczowa. *Poznański czerwiec 1956.* Poznań: Wydawnictwo Poznańskie, 1990.

Mackiewicz, Stanisław. *Historia Polski od 11 listopada 1918 r. do 17 wrzesnia 1939 r.* Warsaw: Głos, 1989.

Majchrowski, Jacek. *Geneza politycznych ugrupowań katolickich: Stronnictwo Pracy, grupa "Dzis i Jutro".* Paris: Libella, 1984.

———. *Silni-zwarci-gotowi: Myśl polityczna Obozu Zjednoczenia Narodowego.* Warsaw: PWN, 1985.

Mann, Michael. *Fascists.* Cambridge: Cambridge University Press, 2004.

Maritain, Jacques. *Nauka i mądrość.* Translated by Marian Reutt. Warsaw: Rój, n.d.

Mazower, Mark. *Hitler's Empire: How the Nazis Ruled Europe.* New York: Penguin, 2008.

Micewski, Andrzej. *Cardinal Wyszyński.* San Diego, Calif.: Harcourt Brace Jovanovich, 1984.

———. *Katolicy w potrzasku.* Warsaw: BGW, 1993.

———. *Współrządzić czy nie kłamać? Pax i Znak w Polsce, 1945–1976.* Paris: Libella, 1978.

Michnik, Adam. *The Church and the Left.* Translated by David Ost. Chicago: University of Chicago Press, 1993.

Michnik, Adam, Józef Tischner, and Jacek Żakowski. *Między panem a plebanem.* Kraków: Znak, 2001.

Misiunas, Romuald J., and Rein Taagepera. *The Baltic States: Years of Dependence, 1940–1990.* Berkeley: University of California Press, 1993.

Naimark, Norman. *Fires of Hatred.* Cambridge, Mass.: Harvard University Press, 2001.

Naimark, Norman, and Leonid Gibianskii, eds. *The Establishment of Communist Regimes in Eastern Europe, 1944–1949.* Boulder: Westview, 1997.

Niedzielko, Romuald, and Bartłomiej Noszczak. "Bolesława Piaseckiego przepustka do wolności." *Przegląd powszechny* 5 (May 2006): 98–107.

Niwiński, Piotr. *Okręg wileński AK w latach 1944–1948.* Warsaw: Oficyna Wydawnicza Volumen, 1999.

Ost, David. *Solidarity and the Politics of Anti-Politics: Opposition and Reform in Poland since 1968.* Philadelphia: Temple University Press, 1990.

Paczkowski, Andrzej. *Pół wieku dziejów Polski, 1939–1989.* Warsaw: PWN, 1998.

———. *The Spring Will Be Ours: Poland and the Poles from Occupation to Freedom.* Translated by Jane Cave. University Park: Pennsylvania State University Press, 2003.

———, ed. *Centrum władzy w Polsce, 1948–1970.* Warsaw: ISP PAN, 2003.

Payne, Stanley. *A History of Fascism, 1914–1945.* Madison: University of Wisconsin Press, 1995.

Petrov, Nikita. *Ivan Serov: Pervyi predsedatel' KGB.* Moscow: Materik, 2005.

Pietrzak, Jerzy. "Prymas Polski kardynał August Hlond a grupa katolików 'Dziś i Jutro.'" In *Komu służył PAX,* edited by Sabina Bober, 93–106. Warsaw: PAX, 2008.

Pilch, Andrzej. *Rzeczpospolita akademicka.* Kraków: Księgarnia Akademicka, 1997.

Plach, Eva. *The Clash of Moral Nations: Cultural Politics in Piłsudski's Poland, 1926–1935.* Athens: Ohio University Press, 2006.

Pobóg-Malinowski, Władysław. *Najnowsza historia polityczna Polski.* Vol. 2, *Okres 1939–1945.* Gdansk: Oficyna Wydawnicza "Graf," 1989.

Polonsky, Antony. *Politics in Independent Poland, 1921–1939: The Crisis of Constitutional Government.* Oxford: Clarendon, 1972.

Porter, Brian. *When Nationalism Began to Hate.* New York: Oxford University Press, 2000.

Radio Wolna Europa. *Prawda o PAX-ie i Piaseckim.* London:, 1968.

Raina, Peter. *Mordercy uchodzą bezkarnia: Sprawa Bohdana P.* Warsaw: Wydawnictwo von Borowiecky, 2000.

Richter, Michael. *Die Ost-CDU, 1948–1952.* Düsseldorf: Droste, 1990.

Rissmann, Martin. *Kaderschulung in der Ost-CDU, 1949–1971.* Düsseldorf: Droste, 1995.

Rogger, Hans, and Eugen Weber, eds. *The European Right: A Historical Profile.* Berkeley: University of California Press, 1965.

Rossino, Alexander B. *Hitler Strikes Poland: Blitzkrieg, Ideology, and Atrocity.* Lawrence: University Press of Kansas, 2003.

Rostworowski, Mikołaj. *Słowo o PAX-ie.* Warsaw: PAX, 1968.

Rothschild, Joseph. *Pilsudski's Coup d'État.* New York: Columbia University Press, 1966.

———. *East Central Europe between the Two World Wars.* Seattle: University of Washington Press, 1974.

Różewicz, Tadeusz. "Świadkowie albo nasza mała stabilizacja." *Dialog,* no. 5 (1962): 5–26.

Rudnicki, Szymon. *Obóz Narodowo-Radykalny: Geneza i działalność.* Warsaw: Czytelnik, 1985.

Schaff, Adam. *Marksizm i jednostka ludzka.* Warsaw: PWN, 1965.

Siemaszko, Zbigniew S. *Narodowe Siły Zbrojne.* London: Odnowa, 1982.

Skwarski, Ryszard. *Za zieloną kurtyną: PAX lat 1975–1982.* London: Polska Fundacja Kulturalna, 1990.

Snyder, Timothy. *The Reconstruction of Nations: Poland, Ukraine, Lithuania, Belarus, 1569–1999.* New Haven, Conn.: Yale University Press, 2003.

Sternhell, Zeev. *Neither Right nor Left: Fascist Ideology in France.* Berkeley: University of California Press, 1986.

Stokes, Gale. *The Walls Came Tumbling Down: The Collapse of Communism in Eastern Europe.* New York: Oxford University Press, 1993.

Stola, Dariusz. *Kampania antysyjonistyczna w Polsce, 1967–1968.* Warsaw: ISP PAN, 2000.

———. "Rok 1968." In *Centrum władzy w Polsce, 1948–1970,* edited by Andrzej Paczkowski, 215–46. Warsaw: ISP PAN, 2003.

Szajkowski, Bogdan. *Next to God... Poland: Politics and Religion in Contemporary Poland.* London: Pinter, 1983.

Szarota, Tomasz. *U progu zagłady: Zajścia antyżydowskie i pogromy w okupowanej Europie.* Warsaw: Wydawnictwo Sic!, 2000.

Szubiński, Rajmund. *Polska broń pancerna, 1939.* Warsaw: MON, 1982.

Śleszyński, Wojciech. "Utworzenie i funkcjonowanie obozu odosobnienia w Berezie Kartuskiej." *Dzieje Najnowsze* 2 (June 2003): 35–53.

Świda, Józef. "Wyjaśnienia dotyczące okresu 1943–1944." *Zeszyty historyczne* 73 (1983): 74–80.

Talmon, J. L. *Political Messianism: The Romantic Phase.* New York: Praeger, 1960.

Taubman, William. *Khrushchev: The Man and His Era.* New York: Norton, 2003.

Taylor, Fred, ed. *The Goebbels Diaries, 1939–1941.* New York: Penguin, 1982.

Tismăneanu, Vladimir. *Stalinism for All Seasons: A Political History of Romanian Communism.* Berkeley: University of California Press, 2003.

Verdery, Katherine. *National Ideology under Socialism: Identity and Cultural Politics in Ceauşescu's Romania.* Berkeley: University of California Press, 1991.

Walicki, Andrzej. *Marxism and the Leap to the Kingdom of Freedom: The Rise and Fall of the Communist Utopia.* Stanford, Calif.: Stanford University Press, 1995.

Wapiński, Roman. *Narodowa Demokracja, 1893–1939.* Wrocław: Ossolineum, 1980.

Wawrzyniak, Joanna. *ZBOWiD i pamięć drugiej wojny światowej, 1949–1969.* Warsaw: Trio, 2009.

Weiner, Amir. *Making Sense of War: The Second World War and the Fate of the Bolshevik Revolution.* Princeton, N.J.: Princeton University Press, 2001.

Weydenthal, Jan B. de. *The Communists of Poland: An Historical Outline.* Stanford, Calif.: Hoover Institution Press, 1978.

Wieczorkiewicz, Paweł. "Walka o władzę w kierownictwie PZPR w marcu 68." In *Marzec 1968: Trzydzieści lat później,* edited by Marcin Kula, Piotr Osęka, and Marcin Zaremba, 1:39–57. Warsaw: PWN, 1998.

Wynot, Edward D., Jr. *Polish Politics in Transition: The Camp of National Unity and the Struggle for Power, 1935–1939.* Athens: University of Georgia Press, 1974.

Załuski, Zbigniew. *Siedem polskich grzechów głównych.* Warsaw: MON, 1962.

Zaremba, Marcin. *Komunizm, legitymizacja, nacjonalizm: Nacjonalistyczna legitymizacja władzy komunistycznej w Polsce.* Warsaw: Trio, 2001.

Zubrzycki, Genevieve. *The Crosses of Auschwitz: Nationalism and Religion in Post-Communist Poland.* Chicago: University of Chicago Press, 2006.

Żakowski, Jacek. *Pół wieku pod włos czyli życie codzienne "Tygodnika Powszechnego" w czasach heroicznych.* Kraków: Znak, 1995.

Żmijewski, Norbert A. *The Catholic-Marxist Ideological Dialogue in Poland, 1945–1980.* Brookfield, Vt.: Dartmouth, 1991

Index

ism, acceptance of, 88–89; national identity, role in definition of, 5; opposition group to contest domestic issues, 83; political influence of, 34; Second Vatican Council (Vatican II), 132–34; social and political activism by, 89–92; unification of, 97

Catholic MPs, 100–101, 110, 152

Catholic political movement and party: attitudes toward, 91–92; clerical control over, 133; formation of, 90–91, 117; friendships and intermarriages in, 93, 210n79; general election, outcome of, 90; military underground, disbanding of, 92–93, 210n76; socialist movement, Catholic component of, 93

Catholics and Catholicism: activism, social and political by Catholics, 82–93; Catholic-fascist-nationalist state, vision of Poland as, xi; Catholic-Marxist dialogue and alliance, 16, 84, 87–89, 97, 102–5, 132–34, 169, 178; Catholic-Marxist-nationalist trinity, 88, 103–5; Catholic-socialist state, 100, 103–5; communist assault on and destruction of, 94–100, 191n7; contributions of Polish Catholics, 166; elections and voting, 90, 117, 209nn62–63; emancipation in Poland, PAX advocacy for, 132–34; end of in Poland, 128; *Essential Issues*, reaction to, 105–10; ethnoreligious identity, 121–23, 184; excommunication threat, 107–8, 109; fascist religious policies, 13; great ideology of, 52; intellectual condition of, 101; Jewish Catholics, 18; Left Catholicism in Europe, 88; militancy and militant Catholicism, 13, 15, 32; moral-political unity, contribution to, 61, 174–75; national identity, central role of, 3, 5, 12, 88, 103–4, 112, 136–37, 139, 183–85; nationalist-Catholic synthesis, 12–13, 19–20, 60–61, 78, 103–4, 121; national renewal of Poland and, 52; OWP support for, 10–11; PAX, response to creation of, 98; PAX allegiance to, demonstration of, 110; Poland as Catholic-fascist-nationalist state, vision of, 3; Polish-led racial-geographical bloc,

62; political Catholicism, fragmentation of, 33–34; political involvement of, 94, 121–24; prevalence of, 82; reform of in spirit of socialism, xi, 162; reform of Poland, role in, 167–68; revisionist assault on by, 124; revolution, support for, 101; rights of Catholics, 90; socialism and Catholic-nationalist support for, xi; social teaching of the papcy, 12–13; Stalinism and, 94; totalitarianism, Catholic, 13

Catholic Social Movement, 209nn63

Ceauşescu, Nicolae, 181

censorship, 35, 151–52, 217–18n71, 226n84

Central Circle of Priests "Caritas" (Centralne Koło Księży "Caritas"), 131–32, 220nn114–115

Central Committee of Organizations for Independence (Centralny Komitet Organizacji Niepodległościowych), 60, 202n32

Centrolew, 14, 26, 62

chauvinism, 112, 140, 141, 153, 155, 156, 161

Chernyakhovsky, Ivan, 74

Christ, non-Jewish ancestry of, 33

Christian Democratic Union (Ost-CDU), 101–2

Christian Democrats: German political culture, participation in, 131, 220n112; government and political system, structure of, 8; OWP partnership opportunity, 10; voting for, 95; Western Europe and ideology of, 78

Christian ideology: Christianity as unifying national religion, 32–33; Christian state and society, establishment of, 16; existentialism, 16; great ideology of, 32; nationalist-Christian ideology, 13; religious nationalism in Europe, 13; universalism, 16

Christian-National Union, 184

Christian Social Association, 165

Christian Social Party, 13

Christus Rex movement, 13, 32, 34

Chrobry, Bolesław, 195n85

Chrobry sword, 1, 26, 195n85

Church and the Left, The (Michnik), 175

Church of the Nuns of the Visitation, 95

Cieszkowski, August, 15

www.ingramcontent.com/pod-product-compliance
Lightning Source LLC
Chambersburg PA
CBHW021853020426
42334CB00013B/316